A JOURNAL OF CONTEMPORARY WRITING

IRISH PAGES

DUILLÍ ÉIREANN

IRISH PAGES is a biannual journal (Spring-Summer, Autumn-Winter), edited in Belfast and publishing, in equal measure, writing from Ireland and overseas. It appears at the end of each six-month period.

Its policy is to publish poetry, short fiction, essays, creative non-fiction, memoir, essay reviews, nature-writing, translated work, literary journalism, and other autobiographical, historical, religious and scientific writing of literary distinction. There are no standard reviews or narrowly academic articles. Irish language and Ulster Scots writing are published in the original, with English translations or glosses.

IRISH PAGES is a non-partisan, non-sectarian, culturally ecumenical, and wholly independent journal. It endorses no political outlook or cultural tradition, and has no editorial position on the constitutional question. Its title refers to the island of Ireland in a purely apolitical and geographic sense, in the same manner of The Church of Ireland or the Irish Sea.

The sole criteria for inclusion in the journal are the distinction of the writing and the integrity of the individual voice. Equal editorial attention will be given to established, emergent and new writers.

The views expressed in IRISH PAGES are not necessarily those of the Editors. The magazine has no editorial or financial connection to the Linen Hall Library or its Directors.

Submissions are welcome but must be accompanied by return postage or an international reply coupon. No self-addressed envelope is required. Reporting time is six months. If work is accepted, a copy on disk may be requested.

Your subscription is essential to the independence and survival of the journal. Subscription rates are £16stg/€26/$24 for one year, or £24/€39/$36 for two years. For postage outside Ireland and Britain, add £4/€6/$5 per year for Europe, or £6/€9/$8 per year for the rest of the world. Visit our website at www.irishpages.org for a subscription form. Credit cards are welcome.

IRISH PAGES
The Linen Hall Library
17 Donegall Square North
Belfast BT1 5GB

IRISH PAGES is designed by Tonic and set in 11.5/12.5 Monotype Perpetua.
It is printed in Belfast by Nicholson & Bass.

This issue has been generously asssisted
by the Arts Councils of Northern and Southern Ireland.

arts council of Northern Ireland

the arts council an chomhairle ealaíon

ISBN 0-9544257-5-8

A JOURNAL OF CONTEMPORARY WRITING

IRISH PAGES

CHRIS AGEE, *Editor*

CATHAL Ó SEARCAIGH, *Irish Language Editor*

SEÁN MAC AINDREASA, *Managing Editor*

EDITED AT THE LINEN HALL LIBRARY IN BELFAST
SPRING / SUMMER 2005

IRISH PAGES

DUILLÍ ÉIREANN

VOLUME 3, NUMBER 1, SPRING / SUMMER 2005

CONTENTS

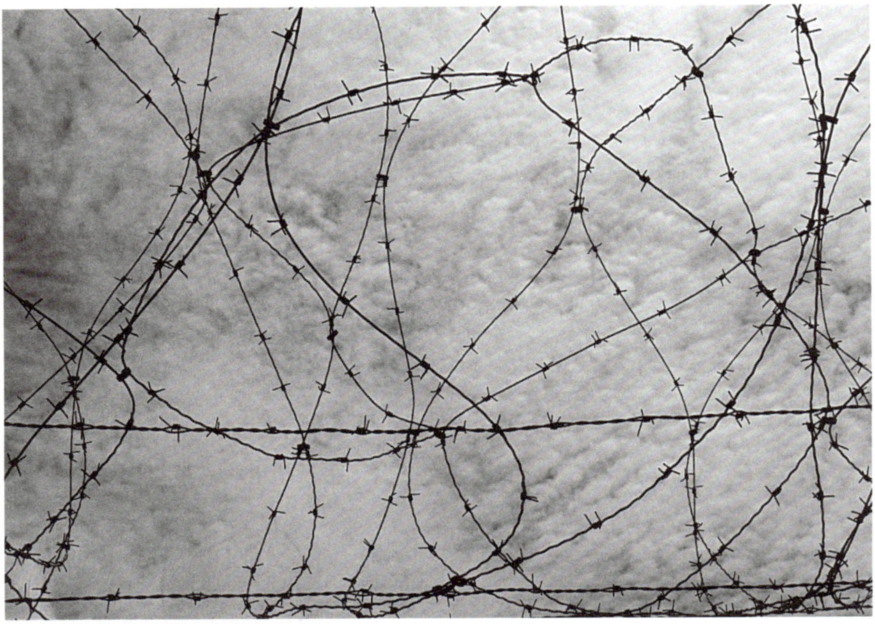

Penal Memory, French Guyana
by Mélina Gacoin

THE VIEW FROM THE LINEN HALL

On the Sociology of Literature

As things are, and as fundamentally they must always be, poetry is not a career but a mug's game. No honest poet can ever feel quite sure of the permanent value of what he has written: he may have wasted his time and messed up his life for nothing.

T.S. Eliot

There is an inescapable indeterminacy about all questions of reputation where literary and intellectual figures are concerned. Membership of the jury is heterogeneous and potentially infinite; the various parts of a writer's oeuvre or achievement may receive different ratings from different categories of reader; it is almost impossible to maintain a clear distinction between questions of merit and the neighbouring territories of celebrity and utility; and at any given moment judgement is almost inevitably contaminated by hearsay, selective recall and cultural lag.

Stefan Collini

Straddling the last half-century, these classic formulations of the Uncertainty Principle of Literature could be said to bracket the contemporary literary world whose outlines emerged after the efflorescence of early twentieth-century Modernism. Such gems of literary folk-wisdom are legion, of course, in the works of twentieth-century writers of all varieties and origins. That self-consciousness alone suggests that "literature" had become a burgeoning cultural formation whose space, autonomy and consolidation grew immeasurably with the spread of mass literacy in the modern period.

Like Heisenberg's principle of the same name in physics, which laid the basis for quantum mechanics, Eliot's purely critical observation can be felt to have, on reflection, an ever-widening gyre of unsettling intellectual consequences. That he of all writers, at the heyday of his own renown, could cast doubt on the appearances of day-to-day reputation-making carries an especial ethical charge. (Perhaps he sensed the inevitable decline in standing that might follow, as it has in some quarters, such critical election by the Modernist *mythos*). Writing in our own day, the critic and essayist Stefan Collini takes up the same quantum-literary insight, and with a few deft strokes, suggests how any empirical demonstration of this indeterminacy principle must involve a sociological approach to literature.

To extend the metaphor, one might add that just as the laws of Newtonian physics, within the sphere of the daily macrocosm, appear unaffected by the quantum microcosm, or at least empirically compatible with it, so the literary world as a major social formation does not seem, at any one historical moment, unduly troubled by the background irradiation of its Uncertainty Principle. Only in this case, it is the daily literary world that might be likened to the microcosm of period relations, and the indeterminacy of reputation to the *longue durée*, or deep structure, of the historical macrocosm. Which returns us, by "a commodious victus of recirculation," to that earlier phrase, *the sociology of literature*: for it is only such a thing (of which literary history is a very limited, and cosseted, sub-set) that can align period relations with historical deep-time, thereby illustrating, empirically, the continual infiltration of indeterminacy through the façade of immediacy – the apparent fixity – of the literary world at one given social moment.

But hold on: a *sociology* of literature? Does such exist, actually, as a branch of scholarship? Is it not simply a catchphrase, a cipher without a developed discipline? Indeed, for that matter, is it even desirable as a field of study, or simply another exercise in arid academic reductionism? For an answer, a benchmarking with the study of religion is instructive.

In the history of ideas, it is an observation of old provenance that the arts in general, and literature in particular, have increasingly proffered a "secular spirituality" in the aftermath of the Enlightenment, and its consequent weakening of the distinct empyrean (or otherworldly *imperium*) of a purely religious transcendence as upheld in the classical Christian tradition. Transcendence having thus been "earthed," some of its otherworldly cultural purchase has been either decanted by spiritual deed-poll, or supplanted by secular advance, so that it is now firmly part of a "profane," this-worldly social space. From the Oxford Movement to the existentialists, from the Romantics to geoliterature, one would be hard-pressed to miss this quintessential direction of literary modernity (albeit one among many others). Certainly, the traditional religious creeds are now well-aware of the convergence and competition manifest in contemporary secular "art-spirituality" generally. (As the American poet Charles Wright succinctly puts it in a poem: "It's a kind of believing without belief we believe in.") Be all that as it may, the premise that modernity has witnessed the partial collapse of traditional religious transcendence, with a consequent deep secularisation of the cultural space inhabited by the arts, noticeable especially in art and music histories, is a staple of the modern social sciences, themselves a product of the secularisation of society they describe.

Apropos religion, there is, of course, a vast sociological literature. One of the *ur*-texts is Weber's *The Sociology of Religion* (1922), whose systematic and comparative overview of the evolution of relations between religion, the socio-economic order and culture generally proved extraordinarily fertile for subsequent scholars. Much of his comparative terminology concerning religious origins, classes, beliefs, ethics, types of consciousness, the major modern faiths, and so forth, remains in popular play, most famously the idea of "the Protestant ethic" and its relation to "the spirit of capitalism" (the subject of another book of 1930). The study of religion is so capacious, in fact, that it has several distinct professional specializations – the sociology of religion, the history of religion, and comparative religion – each with its own structure of focus and methodological approach. And it could hardly be otherwise: the great faiths, those ancient globalisations, and indeed what preceded them in the religion of remote antiquity, have utterly shaped and reshaped the globe, and (obvious to add) continue to do so.

Yet who could doubt that the worldview of "secular modernity" (to use a social-science shorthand) is now rivalling, indeed partly erasing and eclipsing, those antique religious globalisations? Viewed in this way, the role of the "high arts" in secular society, of which "literature" is perhaps the most globally emblematic as a modern "formation," assumes a key sociological frame. Something in our *fin-de-siècle*, turn-of-the-century air suggests a rising participation in, and diffusion of, self-consciously "artistic" activity. A recent research study, surveying the skewered logorrhoea of Internet keywords, floated this nonetheless plausible generalization. (Of course, in earlier tribal, peasant or traditional pre-modern societies, much cognate activity would not have been understood as "artistic," as such, in the modern sense). Apart from the infinite variety of practitioners working within the legacy of a genre or combination of genres, there is even a uniquely contemporary type of Artist, of no fixed genre-abode, a kind of conceptual Johnny Appleseed (at best) or leaden pseudo-clerisy (at worst), moving about the land, on whatever strength of self-designation, planting acts and works of Art in the soil of every conceivable medium, milieu, or venue. That the tone of conceptualism echoes earlier hieratic castes is all too obvious, if seldom remarked upon, though it would be rich material to any thorough-going sociology of "art-spirituality."

All the more striking and extraordinary, then, that no comparable sociology has attached itself, in proportionately lesser terms, to the study of literature. So far as this writer is aware, no self-consciously discrete field of sociological study – of the sophistication and coherence of Weber, Durkheim, Eliade and their successors on religion – exists for the evolution of relations between literature, the social-economic order and culture generally. True, there can be no shortage of writers, scholars, incidental passages, articles, studies, academic territories or preoccupations, and so on, that partly occupy, co-opt or enlighten the parameters of a potential literary sociology. Certain fields of study – orality and literacy studies, Homeric and biblical commentaries, the history of reading, reader-response and media theory, deconstruction, literary history – impinge on it strongly. But even in comparison with the anthropological tenor of ethno-musicology, or whole reams of art history (the role of patronage, the riddle of a style's relation to period), literary sociology of any sort is decidedly thin on the ground. For instance, in one recent classic on the sociology of culture, *Culture* (1981), by the polymathic Raymond Williams, literature only features very sketchily in its groundbreaking exploration of modern cultural "formations."

In short, properly speaking, a more-than-piecemeal, more-than-heavily anecdotal sociology of literature does not yet exist; nor can it, as more than a half-glimpsed field of real importance, without a full muster of interpreters, whether writerly or scholarly.

The absence of a genuine sociology of literature might come as something of a surprise. After all, what we call "literature" could appear as nothing more than the aggregate of literary writers and literary scholars, and surely the theme of literature as a sociological "formation" would be of considerable self-reflexive interest to some of its practitioners? Literary texts are everywhere scrutinized for their social and historical meanings, so why not the social constitution of the literary world itself, it structures and processes, its rules and codes? More generally, why should we assume, in the general absence of this cohesive discourse on context, that the literary formation is immune, as if hermetically and aesthetically sealed, against wider developments in the culture, such as rampant commodification, corporate control, pervasive "status anxiety," the influence of media-born(e) image, mass-marketing's engineering of culture, *et cetera?*

Perhaps it would be too much to speak of a taboo regarding this line of thinking in the literary world, rather than simply *de facto* disinterest, or reticence, when it comes to scrutinizing its own relations with wider society. It might be observed, indeed, that such disinclination is a prime point of initial sociological interest. Clearly, on a broad canvas, issues of collective psychology, professional *esprit de corps* and self-interest are central and inescapable. How these pan out across the major general division of the literary world – between authors of primary texts (the "creative" writers of poetry, fiction, drama and so on: "primary" because they serve as the subject of other writings) and those of secondary texts (critics, scholars, academics, journalists: "secondary" because they presuppose the primary genres in any discussion of them) – will, of course, differ considerably in emphasis.

For primary writers, there is little enough incentive to look closely at the sociological dimension of their genres. On the one hand, amongst those who are celebrated by the reputation-making of period relations, there is, moreover, a distinct *disincentive*. Reputation and, even more, fame tend, of course, to engender a public mystique, and even for its beneficiaries the processes involved can seem somewhat opaque and mysterious. Published investigation of those processes could only lessen that mystique and that mystery, to no obvious benefit of reputation, which seems, unusually, the precise intent of Eliot's reflection above. It is often noticeable, though, that a certain class of very great writer, like a certain class of mystic, possesses a modesty equal to the achievement in question. (In contrast, like Big Oil or Big Pharma, Big Ego in things literary should prompt, *ipso facto*, vigilance and scepticism: not only as a potential flaw-in-the-glass, but for the note of sociological naiveté, or hubris.)

On the other hand, among those who are less in receipt of the reputation-making of period relations, especially if they aspire in that direction (as pretty much all dedicated writers do, to some degree), there can be many politic reasons to steer clear of the sociological tack. They may fear queering their own reputational pitch, being seen to suffer from sour grapes, or showing insufficient deference to the reigning tastes, elders and peers, or model of career progress. Alternatively, they can default from period reputation-making to the rum sociology of downtrodden literary clichés, seeing conspiracies in established tastes, finding self-protective refuge in the sects and sub-groups of overblown style- or identity-shibboleths, and the like. Either way, the inhibitions are many and varied. But what lingers in the mind is the degree to which this sociological reticence covers primary writers *across the board*. A kind of hegemony seems to be at work, not so much as a set of ideas, as an absence of a crucial perspective.

For the authors of secondary texts, much in the grain of literary criticism militates against the sociology of literature. Literary critics are trained in the internal dynamics of the textual and their spot-in-time relations with the world, rather than the generalized pattern-making characteristic of the social sciences, which involve a very different intellectual orientation. For all its scholarship, the literary Academy is also prone to cultural lag, specialist focus, control-freak partisanship of schools and tastes, the career dynamics of intellectual fashion, and all-sorts theoretical interactions. Not being practising literary artists themselves, many academics evince a displacement of aspiration *manqué* towards a chosen few, attaching their critical dinghy to the great schooners of the period or recent past, forgetting that each one began in some unknown boatyard. In particular, what a certain type of go-along academic and critic hears, like the drone of an interfering static, is the powerful seduction of reputation alone, as a strategy of self-validation for a lack of certainty or competence in inner judgement. All this suggests that the literary Academy is ill-suited to the sociological approach, whilst itself being an extraordinarily fertile field for its application.

A culminating difficulty concerns the sheer conceptual complexity involved in any sociology of literature. Delineating the interplay between the realm of ideas and the realm of social events is a notoriously intractable problem in both philosophy and the social sciences. Vulgar Marxism, with its ludicrous talk of "superstructure and base," helped discredit last century's attempt and, *faute de mieux*, nothing much has stepped into the sociological gap. At the same time, for the literary artist no less than the religious believer, there is a natural reluctance to see the essential interiority of one's practice subjected to an outward gloss, as if flipped inside out, like the torque of a Mobius strip.

But whatever the concatenation of reasons, the absence of a literary sociology assumes its full importance when one considers the actual scale of "the literary world," broadly conceived. It is now, indubitably, a massive global "formation". It comprises a sizeable literary sector of publishing and the book trade, and associated extensive publicity and PR; has a huge presence in the university (both academics and creative writers); and supports a vast array of periodicals and e-journals of all stripes. It commands considerable presence in both the print and electronic media. Increasingly in recent decades, it has seen the flourishing of its own autonomous milieus of readings, festivals, prizes, arts organizations, newsletters, and writers' groups. To say nothing of the truly epic horde of practitioners who might be said to belong to "the literary world," however tightly its definition is drawn. If much of this is easily seen in detail, the totality of the literary formation, and the way its structures relate to the wider culture, are far less forthcoming.

Consider, for instance, the impact of global population on the contemporary literary formation, a curiously unexplored topic. When Eliot published *The Waste Land* (1922), world population stood at about one billion; it is now nearly six times that. The global publishing world alone, let's reflect, has grown exponentially. That must mean a bigger literary world in every sense: more authors and reading, more reputation and reception. At the same time, the field to be filtered in English alone goes beyond anyone's ken. Is this the sociological background to the Western explosion of high-class publishing filler, or to the widespread feeling that an unprecedented mass-media machine is constantly encroaching on the older prerogatives of "a whole culture, the literate one" (Michael Hamburger, p. 223 of this issue)?

To paraphrase the Slovenian philosopher Slavoj Zizek, hegemony can only fully exist in the absence of any consciousness of it. That is to say, hegemony reverts to mere empowerment, whether of an idea or social relation (typically both together), as soon as its invisible dominion is unmasked by a countervailing awareness. Given its colossal expansion, something of this truth must increasingly haunt the contemporary literary formation. For it is an egregiously unreflective view to identify "literature" with simply what we cherish in it: talent, achievement, craft, knowledge, significance, wisdom, and other incarnations or intimations of "permanent value." The landscape of the literary world is also, pre-eminently, a kind of barony of power relations in the widest sense. The vassals of this barony – or series of national baronies – include status, hierarchy, reputation-making, canon-formation, the manipulation of taste, money, celebrity, utility, and a host of other extra-literary pawns. Power exists in all human relations: it must therefore in "literature."

But, lo and behold, it is precisely at this sociological point that the knight-errant Eliot arrives before the portcullis, and the Uncertainty Principle of Literature enforces its full quantum power. On the critical watchtowers, the archers and gatekeepers are amazed. For history is tough, and its future use of any present "literature," in the sense of the writing itself, will constitute the natural selection of posterity. To a high degree, its criteria of "permanent value" may not be ours. Above all, posterity has literally no use for the period relations of extra-literary power, no interest in the barony of careerism, of success *per se*. Rather, as literary history endlessly confirms, the landscape of the contemporary barony will be dissolved and reassembled by posterity's understanding and estimation of the writing alone.

Thus the literary barony finds its hegemony and mystique eroded by sociological consciousness, since the latter is really a kind of critical foreshadowing, or inkling in the present, of the future arrival of the Uncertainty Principle. A *sociology of literature* matters, precisely, because it clarifies the period relations of the literary world, and so correlates them to the historical long-term, to how and why "permanent value" survives. In this sense, the sociological approach to literature assumes that "permanent value" is far too important a question to be left to the Newtonian relations of the literary world.

The literary world, or "literary scene," might be analogised to just that: a "scene-structure," in the dramatic sense. Only the writing itself, its coming-into-being, exists off stage, in the cloud-chamber of the imagination. Once a text is put forward for public consumption, it finds itself, willy-nilly, in the middle of a scene-structure of publishers, publications, editors, critics, academics, readerships, *et al*. Each part of the structure has its own internal dynamics, interactions with the other parts, and structural debts to the audience beyond the proscenium, from the front stalls to the gods. All the aforementioned vassals are on stage in full force.

As a result, the established literary stage-plan tends by its nature to be unwelcoming to the literary iconoclast, unconventional troubadour, or independent spirit wandering through the props and backdrops without due homage to the existing period scenery. And for the same reason, much of the actually-existing literary world inculcates subtle forms of stylistic or intellectual imitation, a kind of artistic socialization, which often proves, in the long-term, highly inimical to "permanent value". Many other such general literary tendencies, or "rules" (exceptions taken as read), can be clarified and coordinated by the quanta of sociology, which is one reason why so many of

Eliot's essays have weathered so well.

Our contemporary literary proscenium is, of course, the culmination of a long historical evolution, reaching back beyond even Guttenberg, to the medieval and classical manuscript cultures. But it has also tremendously altered, as previously suggested, over the past century. What, then, are the most salient territories of this change brought up to our own day?

In his fascinating personal reflection on over sixty years of British literary life, "Afterthoughts on the Mug's Game" (p. 220), Michael Hamburger enumerates a number of major sociological "tendencies," including the change he deems the greatest:

> The most drastic change since T.S. Eliot's lifetime is the degree to which electronic media have replaced the written word – and the spoken word, for that matter, where it has become a gabble in competition with the abbreviati of those media, because time is money. The effect of this on generations that receive most of their knowledge not from immediate experience, nor from original texts, but from the television screen or from computers is so blatant that it needs no elaboration here. Its effect on poetry – its reception, if not its production – is not only a psychic one, in that more and more young people have grown incapable of sustained attention to anything whatever, other than images and sounds projected for instant consumption or instant distraction – distraction from what?, one begins to ask oneself – but a practical one that extends to the non-career ... Needless to add, the question of "permanent value" does not arise at all in media that are random, insatiably and indigestibly cumulative, conveying information about this, that and anything without end.

In terms of the literary "scene-structure," in other words, this represents the creation of a whole new space, not so much another façade or drop-curtain, but a veritable orchestra-pit, whose warm-up sounds and little airs continually fill the entire proscenium.

Self-evidently, older writers have the benefit of the long-term view. Maybe this is why another long-standing British literary figure, Al Alvarez, says something cognate in *The Writer's Voice* (2005), remarking on how the cult of personality and "being known" in the literary world has mushroomed since the Beats. Is there some subterranean link between this general growth in publicity and the thesis of the philosopher Alain de Botton that the advanced Western economies are now characterized by an unique superaddition of "status anxiety"? Or a further link with the impression, impossible to suppress, that the same societies somehow privilege doing good in the sense of feeling good, rather than doing good in the sense of actual justice, as Live Eight so perfectly illustrated?

Though the ubiquity of these abbreviati (electronic, PR, print) now makes them so obvious as to be nearly invisible, the consequences for the literary world of what might be dubbed the Big Media Machine are enormous and undeniable. Cumulatively, Big Publicity has engineered a shift in the centre of literary gravity, a displacement of critical locus away from the prerogatives and standards of a traditionally more independent literary territory – that is, towards itself, and an attendant culture of celebrity, both of which cascade into literary milieus massaged and messaged by said Media Machine, such as culture shows on television and radio, the programming of readings and festivals, and even newspaper review pages that still evince literate resistance. Thus the orchestra-pit, rather than the proscenium, becomes increasingly the place where reputation *appears* to exist, and indeed, in a certain momentary and carnivalesque sense, *does* exist; though in the long-term, owing to an application of the Uncertainty Principle – the inevitable divergence of outer and inner judgements – this media masque does not constitute final proof of the enduring criterion, the writing itself.

A barometer of this particular change in the literary weather is the way fiction is becoming highly porous to media figures. Journalists, politicians, performing artists and others from the celebrity limelight appear able to land publishing contacts for novels of largely minimum literary value. Still more revealing than the amounts offered or the attention generated is the degree to which these "media writers" assume instant personal-creative access to a genre with a long imaginative history in which, for the most part, they have read little or nothing. However, as Joseph Brodsky once remarked, all original styles tend to begin in either emulating or contradicting preceding ones. Is it possible to emulate or contradict No Style, without falling into clichés of the day? No doubt some of these limelight novels will be competent, and occasionally distinguished, and a few may even attain to "permanent value".

Still, it would be quite dishonest not to finger the essentially profit-driven circularity of such "media fiction": prior reputation begets contract begets ready-made reception begets bank balance. It is certain that many of these novels, had they not come, for instance, from a Taoiseach's daughter, would be languishing in the slush-piles of the publishers now touting them as the *dernier cri*. As pieces of writing, most are, in truth, cultural zeroes in an accountant's ledger, the slick penny-dreadfuls of our media-driven period.

Fiction, though, is merely the exemplar of a publishing strategy now gaining momentum. Such celebrity writing trades on the traditional prestige of style-labels like "fiction," but is essentially outside the loop of the literary world in the sense of having any meaningful connection with "a whole culture, the literate one, in which literacy was bound up with an awareness of the past – a selected past, therefore 'elitist' in the terminology of those who confuse class resentments with considerations of quality" (Hamburger, p. 223). In a classic social manoeuvre of the sort that enraged Enlightenment *philosophes*, celebrity authors parley their pre-existing "status" into further cultural preferment. Hype and short-termism are revealed as a social tautology in which quack "literary" products, like the "Shakespeare" performance in *Huckleberry Finn*, are transformed into profits. Top-down publicity from publishers which issue both serious and populist titles further enforces the Pavlovian confusion of taste.

To the Big Media Machine must be added, then, the question of money. Or rather, as it is specific to our day, the rise and rise of Big Money publishing corporations in the larger advanced economies. (In many smaller polities or languages, such as in Eastern Europe, the role of Big Money in the publishing world is negligible in comparison.) Just as the salaries of footballers have soared in recent decades, so the sums available for, say, quality Anglophone fiction are beyond comparison with a half-century ago (not to mention those available for "popular" fiction). The novelist Arundhati Roy, who sold her Indian-published novel *The God of Small Things* (1997) to Harper Collins, subsequently reflected on the illustrative significance of the vast sums available even for serious literary fiction. Roy is also an environmental activist of considerable courage, and she likened the money of Western publishing to a huge pipeline circulating the globe, its spigots suddenly bestowing wealth on a selected few, in a way that parallels the general inequity of the global system. Surely the admixture of a certain proportion of literary success with an enormous financial reward must have some influence on the whole tenor of the literary culture, over time at least?

The alternative, no creative or ethical influence at all, seems an impossible idea. Every honest writer understands the role of position, context, life-situation in one's writing – in a word, *perspective*. That changes in circumstances or sensibility entailed by the altered perspectives of success can sometimes re-route the subsequent work is a commonplace in all the arts. Without succumbing to the notion that there was ever a golden age of frugal literary economics, or that individuals are social puppets, one is entitled to wonder about where the Great Western Pipeline will progressively take the literary formation, and indeed the culture as a whole. Even after the success of his late political novels, Orwell (1903-1950) could never have expected recompense equivalent to that on offer today.

Big Media and Big Money: these are the dynamic duo of our literary Gotham, mirroring the symbiosis of mass production and mass marketing that drives industrial society as a whole. (In purely economic terms, a *best seller* is simply this symbiosis writ large). The overall result in the larger advanced economies of Europe and North America is the existence of a highly centripetal literary economics. At its heart, the "corporate monoculture," as it might be called, is a sort of dominant bloc, or evolving formation, consisting of all sorts of interlocking factors: the agent/publisher/media apparatus of publicity; prizes and awards; editorial insider-trading; literary group-think; imprint prestige; fashions of collective taste; historical style-tones – to name some of those most subject to anecdotal comment. But to the extent that taste is "embedded" in any one particular socio-economic milieu, literary history leaves no doubt that its discriminations become highly unreliable. Although capacious in many senses, the literary monoculture of large publishing corporations is unquestionably such a milieu, shaped by a host of bottomline considerations.

That much of the best writing in all genres still issues from this centripetal economics is not in question. But social formations are never fixed. The Big Money Medici might become less capacious and enlightened, the corporate environment cheaper and nastier. (Let us call it the Dan Brown future). In two or three generations of executives, it could have spawned a bastard progeny, even less interested in "a whole culture, the literate one," even more prone to the logic of media circularity. There is good reason to think that the advanced economies are on the precipitous cusp of globalization's downward spiral.

As the case of "media fiction" demonstrates, there is already an expanding Soviet-style disconnect between image and actuality, a Potemkin village of mass-marketing behind which there is simply empty literary space. Into the gap between achievement and preferment can flow all manner of extra-literary power under corporate patronage. And due to the confusion between this media simulacrum and a literary world still partly defined by things like Eliot's "permanent value," "an awareness of the past," or "considerations of quality," the potential for further monoculture – at the expense of a healthy and independent ecology for what we cherish in literature – remains great indeed.

Chris Agee

The second half of this essay, "On the Sociology of Reputation," will appear in the next issue of this journal (Vol 3, No 2: "The Media").

IN PRAISE OF SPACE

Tim Robinson

The step that isn't there.

THE IRISH PAGES ANNUAL LECTURE
(2004)

I can begin by reporting to you what is at the centre of the Earth, as I visited it, or a place that felt close to it, not long ago. In a vast cavern there is an altar, or a tomb. Circular, some fifteen feet across, six or seven feet high, dome-shaped, smooth, ivory-coloured. An umbilicus, perhaps. The way into this place is in the French Pyrenees. A river, the Ariège, has cut a deep cliff-sided valley almost from the crest of the mountain range down towards Toulouse; a train takes you up this valley, stopping at the medieval towns and villages of the ancient duchy of Foix. I got off at Tarascon, and the next day, a Sunday, walked a few miles further up the valley to visit a cave said to be the largest in Europe, La Grotte de Lombrives. I had expected there to be a queue for the guided tour, but as it happened no-one else turned up, and so the guide, a girl university student on a holiday job, led me up the zigzag trail to the portal of the cave, which was like a great quarry sunk obliquely into the hillside. These caves of the Pyrenees were bored through the limestone by underground rivers long before the present-day valleys such as that of the Ariège were carved into the layers of rock, so that in places one can see a cave opening high on a cliff face, and a matching opening on the opposing cliff, and imagine that long-gone river thundering across the sky above the road and the railway. At the bottom of the cave entrance my guide unlocked a door in a metal barrier and clicked on a light switch. We were in a tunnel the size of a subway. We literally trotted along it, over a water-worn rock floor, for nearly a mile, pausing to admire strange formations of drip-stone and to glance down dark branching perspectives. The girl recited the legends of the cave to me with great earnestness. The last great cavern looked like a cathedral that had been turned inside out. Almost invisible in the gloom far above us its steeple hung from the ceiling, an immense stalactite, and on the floor below it stood the answering stalagmite, formed of the calcium carbonate deposited by drop after drop of water over unimaginable silent millennia. This is the altar and tomb or omphalos that felt to me at that moment to mark the very centre of the Earth. It is indeed an altar; Roman cult objects have been found around it. And it is a tomb, that of Pyrène, the goddess of these mountains. My guide told me that Hercules once had a love-affair with the princess Pyrène, but then was called away to his labours. Finding herself pregnant, she fled her father's court. When she was attacked by a bear she cried out, and Hercules heard her and came running from the other end of the Mediterranean, but was to late to save her. So he carried her body deep into the mountain, and buried it here.

Just beyond this tomb one comes to the shore of an underground lake. The smooth motionless water surface disappears in darkness under a lip of rock. It reminded me strongly of the most exciting day of my early childhood, during a family holiday in Wales, when my father led us through woods to a water-filled cave entrance. We skirted round an adder sunning itself on the woodland path, we heard woodpeckers high in the foliage, we wondered at the great horizontal blade of water entering into the rock, an Excalibur. The outing so excited me that I could hardly wait to get home again so that I could start a diary. And the reason I wanted to record that day was to give myself the pleasure of quoting lines my father often intoned, from Coleridge:

Where Alph, the sacred river, ran
Through caverns measureless to man,
D
o
w
n
to a sunless sea.

All that, the first stirrings of my longing to be an artist, a writer, to travel and see strange places, came back to me there, standing by the shore of that cave-lake in the Pyrenees. I flung a coin as far as I could into the still water, and made a wish, the usual one, and then we turned and trotted back through the grey tunnels to where the sunlit vegetation was a dazzling glory of gold and green in the cave portal.

That excursion was dreamlike: the companionship of the light-footed girl, the sudden recursion to a crucial moment of childhood, the visit to the dark truth at the centre of things. The whole escapade was so far outside the run of my life that I haven't been able to make use of it till now, when I'm looking for the overall theme of the various works and quirks that have possessed me, and trying to capture ideas partially expressed in my writings and artworks here and there, hoping to give them some objective validity and interpersonal standing. Space – the theme could scarcely be more general and omnipresent. Spaces and their echoes, to bring it nearer to experience. That journey into the Earth took place in an echoing space – and in recounting it I've deliberately set the echoes flying, mythological, literary, oneiric, sexual. But echoes need solids to rebound from. We construct places, the sociologists and ethnologists tell us; we build them out of memories and habits and language, we summon them into existence or out of oblivion with the magic power of a placename. But underlying places are spaces, which have their own mode of being, quite independent of our wills and desires. And underlying all particular spaces is Space, the sort and shape of Space this Universe exists in and perhaps one should say consists of.

Before I turn to that all-embracing mystery, Space itself, I'll look briefly at other terrestrial situations that induce what I call topographical experiences, experiences essentially dependent on the general topographical features of one's surroundings rather than the particulars of a place; I'll be autobiographical in conveying them – the pressures of memory give me access to them in their richness and fullness, and keep me from straying into the schematic - but everyone will recognise them. The cave is one such generality; whatever its dimensions and dangers and legends, being in a cave is to be in an emptiness surrounded by impenetrable solidity. The opposite of that would be standing on a small moon, a solid volume surrounded by emptiness, and the nearest any of us is likely to get to that is being on a small island. Life has been extraordinarily generous in giving me the time to explore a small island to my heart's content, an island of exceptional and strange beauty, of interest from the points of view of all the -ologies – it has even had a professional ontologist visiting it regularly, using it as an example in his philosophical texts. The ontology, the mode of being, of this island is as clear as that of a crystal: its solidity is palpable underfoot, its surrounding emptiness of sky and sea is visible and sensible from all points; it is a foothold of habitability in the midst of a rampant wilderness.

The island in question is the largest of the three Aran Islands, vulgarly called Inishmore; its real name is Árainn. It is remarkable for its fissured limestone formations, its flora and birdlife, its prehistory and history, language and folk-ways, its iconic standing in the ideology of the Irish cultural revival. All these factors are heightened by its being an island, visibly a totality. One can walk round it in a day – it would be a gruelling walk and I've never done it, but the islanders used to do so at Easter, praying at all the churches and holy wells on the way. So the shape of the island ordains the sacred rite of its own celebration. Perhaps the possibility of walking round it in a day defines the concept of a small island. It took me 282 pages to describe walking round Árainn, but the act itself, the completion of that act, the closing of the circuit, on any small island, imposes a shape on the experience, so that later on the shape may be all that one remembers of it.

These great structural generalities of the island experience are presented in unforgiving harshness by Árainn. Being so much a bare stone, hiding nothing of its outlines in shadowy woods or soft hedgerows, sometimes apparently threatened with annihilation by the turbulent vastness of waves and clouds all around it, Árainn insists on its island status. But it also exemplifies in the highest degree a contrary feature of landscape. Caught up by that dramatic and dramatising maritime light, interrogated by it, Árainn is revealed as being composed of tiny details, as precise and as intricated as the works of an old watch. As a visual artist it had failed me to express this dual nature of landscape, the construction of its grandest unities out of incalculably many and various flecks and dots; I had to turn to prose, and lengthy works, to begin to model this relationship of overarching simplicities and inexhaustible minutiae in the structure of landscapes, which is a mere hint and forerunner of the interdependence of cosmos and microcosm I'll mention later on. Each one of the little fields of Árainn is so precisely defined by walls of equally individuated shapes of stone, that it offers itself as a place, as full of its own past as a room in a long-lived-in house. It probably has a name; many of the fields of Aran do. If you do not know its name it regards you mutely, asking you to find it out, or invent it. Placenames are the lingua franca of the zone of reality I have called the echosphere, the regime of echoes in which we address the habitable world and imagine that it addresses us in return. Since I've written so obsessively about it elsewhere I'll not go into the role of placenames now, except to say that the placename can be the incantation that turns a tract of space, a mere location, into a place. Also, and perhaps too extravagantly, that the totality of the world's placenames constitutes humanity's full address; if we knew it we would know where we are.

"Location" – perhaps that is a concept one could usefully situate between those of space and place. I'm thinking of the word as used by a traffic-controller or a bomb targeter. The location of such and such a person or vehicle is so many miles north of some fixed reference point, or at so many degrees of latitude and longitude; a location is a position defined in terms of some accepted or enforced system of coordinates, such as the National Grid. The location of the cottage we rented for many years in Árainn is L 85 11, the L identifying the 100-km square in which it lies, and the numbers being eastings and northings within that square. Nothing could be more remote from the well-worn and well-loved oddities of our home, with its creaky staircase and dented brass doorknobs, than that bleak alpha-numerical formula. But since in those years I was engaged in making a map of the Aran Islands, including our dwelling, the lines of the National Grid, running exactly north-south and east-west, became familiar and useful presences to me; I could feel where they cut across the islands. Our garden path ran nearly but not exactly north-south, and when we were at work in the garden, its principal directions were those of the path and of the earth ridges at right angles to the path. Recently I turned up a ragged and rain-spotted leaf of paper on which I'd kept a sketch-map record of the vegetables we grew in those ridges – cabbages, courgettes, chives – those thirty years ago. I made a print out of it by superimposing it on a representation of the lines of the National Grid, the blotchy old diagram of the garden being set squarely in the picture space, and the rigidly precise grid therefore thrown slightly askew – to celebrate perhaps a little victory of the homely, the beloved and the memorious, over the totalitarianism of location.

From the back of our house in Árainn we could look out onto flat sheets of limestone, riven by parallel fissures, which receded from us in a vanishing perspective. If we followed this direction written in stone, crossing a few low field walls on the way, we would come to an edge, where the ground stops as it were between one step and the next, and the Atlantic Ocean lies far below. This brings me abruptly to my next topographical sensation, that of the clifftop. Abstract away all the sensory embellishments, the crash and surge and glimmer and glamour of the ocean, the trillion madly semaphoring wavelets, the screech of the falcon, the salty breeze. Here you are; one step more is death; it's a horror and a temptation. Metaphysical parallels are diagrammatically clear. The firm ground ends in thin air; reality exists in unmediated neighbourliness with the void. If you shout here, no echo comes back. There is a projecting spur of rock like a diving-board on the lip of Árainn's highest cliff, which is of all parts of the island the remotest from villages and paths. It is called An Troigh Mhairbh, or An Troigh Mharfach, the deadly step. At the end of it is 'the step that isn't there,' according to island and Connemara folklore about it. Now, in the old days a few islanders used to make a living by killing cormorants and guillemots on the ledges of these three-hundred-foot cliffs. At dusk the village lads would lower the *ailleadóir* or cliffman on a rope, and leave him crouched in on a ledge overnight. When the birds had come in to roost he would creep along and strangle them silently one by one with his bare hands. At dawn the lads would come over to the cliffs again and haul him up, rigidified into his kneeling position by cold and cramp. The cliffman's experiences at night on the cliff face must have been of shamanic intensity. One of the last of them, when he was too old to go down the cliff any more, used to come across the island to An Troigh Mharfach, and walk out to stand on the very end of it. To look down would have been fatal; his visual field must have been filled with nothingness, scored across by the horizon. Imagine him standing there; imagine the purity, the utter solitude, of his experience.

Now, let me idealise this stance, alone in thin air, even further, and make it the point of entrance into an abstract geometrical space. Let the old man's footprint on the rock shrink to a point, a nothing; let the thin air all around him become thinner and thinner, infinitely thin. Abolish gravity, and impenetrability, and all traces of the physical. How many angels can dance on the head of a pin? We smile at this example of medieval theological riddling, but in fact it's a step in a profound investigation of the concept of space. The head of a pin is not quite nothing; it has a tiny area. Could a million angels dance on it? A millionth of that area is also not quite nothing; therefore a million angels could dance on that millionth part of the head of a pin; angels are able to do these things. And so on, indefinitely. Is space infinitely divisible? What we are conceiving here is a space of a particular sort, a continuum. The ancient Greeks saw the pitfalls of such an idea; the paradoxes of Zeno such as the riddle of Achilles and the tortoise raised doubts about the continuum that were only laid to rest by Dedekind and Cantor and other great mathematicians of the late nineteenth century. So we will take it that the space I am now going to juggle in is coherent. It is the space of Euclid's geometry. It has the familiar three dimensions; one can associate every point in it with three numbers, its coordinates, just as every point on a map can be specified by two numbers read off a grid. It is hospitable to the cube, the tetrahedron and the other platonic solids, also to the perfect sphere. One can step from point to point of it, with the freedom of an angel. It is very beautiful in a crystalline way; some find it chilling. I'll essay a demonstration in it. Imagine a plane, a flat surface, cutting through this space; imagine another plane meeting it; the two intersect along a straight line, as two pages of a book meet in the spine. In general, two planes intersect in a line. Now let a third plane cut across them both; all three meet in a single point, as for instance in a room two walls and the ceiling meet in a single corner. Two planes meet in a line; three planes meet in a point. Those are the most basic of facts about this space.

Now imagine a sphere, and a plane cutting through it; the cross-section of the sphere is a circle. So one way to specify a circle, in this three-dimensional space, would be to say it lies on such and such a sphere and on such and such a plane. Suppose I balance a sphere in one hand, and a sphere in the other, and bring them together until they interpenetrate. The intersection is a circle; one can imagine a plane slicing through the spheres, with this circle lying on it. So if two spheres intersect there is a plane through their intersection; I'll call it their common plane.

Let there be two circles in space. (Let there be! This space is responsive to godlike or angelic gestures!). Two circles may or may not be interlinked. If each circle is defined by the sphere and the plane it lies on, what are the conditions, in terms of these spheres and planes, for the circles to be interlinked? Obviously if the two spheres are far apart the circles on them cannot be interlinked; so one condition is that the spheres intersect and have a common plane. Also, if the circles lie on parts of the spheres not involved in this intersection, they will not be interlinked; each circle has to penetrate into the sphere of the other circle. Therefore the planes on which they lie cut through the common plane of the spheres, within the circle of intersection. Finally, if those two planes' intersections with the common plane do not themselves cross within the circle of intersection, the two circles will not be interlinked. Hence, the circles will be interlinked if and only if their planes and the common plane of their spheres all meet at a point inside the spheres.*

Perhaps it is over-ambitious of me to try to demonstrate this by waving my hands. But let it stand before you as an elegant result, for I remember it fondly from my days as a maths student. I love mathematics and in particular geometry, but I was never good enough at it to call myself a mathematician; nowadays I "dabble" in mathematics as people used to "dabble" in the occult. The theorem I have described in fact marks one of the few occasions I showed a flicker of geometrical wit, and by great good fortune it came to me in the final exam, and made the difference between me getting a second-class degree and the third I probably deserved. One of the questions on the paper was about whether on not two given circles were interlinked; I had no idea how to proceed, until I suddenly saw this crystalline configuration of the two spheres and the two planes meeting the common plane crosswise, which reduced the question to a bit of calculation - which I probably got wrong; but never mind, I'd intuited its geometrical essence. So this thoroughly abstract space can be a space of experience; one can make forays into it and come back with truths about it. And insofar as it is also a representation of real space, the actual space we inhabit, those truths also hold for actual spherical objects, plane surfaces and the like.

But then, perfect spheres, platonic solids and the other glorious denizens of Euclidean geometry are rare in reality and especially in our mundane and sublunary world. Even circles are not common. Almost the only circular forms we see in nature are the sun, the arc of the rainbow, and the iris of the eye, and it is remarkable that the geometry of the rainbow is such that the centre of the rainbow's arc, and the eye that sees it, and the sun that causes it, all lie on a straight line; i.e. the rainbow is a most striking intrusion of pure geometry into its usually highly ungeometrical setting of clouds and rain showers and sea and mountains. These non-platonic forms seem to demand quite another sort of geometry for their spatial description. As a child I used to love exploring the outline of cumulus clouds, and imagine myself clambering up their silvery flanks; I was disappointed on my first aeroplane flight by the way these delicate and precise margins dissolved into mist as one approached. Even today it is a compulsion with me, when looking idly at a tree or a hawthorn bush, to begin tracing its outline with my eye, trying to see as many as possible of its salients and reentrants, down to the limits of vision. At first glance a cumulus cloud is a great dome; at second glance one notes that it is composed of a number of lesser domes fused together; on a third glance, each of these lesser domes is seen to comprise several even smaller ones, and so on for several steps, before the eye become confused and weary. Similarly for the madly zigzagging silhouette of a hawthorn bush against a winter sky. At each of these levels, a unit of some sort, when closely examined, is revealed to be made up of smaller units which themselves have the same general structure as the whole. Euclid's geometry is not going to help us describe or conceptualise or idealise such forms, which are those omnipresent in nature. But in the 60s of the last century the mathematician Benoit Mandelbrot developed a sort of geometry more relevant to these natural forms. He began by studying the geometry of coastlines, and found that it was impossible to assign a length to, for instance, the west coast of Ireland. We can say that from Malin Head to Mizen Head is about 300 miles as the cormorant flies, but if we take into account just the major bays and headlands the distance along the coast is much longer than that, and if we take notice of every little creek visible on large-scale maps the result is hugely bigger again. The finer the detail one includes in the measurement, the larger the result – and to stop taking account of detail, at any level down to the molecular, is to impose an arbitrary and unnatural limitation. Hence the length of a coastline tends toward the infinite, the more closely one attends to its particulars. Also, a map of any typical stretch of it looks more or less the same, in its general characteristics, as the map of the whole of it, or of a tiny portion of it; as Mandelbrot put it, these forms are self-similar, over a huge range of scales. Shown a map of an unfamiliar coastline, one could not tell whether it represented the side of a continent or the side of a rockpool. So, here are two features of natural forms indescribable in the terms of ordinary geometry; they are self-similar, and their lengths or areas increase indefinitely the more carefully they are measured. Mandelbrot thus inaugurated what he called the geometry of "fractals," the geometry of these fractured shapes. He and other pioneers of this geometry have concocted idealised versions of such natural forms; a simple one is a symmetrical shape called from its inventor the Koch snowflake. It could be the idealisation of the hawthorn bush I mentioned earlier. Start with a triangle, a three-pointed shape, add an extra point to the middle of each of its sides to make a six-pointed star, add smaller points to each of its twelve straight edges; it now has twenty-four straight edges, add a point to each of them... and so on until the end of time. Consider it done, as by an angel: what we have is a closed outline that is longer than any line, and yet does not fill in an area; it isn't one-dimensional and it isn't two-dimensional, but something in between. Mandelbrot shows how to redefine the concept of dimensions, so that we can say that this particular Koch snowflake has a dimensionality of a little more than one and a quarter, that a typical coastline has a dimensionality of 1·2, that the surface of a cumulus cloud or of a forest might have a dimensionality of two and a bit. Is this weird new geometry adequate to the richness of nature? Not by an infinity of infinities! Let us return to the real world.

One spring day a few years ago the British Lichen Society paid a visit to Connemara. Because of the purity of our air, and the damp, mild Atlantic weather, Connemara's lichens are outstanding in variety and luxuriance; there are about 700 species, and the commoner sorts occur in unusual numbers. I know nothing about lichens, so I joined the Society on an excursion to the richest of Connemara's lichen sites, Derryclare Wood, a small forest largely of oaks, growing in a hollow along a lake shore on the sheltery side of the Twelve Pins. Since this forest is mentioned in visitors' accounts from the 1830s it is mainly aboriginal, and many of its trees are huge and ancient. I was almost the last of the group to reach the wood as I'd lingered to help an elderly person over some wire fences, and when at last I reached the edge of the forest and looked down into the first of its shadowy glades, expecting to see the others rambling around it, I was surprised to find it silent and empty. Then I realised that the lichenologists were all there, each one standing stock still with his or her forehead close to a treetrunk, examining specimens through magnifying glasses. The sight was for a moment magical, a folktale of disappearance into an enchanted forest. Then someone stirred, and the spell was broken. Several of them showed me what they had been looking at: diamond dusted velvets and plushes, patches of grey silk scrawled with maps of unknown lands; groups of minute disc-shaped structures like jam tarts for a fairy tea-party. Then, as the lichenologists dispersed on their separate specialist quests, I too wandered through the wood, scrambling over tree branches that seemed weighted down by great beards of moss, revelling in the neo-natal dampness of the April morning and the flux of growth around me. The complexity of such spaces enthrals me, the density of form, the interleaving and mutual penetration of endless fractal hierarchies. If I have spent more days than I like to confess in the hazel scrub of the Burren and the furzy fields of Connemara, the search for archaeological remains or rare plants or blackberries was only an excuse; the repeated but never stale revelation of the richness of being was my occasional reward. My raptures in thickets have been as near to a *participation mystique*, a dissolution of self, in the plenum of nature as I would care to go. In the wood of Derryclare, the lichenologists' magnifying glasses pointed my attention towards the ever smaller, the undersides of leaves, the channels in bark, the crusts of lichens that grow on other lichens. I came home with pages of indecipherable notes and the Latin names of species, useless to me now as a source of information but resonant with the hum of proliferating forms.

I'll pursue this line of thought further down the scale of distances, as it soon brings us to realms that baffle the imagination and so are rarely visited by consciousness, unlike interstellar cosmic space. After all, every time we step out onto a lawn on a starry night, or see the full moon sail free of a cloud's edge, we involuntarily draw a breath of cosmic space. The old cliffman standing on the end of the Deadly Step enjoyed a space of thin air that, one could say, abuts immediately onto cosmic space. So I shall say no more about that, and instead look briefly and cautiously into microcosmic space. And I mean real space, not the abstract space of geometry we entered earlier. In that purely conceptual space of the continuum, it is easily said that millions of millions of angels can dance on the head of a pin; but is real space infinitely subdivisible in this way? It seems not. There is a smallest length. It is called the Planck length, after its discoverer, Max Planck, one of the intellectual giants who gave us quantum theory early in the last century. Planck arrived at an estimate of this length by considering three important constants of physical theory. As we all vaguely know, an unavoidable uncertainty creeps into all measurements down at the subatomic scale; Planck's constant is a measure of that uncertainty; it is minute. And then as well as the three known forces of atomic theory there is gravity, an all-pervasive but very weak force; another constant, Newton's constant, is a measure of its strength. Finally there is the speed of light, a fundamental universal constant. Now Planck by a bit of arithmetical fiddling around with these three constants calculated a length, below which the very concept of length breaks down. To say that this length is very small is the hugest of understatements. It is about a thousandth part of a millionth part of a millionth part of a millionth part of a millionth part of a millionth part of a centimetre. How small is that, compared to other small things? The following mental process might be called "walking the Planck". An atom is very much smaller than the smallest fleck of dust one can see, say a million times smaller; an atomic nucleus is thousands of times smaller than an atom; an atomic particle such as a proton is thousands of times smaller than a nucleus, and at that stage one has hardly begun to get down to the Planck length, which is a million million billion times smaller than a proton. Beyond that is – what? The old cliffman, if I shrank him down until he could stand on the end of the Planck length, would call it "the step that isn't there." The theories propounded over the last decade or two about the structure of space and time at that level are so bizarre, ferociously abstruse, various and fleeting, that I cannot begin to describe them; in any case I do not understand their technicalities and my only access to them is through the exciting metaphors employed in semi-popular expositions written by some great scientists working in this field: Michio Kaku, Brian Greene and others. Below the Planck length, it seems, lies primordial chaos, momentary eruptions of enormous energies, fissures in spacetime itself, tunnels linking our universe to countless others, six or seven new dimensions rolled up so tight that all the power our civilisation could ever generate would be unable to penetrate them. The "quantum foam," as one of the cosmologists has called it, in which these hypothetical, not to say improbable, forms disport themselves is the sea our cliffman would look down into from his perch on the Planck length. All that exists emerges from this sea, for good or ill. And that includes us, which is why, without claiming to make it comprehensible, I want to bring the existence of this appalling and entrancing sea that underlies space – not an *Urgrund*, a sound foundation, but an endlessly creative uncertainty – into our consciousness.

I have said nothing about the ill arising from space in this talk – nothing about space as trap, torture chamber, tomb, the space we cannot get out of because we are it. That would be more than sufficient unto some other day. For now I'll end with a mere mention of one of the speculations of contemporary quantum mechanics: string theory, the suggestion that the ultimate constituents of matter are loops and strands, of Planck-length minuteness, whose various modes of vibration and rotation give rise to all the properties of elementary particles, and so of all of us. The Pythagorean dream of mathematical and musical harmonies underlying all nature, including our nature, has been redreamed.

I began at the centre of the earth, or near it; and it is right that as inhabitants and dependents of the globe we should carry its centre in our consciousnesses, even if in the vastness of the galaxies it is but a local and provincial centre. I ended with the end of space, which, mysteriously, lies at the centre of everywhere. Space: for its oddities, incomprehensibilities and glories, I commend it. And I commend you to it.

* (When delivering this talk I indicated planes and spheres by gestures. For the printed version I tried to draw a diagram of the construction described, but ran into problems, the reason for which is interesting. A sweeping cutting motion of the hand can install a plane in someone's imagination, and this plane can be of indefinite or infinite extent, totally bisecting space but not obscuring whatever lies on either side of it. But to show such a plane in a drawing is impossible; one has to indicate it by showing the boundary of a part of it, such as a rectangle. That burdens the diagram with four lines per plane, that is, twelve lines for the three planes of the construction, none of which have any role in the proof, not to mention the three lines in which the planes intersect in pairs. The result is baffling to the eye even before one has tried to indicate by shading, etc., which parts of which planes lie behind other planes, from the point of view of the reader. None of these disadvantages arise with a purely mental construction. I was pleased to be reminded that the geometrical imagination far exceeds the visual imagination.)

The Second Annual Irish Pages Annual Lecture was delivered on 5 November, 2004 as part of The Belfast Festival at Queen's. The invited speaker alternates between an Irish and overseas contributor to an earlier issue of the journal.

Tim Robinson, cartographer, naturalist and writer, lives in Roundstone, Co Galway. His two-volume Stones of Aran *(The Lilliput Press) appeared in 1986 and 1995. His most recent book is a collection of fictions,* Tales and Imaginings *(The Lilliput Press, 2002). The first volume of his Connemara trilogy will be published by Penguin Ireland in 2006.*

FIVE POEMS

Seamus Heaney

HOME FIRES

1 *A Scuttle for Dorothy Wordsworth*

Dorothy young, jig-jigging her iron shovel,
Barracking a pile of lumpy coals
Carted up by one Thomas Ashburner,
Her toothache so ablaze the carter's name
Goes unremarked as every jolt and jag
Backstabs her through her wrist-bone, neck-bone, jaw-bone.

Dorothy old, doting at the flicker
In a brass companion set, all the companions
Gone or let go, their footballs on the road
Unlistened for, that sounded once as plump
As the dropping shut of the flap-board scuttle-lid
The minute she'd stacked the grate for their arrival.

2 *A Stove Lid for W.H. Auden*

The mass and majesty of this world, all
That carries weight and always weighs the same ...

The mass and majesty of this world I bring you
In the small compass of a cast-iron stove lid.
I was the youngster in a Fair Isle jersey
Who loved a lifter made of stainless steel,
The way its stub claw found its clink-fast hold,
The fit and weight and danger as it bore
The red hot solidus to one side of the stove
For the fire-fanged maw of the fire-box to be stoked,
Then the gnashing bucket stowed.
So one more time
I tote it, hell-mouth stopper, flat-earth disc,
And replace it safely. Wherefore rake and rattle,
Watch sparks die in the ashpit, poke again,
Think of dark matter in the starlit coalhouse.

STERN

in memory of Ted Hughes

"And what was it like," I asked him,
"Meeting Eliot?"
"When he looked at you,"
He said, "it was like standing on a quay
Watching as the prow of *The Queen Mary*
Came towards you, very slowly."

Now it seems
I'm standing on a pierhead watching him
All the while watching me as he rows out
And a wooden end-stopped stern
Labours and shimmers and dips,
Making no real headway.

PIT-STOP NEAR CASTLETOWN

Robert Lowell's incomparable high
What? Pitched voice? Destiny? Mania and style?
Under midnight beeches billowing darkly

We made our pit-stop about half a mile
From the demesne gates, pissing like men
Together and apart against the wall.

"A large, undangerous drinker," he called Larkin,
But not undangerous he. His forthright stroan
Went glittering like a foil, Marlovian,

As shoulder to shoulder, before we got back in
He intimated he'd probably not be
Returning to Caroline. The headlights shone

Level into a whipped-up swirl and eddy
Of roadside leaves – "like ghosts from an enchanter
Fleeing!" O irremediably

Literary, first-striking Cal, two months later
At your memorial arranged by Caroline
I said that the cabbie who'd ferried you to the door

And waited to be paid already had been
Paid in the coin of language, that East River was Styx
And so on, rising to the occasion

Perhaps too highly. Mary McCarthy's verdict –
As reported back to me, at any rate –
Took my rhetoric and wrung its neck:

"The biggest cover-up since Watergate."

SAW MUSIC

Barrie Cooke has started to paint "godbeams,"
Vents of brightness that make the light of heaven
Look like stretched sheets of fluted silk or rayon
In an old style draper's window. Airslides, scrims

And scumble. Columnar sift. But his actual palette
Is ever sludge and smudge, as if a shower
Made puddles on the spirit's winnowing floor.
What it reminds me of is a wet night

In Belfast, around Christmas, when the man
Who played the saw inside the draughty doorway
Of a downtown shop, in light from a display
Of tinselled stuffs and sleigh bells blinking neon,

Started to draw his bow across the blade.
The stainless steel was oiled or vaselined,
The saw stood upside down and his left hand
Pressed light or heavy as the tune required

Flop-wobble grace note or high banshee whine.
Rain spat upon his threadbare gaberdine,
Into his cap where the occasional tossed coin
Basked on damp lining, the raindrops glittering

Like the saw's greased teeth his bow caressed and crossed
Back across unharmed, the bellied metal
Dirtily lit as the nightsky over Belfast
Shining up out of an oily puddle.

AFTER DARK

"After dark"
should mean it's morning
but this the language
disallows.

Homunculus
from the age of blackout,
skylight pupil
reflected back

off night-backed glass,
I watch my words
and a starship-placid,
lit-up dredger

anchored out
near the Bailey Light.
It pinpoints dark.
It doesn't blink.

A star-wars satellite,
crossing, does,
time and again.
I jot and husband.

Seamus Heaney was awarded the Nobel Prize for Literature in 1995. His most recent volume is Finders Keepers: Selected Prose 1971-2001 *(Faber, 2002).*

CÚIG DÁNTA

Cathal Ó Searcaigh

AINGEAL AN TSOLAIS

Nuair a shiúil tú thar an tairseach, a ghile an tsolais,
bhí aoibh áthais ar bhéal an dorais. Léim
an chathaoir mhór as a seasamh tromaosta
agus thug sí trí choiscéim scléipe i d'araicis.
Nuair a labhair tú, a bhéal milis an aoibhnis,
chlaon na cupáin a gcuid cluasa cré i do threo
agus d'éist go beo le gach glinnfhocal binn a shnigh
ó do theangaidh. Chuir tú aoibh go dtí na cluasa orthu, a chroí.

Nuair a bhain tú díot do chuid éadaigh, a ghile na háilleachta,
thit na scátháin i ngrá leat láithreach. Bhí siad splanctha
i do dhiaidh ag iarraidh tú a mhuirniú is a shealbhú go buan.
Nuair a sheas tú ag déanamh aoibhnis i gcroílár
an urláir bhíog an sú i bhféitheoga an tseanchachtais
agus tháinig seasamh ann arís le tréan macnais.
Nuair a shín tú siar, nuair a chlutharaigh tú, a chroí,
i measc na bpiliúr, lig an leabaidh osna pléisiúir.

Nuair a ghealaigh tú chugam ón leabaidh, las
a raibh istigh ionam, a raibh faram. D'aoibhnigh
an chuimhne ba dólasaí i m'aigne. Tháinig ruaithne
ghréine i ngnúis liath an lae agus luisne ghlas
i gcraobh lom an gheimhridh le taobh na fuinneoige.
Nuair a d'fháisc tú do lámha thart orm go bláfar
chumhraigh mo chraiceann agus tháinig bláth bán na féithleoige
i réim ar mo mhéara. Líon an seomra le cumhracht an tsamhraidh.

Nuair a mhuirnigh tú mé le barróga. le póga, d'éirigh
buíoga an chinn óir ina scaotha glémhaiseacha ó mhuine
mo ghabhail agus mheidhrigh an leabaidh, lena gcuid spraoi.
Nuair a dhlúthaigh tú liom, a chroí, do theangaidh ghréine
ag taitneamh i mo bhéal, ag soilsiú i mo shúile, ag grianú mo bhrollaigh,
bhorr an solas i ngach ball de mo bhallaibh ionas go raibh mo chorp
go huile ina ghile glanghuthach, a theanga aibí féin faighte
go groí ag gach féith agus géag; ag gach cuisle agus cnámh.

Nuair a shín tú síos liom, a ghile na ngrást, cneas
le cneas, nuair a líon tú mé le gríos glórmhar do ghrá,
phléasc mé ina spré solais, las mé ina splanc thintrí.
An uair sin, mé lán de bhruth na huilechumhachta
dá dtiocfadh Dia chugat, a aingeal an tsolais, do chiontú
lena Chré cúng crábhaidh as a bheith sáite ionamsa
i bhfeis mais an áthais, d'fhógróinn go híochtar Ifrinn é.
Ansin loiscfinn é. loiscfinn é, a chroí, i gcaorthine teasbhaigh.

SEARC

1

Deora drúchta
Ag aoibhniú chugam go líofa
Ó bhláth buí an tsiolastraigh
maidin i Mín a' Leá.

Ar a laghad
d'fhan siadsan níos faide
ná tusa, a ghrá, a d'imigh
gan oiread is focal a rá.

2

Inniu tá gaoth ghéar
an Earraigh ag scaipeadh
bláthanna na gcrann silíní
anseo i mo gharraí.

Níor chuir an scaradh leatsa
a oiread cumhaidh orm, a chroí,
agus a chuir scaradh na mbláth
inniu orm sa gharraí.

3

Am marbh na hoíche –
splanc thoirní
ag lasadh an tí seo
ina mairim go huaigneach.

Dá dtiocfá arís chugam,
tusa, atá lán de theaspach
na hóige. Dá dtiocfá arís,
a chroí, go fiú an fad sin …

SÉASÚIR

1

Anseo agus caoinsolas na Bealtaine
ag lasadh na maidine, tá
domhan drúchta os mo choinne
ag spréacharnaigh go lách.

Tá seilide ag sní fríd an fhéar
ag biorú a chuid aeróga go tapaidh,
ag fiosrú a bhealaigh. De réir
mar atá sé ag gabháil chun tosaigh,

rian glé fágtha ina dhiaidh aige, tá
sé ag mothú an tsaoil atá lena mhian
go fiafraitheach, fiosrach, foighneach,
ag déanamh a chuid bheag féin go dian

de dhán seo na dea-mhaidine. A airdeallaí
bheag na n-adharc, a theagmhálaí an drúchta,
is grástúil raon mo shúl, mo shamhlaíochta
a bheith i bpáirtíocht leatsa sa tsolas

an mhaidin ghlasuaine seo sa tsíoraíocht.

2

Tá na fámairí imithe i gcéin;
an chuach agus an traonach
imithe ó dheas chuig an teas
ach tá tusa anseo go fóill
a spigeoigín, ag déanamh ceoil
ar thairseach lom na Nollag.

Tá mise agus tusa linn féin
ag canadh go teasaí, amhráin bheaga bhroinndearga uchtaigh
a choinníonn caor sa chroí
i ndúlaíocht seo an gheimhridh.

CLAOCHLÓ

Nuair a chan tú m'ainm, a chroí.
i nbogosnaí an cheana, ní m'ainmse a bhí
ann níos mó ach bláth an tsiolastraigh
ag buíú i mbéal na gaoithe.

Nuair a theann tú mé le do chroí
i mbarróg fhiáin an ghrá, chan mise a bhí
ann níos mó ach sruthán samhraidh
ag brúchtadh is ag briseadh bruaigh.

CLAOCHLÚ

An seo tírdhreach m'anama atáthar a thaibhreamh
i bhfís domh anois tráthnóna beag seo an tsolais bháin;
an dúiche rúin seo atáthar a nochtadh as na duibheagáin?
Nuair a fhéachaim síos tchím iad go soiléir ag soilsiú
ansiúd san áit is uaigní i mo chroí, san áit is sia i mo stuaim,
na garbhchríocha ina mbeathaím, ina mbuanaím.

Anois is léir domh tailte fáin ar a bhfásann go binn
focla fraoigh, ina gcluinim comhrá ciúin cíbligh.
I dtobainne, tá mé ag sní thar teorainn mo chraicinn,
ag síneadh i gcóngar mo chinn, ag fairsingiú

i mbithchríoch m'inchinne. Anois tá talamh
míntírithe mo chéille ag gabháil i bhfiántas, ag tiontú
arís ar a dhúchas cíbe. Mar chomharthaí feasa
tá giolcaí ina gcolgsheasamh ar chosáin mo chuimhne, mo
threorú isteach i ríocht rúin no chinniúna ...
Ní mise an mise a bhíodh ar eolas agaibh, a chairde cléibhe.
Nuair a labhrann sibh liom anois ní mise a thugann freagra
ach a bhfuil ionam de theangaidh bheo an tsléibhe.
Labhraim libh i gcumhracht raideoige, i bport na fuiseoige.
Anois le teacht na hoíche, lorgaigí san áit ina raibh mé ...

ceannabháin ag séideadh i mbéal na gaoithe.

ANGEL OF LIGHT

When you step over the threshold, bearer of light,
the mouth of the door grins so widely
and the old armchair leaps from its straight-
backed stance and dances three reel steps towards you.
When words fall from those honeyed lips
cups stretch their delph ears forward, listening closely
to every sweet sound, every luscious vowel
rolling off your tongue. You give them delight.

When you take off your clothes, bearer of beauty,
the gilded mirror is blinded, and if you step away
it flashes and sparkles to make you turn and stay.
Waiting there, causing wonder from the centre of the room
makes the sap in the veins of the withered cactus stream
until it's standing upright and wanton again.
When you lie down, my love, and make yourself comfy
the fluffed pillows sigh softly with pleasure.

When you smile towards me from my lonely bed
all that's in me brightens and every painful memory
slowly gladdens in my soul. A cheerful presence
dawns on the day's grey face and a spring green
blooms on my garden's wintered trees.
When you touch me so tenderly my skin sweetens
and yellow blossoms flower from these fingertips.
The room fills with the full fragrance of summer.

When you caress me with hugs and kisses
a bunting of yellowhammer rises
from the thicket of my crotch, and the lumpy mattress
frolics with your fun. When we embrace,
your sunny tongue lightens my mouth, brightens
my eyes, softens my weary chest. Sunlight flows
through each inch of my body and those low tones
reach every sinew, every limb, every tired bone.

When you lie with me, bearer of grace, flesh
against flesh, filling me with the heated embers
of glorious loving, I explode in lightning bolts,
sparkle in fireworks until I'm filled with the power
of omnipotence. If God should appear, angel of light,

carrying the conviction of the Creed, spurning our delight
in our deeds, I'd send him to the depths of Hell.
There he'd burn, he'd burn, my love, in raging ardour.

LOVE

1

Droplets of dew
with polished smiles
linger on the wild-yellow iris
morning in Mín a' Leá.

At least, my love,
they stay longer
than you, who wandered away
without the trace of a word.

2

Today a slicing
spring wind scatters
blossoms from the cherry tree
here in my garden.

Your scarpering off
didn't cause as much sadness, darling,
as the scattering of these flowers
today in the garden.

3

In the dead of night
thunderbolts
light up this house
where I live in loneliness.

If you came back to me,
you, full of the vigour
of youth, if you came back,
my love, even for the flash of a lightning bolt ...

Translated, from the Irish, by Denise Blake.

SEASONS

1

Here, and the gentle light of May
lighting the morning, there's
a world of dewfall before me
sparkling kindly.

There's a snail creeping through the grass
pointing his aerials quickly,
asking directions. As
he heads forward,

a bright trail behind him, he's
feeling the world of his delight
questingly, curiously, patiently,
busy at his own little part

of this good morning's poem. Little
horned vigilante, little dewy go-between,
full of grace is the path of my eye, of my imagination
to be joined with you in the light

this bright green morning in eternity.

2

The summer visitors are long gone;
the cuckoo and the corncrake
flown south to the heat
but you're still here
little robin, making music
on the bare threshold of Christmas.

Me and you on our own
singing lustily the little
red-breasted songs of hope
that keep fire in the heart
in these depths of winter.

METAMORPHOSIS

When you sang my name, darling,
in the soft sighs of love, it wasn't mine
any longer but the iris flower
yellowing in the teeth of the wind.

When you held me to your heart
in a wild hug of love, it wasn't me
any more but a summer stream
leaping up and bursting its banks.

METAMORPHOSING

Is this the landscape of my soul that shows itself
in a vision on this late evening of the white light –
this secret country appearing from the dark abysses?
When I look down, I see them shining yonder, clearly
in my heart's loneliest place, place furthest from prudence,
the highlands where I feed, where I multiply.

Now I see fallow lands where grow sweet-sounding
heathery words, where I hear quiet sedgy conversation.
Suddenly, I'm filtering beyond the limits of my skin,
stretching to easy reach of my head, spreading out
in the eternal boundary of my mind. Now the reclaimed
land of my senses is running wild, turning
again to her own sedgy places. Like beacons
the reeds are upright on the paths of my memory,
guiding me into the secret kingdom of my destiny …
I'm not the *I* you used to know, dearest friends.
When you speak to me now, it's not the *I* that answers
but all that's in me of the living mountain language.
I speak to you in sweet bog-myrtle scent, in the lark's tune.
Now, with the dark coming down, look for me where I was …

bog-cotton blowing in the teeth of the wind.

Translated, from the Irish, by the Managing Editor and Editor.

Cathal Ó Searcaigh is the Irish Language Editor of this journal. His most recent volumes are Séal Neipeal *(Cló Iar-Chonnachta, 2004), an account of his time in Nepal, and* By the Hearth at Mín a' Leá *(Arc, 2005), a selection of English translations of his poetry.*

THE ROOM

William Trevor

A soreness.

"Do you know why you are doing this?" he asked, and Katherine hesitated, then shook her head, although she did know.

Nine years had almost healed a soreness, each day made a little easier, until the balm of work was taken from her and in her scratchy idleness the healing ceased. She was here because of that, there was no other reason she could think of, but she didn't say it.

"And you?" she asked instead.

He was forthcoming, or sounded so; he had been attracted by her at a time when he'd brought loneliness upon himself by quarrelling once too often with the wife who had borne his children and had cared for him.

"I'm sorry about the room," he said.

His belongings were piled up, books and cardboard boxes, suitcases open, not yet unpacked. A word processor had not been plugged in, its flexes trailing on the floor. Clothes on hangers cluttered the back of the door, an anatomical study of an elephant decorated one of the walls, with arrows indicating where certain organs were beneath the leathery skin. This grey picture wasn't his, he'd said when Katherine had asked; it came with the room, which was all he had been able to find in a hurry. A sink was in the same corner as a wash-basin, an electric kettle and a gas-ring on a shelf, a green plastic curtain not drawn across.

"It's all a bit more special now that you're here," he said.

When she got up to put on her clothes, Katherine could tell he didn't want her to go. Yet he, not she, was the one who had to; she could have stayed all afternoon. Buttoning a sleeve of her dress, she remarked that at least she knew now what it felt like to deceive.

"What it had felt like for Phair," she said.

She pulled the edge of the curtain back a little more so that the light fell more directly on the room's single looking-glass. She tidied her hair, still brown, no grey in it yet. Her mother's hadn't gone grey at all, and her grandmother's only when she was very old, which was something Katherine hoped she wouldn't have to be; she was forty-seven now. Her dark eyes gazed back at her from her reflection, her lipstick smudged, an emptiness in her features that had not to do with the need to renew her make-up. Her beauty was ebbing – but slowly, and there was beauty left.

"You were curious about that?" he asked. "Deception?"

"Yes, I was curious."

"And shall you be again?"

Still settling the disturbances in her face, Katherine didn't answer at once. Then she said:

"If you would like me to."

Outside, the afternoon was warm, the street where the room was – above a betting shop – seemed brighter and more gracious than Katherine had noticed when she'd walked the length of it earlier. There was an afternoon tranquillity about it in spite of shops and cars. The tables were unoccupied outside the Prince and Dog, hanging baskets of petunias on either side of its regal figure and a Dalmatian with a foot raised. There was a Costa Coffee next to a Pret à Manger and Katherine crossed to it. "*Latte*," she ordered from the girls who were operating the Gaggia machines and picked out a florentine from the glass case on the counter while she waited for it.

She hardly knew the man she'd slept with. He'd danced with her at a party she'd gone to alone, and then he'd danced with her again, holding her closer, asking her name and giving his. Phair didn't accompany her to parties these days and she didn't go often herself. But she'd known what she intended, going to this one.

The few tables were all taken. She found a stool at the bar that ran along one of the walls. *Teenagers' Curfew!* a headline in someone else's evening paper protested, a note of indignation implied, and for a few moments she wondered what all that was about and then lost interest.

Phair would be quietly at his desk, in shirtsleeves, the blue flecked shirt she'd ironed the day before yesterday, his crinkly, gingerish hair as it had been that morning when he left the house, his agreeable smile welcoming anyone who approached him. In spite of what had happened nine years ago, Phair had not been made redundant, that useful euphemism for being sacked. That he'd been kept on was a tribute to his success in the past, and of course it wasn't done to destroy a man when he was down. "We should go away," she'd said and remembered saying it now, but he hadn't wanted to, because running away was something that wasn't done either. He would have called it running away, in fact he had.

This evening he would tell her about his day, and she would say about hers and would have to lie. And in turn they'd listen while she brought various dishes to the dining-table, and he would pour her wine. None for himself because he didn't drink any more, unless someone pressed him and then only in order not to seem ungracious. "My marriage is breaking up," the man who'd made love to her in his temporary accommodation had confided when, as strangers, they had danced together. "And yours?" he'd asked, and she'd hesitated and then said no, not breaking up. There'd never been talk of that. And when they danced the second time, after they'd had a drink together and then a few more, he asked her if she had children and she said she hadn't. That she was not able to had been known before the marriage and then became part of it – as her employment at the Charterhouse Institute had been until six weeks ago, when the Institute had decided to close itself down.

"Idleness is upsetting," she had said while they danced and had asked the man who held her closer now if he had ever heard of Sharon Ritchie. People often thought they hadn't and then remembered. He shook his head and the name was still unfamiliar to him when she told him why it might not have been. "Sharon Ritchie was murdered," she'd said, and wouldn't have without the few drinks. "My husband was accused."

She blew on the surface of her coffee but it was still too hot. She tipped sugar out of its paper spill into her teaspoon and watched the sugar darkening when the coffee soaked it. She loved the taste of that, as much a pleasure as anything there'd been this afternoon. "Oh, suffocated," she'd said when she had been asked how the person called Sharon Ritchie had died. "She was suffocated with a cushion." Sharon Ritchie had had a squalid life, living grandly at a good address, visited by many men.

Katherine sat a while longer, staring at the crumbs of her florentine, her coffee drunk. "We live with it," she had said when they left the party together, he to return to the wife he didn't get on with, she to the husband whose deceiving of her had ended with a death. Fascinated by what still was lived with, an hour ago in the room that was his temporary accommodation her afternoon lover had wanted to know everything.

On the Tube she kept seeing the room: the picture of the elephant, the suitcases, the trailing flexes, the clothes on the back of the door. Their voices echoed, his curiosity, her evasions and then telling a little more because, after all, she owed him something. "He paid her with a cheque once, oh ages ago. That was how they brought him into things. And when they talked to the old woman in the flat across the landing from Sharon Ritchie's she recognised him in the photograph she was shown. Oh yes, we live with it."

Her ticket wouldn't operate the turnstile when she tried to leave the Tube station and she remembered that she had guessed how much the fare should be and must have got it wrong. The Indian who was there to deal with such errors was inclined to be severe. Her journey had been different earlier, she tried to explain; she'd got things muddled. "Well, these things happen," the Indian said and she realised his severity had not been meant. When she smiled he didn't notice. This is his way too, she thought.

She bought two chicken breasts, free-range, organic; and courgettes and Medjool dates. She hadn't made a list as she usually did, and wondered if this had to do with the kind of afternoon it had been and thought it probably had. She tried to remember which breakfast cereals needed to be replenished but couldn't. And then remembered Normandy butter, and Braeburns and tomatoes. It was just before five o'clock when she let herself into the flat. The telephone was ringing and Phair said he'd be a bit late, not by much, maybe twenty minutes. She ran a bath.

The tips of his fingers stroked the arm that was close to him. He said he thought he loved her. Katherine shook her head.

"Tell me," he said.

"I have, though."

He didn't press it. They lay in silence for a while. Then Katherine said:

"I love him more, now that I feel so sorry for him too. He pitied me when I knew I was to be deprived of children we both wanted. Love makes the most of pity, or pity does of love, I don't know which. It hardly matters."

She told him more, and realised she wanted to, which she hadn't known before. When the two policemen had come in the early morning she had not been dressed. Phair was making coffee. "Phair Alexander Warburton," one of them had said. She'd heard him from the bedroom, her bath water still gurgling out. She'd thought they'd come to report a death, as policemen sometimes have to, her mother's or Phair's aunt's, his next of kin. When she went downstairs they were talking about the death of someone whose name she did not know. "Who?" she asked and the taller of the two policemen said Sharon Ritchie and Phair said nothing. "Your husband has explained," the other man said, "that you didn't know a Miss Ritchie." A Thursday night, the eighth, two weeks ago, they said: what time – could she remember – had her husband come in?

She'd faltered, lost in all this. "But who's this person? Why are you here?" And the taller policemen said there were a few loose ends. "Sit down, madam," his colleague put in and she was asked again what time her husband had come in. The usual misery on the Northern Line, he'd said that night, the Thursday before last. He'd given up on it, as everyone else was doing, then hadn't been able to get a taxi because of the rain. "You remember, madam?" the taller policemen prompted, and something made her say the usual time. She couldn't think; she couldn't because she was trying to remember if Phair had ever mentioned Sharon Ritchie. "Your husband visited Miss Ritchie," the same policeman said and the other man's pager sounded and he took it to the window, turning his back to them. "No, we're talking to him now," he mumbled into it, keeping his voice low but she could hear. "Your husband has explained it was the day before," his colleague said. "And earlier – in his lunchtime – that his last visit to Miss Ritchie was."

Katherine wanted to stay where she was now. She wanted to sleep, to be aware of the man she did not know well beside her, to have him waiting for her when she woke up. Because of the heat-wave that had begun a week ago, he had turned the air-conditioning on, an old fashioned contraption at the window.

"I have to go," he said.

"Of course. I won't be long."

Below them, another horse-race had come to its exciting stage, the commentary faintly reaching them as they dressed. They went together down uncarpeted narrow stairs past the open door of the betting shop.

"Shall you come again?" he asked.

"Yes."

And they arranged an afternoon, ten days away because he could not always just walk out of the office where he worked.

"Don't let me talk about it," she said before they parted. "Don't ask, don't let me tell you."

"If you don't want to."

"It's all so done with. And it's a bore for you, or will be soon."

He began to say it wasn't, that that was what the trouble was. She knew he began to say it because she could see it in his face before he changed his mind. And of course he was right; he wasn't a fool. Curiosity couldn't be just stifled.

They didn't embrace before he hurried off, for they had done all that. When she watched him go it felt like a habit already, and she wondered as she crossed the street to the Costa café if, with repetition, her afternoons here would acquire some variation of the order and patterns of the work she missed so. "Oh, none at all, " she'd said when she had been asked if there were prospects yet of something else. She had not said it was unlikely that again she'd make her morning journey across London, skilful in the over-crowded Tube stations, squeezing on to trains that were crowded also. Unlikely that there'd be, somewhere, her own small office again, her position of importance, and generous colleagues who made up for a bleakness and kept at bay its ghosts. She hadn't known until Phair said, not long ago, that routine, for him, often felt like an antidote to dementia.

She should not have told so much this afternoon, Katherine said to herself, sitting where she had sat before. She had never, to anyone else, told anything at all, or talked about what had happened to people who knew. I am unsettled, she thought and, outside, rain came suddenly, with distant thunder, ending the heat that had become excessive.

When she'd finished her coffee Katherine didn't leave the café, because she didn't have an umbrella. There had been rain that night too. Rain came into it because the elderly women in the flat had looked out when it was just beginning, the six o'clock news on the radio just beginning too. The woman had remembered that earlier she had passed the wide-open window half a flight down the communal stairway and went immediately to close it before, yet again, the carpet was drenched. It was while she was doing so that she heard the downstairs hall door opening and footsteps beginning on the stairs. When she reached her own door the man had reached the landing. "No, I never thought anything untoward," she had later stated apparently. Not anything untoward about the girl who occupied the flat across the landing, about the men who came visiting her. "I didn't pry," she said. She had turned round when she'd opened her front door and had caught a glimpse of the man who'd come that night. She'd seen him before, the way he stood waiting for the girl to let him in, his clothes, his hair, even his footfall on the stairs: there was no doubt at all.

The café filled up, the doorway crowded with people sheltering, others queuing at the counter. Katherine heard the staccato summons of her mobile phone, a sound she hated, although originally she'd chosen it herself. A voice that might have been a child's said something she couldn't understand and then repeated it, and then the line went dead. So many voices were like a child's these days, she thought, returning the phone to her handbag. "A fashion, that baby telephone voice, " Phair had said. "Odd as it might seem."

She nibbled the edge of her florentine, then opened the spill of sugar. The light outside had darkened and now was brightening again. The people in the doorway began to move away. It had rained all night the other time.

"Nothing again?" Phair always enquired when he came in. He was concerned about what had been so arbitrarily and unexpectedly imposed upon her, had once or twice brought back hearsay of vacancies. But even at his most solicitous, and his gentlest, he had himself to think about. It was worse for Phair and always would be, that stood to reason.

Her mobile telephone rang again and his voice said that in his lunch hour he'd brought asparagus because he'd noticed it on a stall, looking good and not expensive. They'd mentioned asparagus yesterday, realising it was the season: she would have bought some if he hadn't rung. "On the way out of the cinema," she said, having already said that she'd just seen *La Strada* again. He'd tried for her an hour ago, he said, but her phone had been switched off. "Well yes, of course," he said.

Six months was the length of an affair that took place because something else was wrong: knowing more about all this than Katherine did, the man she met in the afternoons said that. And, as if he had always been aware that he would, when a little longer than six months had passed he returned to his wife. Since then, he had retained the room while this reunion settled – or perhaps in case it didn't – but his belongings were no longer there. The room looked bigger, yet dingier, without them.

"Why do you love your husband, Katherine? After all this – what he has put you through?"

"No one can answer that."

"You hide from one another, you and he."

"Yes."

"Are you afraid, Katherine?"

"Yes. Both of us are afraid. We dream of her, we see her dead. And we know in the morning if the other one has. We know and do not say."

"You shouldn't be afraid."

They did not ever argue in the room, not even mildly, but disagreed and left it there. Or failed to understand and left that too. Katherine did not ask if a marriage could be shored up while this room was still theirs for a purpose. Her casual lover did not press her to reveal what she still withheld.

"I can't imagine him," he said, but Katherine did not attempt to describe her husband, only commented that his first name suited him. A family name, she said.

"You're fairly remarkable, you know. To love so deeply."

"And yet I'm here."

"Perhaps I mean that."

"More often than not, people don't know why they do things."

"I envy your seriousness. It's that I'd love you for."

Once, when again he had to go, she stayed behind. He was in a hurry that day; she wasn't quite ready. "Just bang the door," he said.

She listened to his footsteps clattering on the boards of the stairs and was reminded of the old woman saying she had recognised Phair's. Phair's lawyer would have asked in court if she was certain about that and would have wondered how she could be, since to have heard them on previous occasions she would each time have had to be on the landing, which surely was unlikely. He would have suggested that she appeared to spend more time on the communal landing than in her flat. He would have wondered that a passing stranger would have left behind so clear an impression of his features, since any encounter there had been would have lasted hardly more than an instant.

Alone in the room, not wanting to leave it yet, Katherine crept back into the bed she'd left only minutes ago. She pulled the bedclothes up although it wasn't cold. The window curtains hadn't been drawn back and she was glad they hadn't. "I didn't much care for that girl," Phair said when the two policemen had gone. "But I was fond of her in a different kind of way. I have to say that, Katherine. I'm sorry." He had brought her coffee and made her sit there, where she was. Some men were like that, he said. "We only talked. She told me things." A girl like that took chances every time she answered her doorbell, he said; and when he cried Katherine knew it was for the girl, not for himself. "Oh yes, I understand," she said. "Of course I do." A sleazy relationship with a classy tart was what she understood, as he had understood when she told him she could not have children, when he'd said it didn't matter, although she knew it did. "I've risked what was precious," he whispered in his shame, and then confessed that deceiving her had been an excitement too. Risk came into it in all sorts of ways; risk was part of it, the secrecy of concealment, stealth. And risk had claimed its due.

The same policemen came back later. "You're sure about that detail, madam?" they asked and afterwards, countless times, asked her that again, repeating the date and hearing her repeat that ten to seven was the usual time. Phair hadn't wanted to know – and didn't still – why she had answered as she had, why she continued to confirm that he'd returned ninety minutes sooner than he had. She couldn't have told him why, except to say that instinct answered for her, as bewilderment and confusion had when first she'd heard the question. She might have said she knew him as intimately as she knew herself, that it was impossible to imagine his taking the life of a girl no matter what his relationship with her had been. There was – she would have said if she'd been asked – the pain of that, of their being together, he and the girl, even if only for conversation. "You quarrelled, sir?" the tall policeman enquired. You could see there'd been a quarrel, he insisted, no way you could say there hadn't been a disagreement that got out of hand. But Phair was not the quarrelling sort. He shook his head. In all his answers he hadn't disputed much except responsibility for the death, had not denied he'd been a visitor to the flat, gave details as he remembered them, accepted that his fingerprints were there, while they accepted nothing. "You're sure, madam?" they asked again, and her instinct hardened, touched with apprehension, even though their implications were ridiculous. Yes, she was sure, she said. They said their spiel and then arrested him.

Katherine slept and when she woke did not know where she was. But only minutes had passed, less than ten. She washed at the basin in the corner, and slowly dressed. When he was taken from her, in custody until the trial's outcome, it was suggested at the Institute that they could manage without her for a while. "No, no, " she had insisted. "I would rather come." And in the hiatus that followed – long and silent – she had not known that doubt began to spread in the frail memory of the elderly woman who in time would be called upon to testify to her statements on oath. She had not known that beneath the weight of importance the old women was no longer certain that the man she'd seen on that wet evening – already shadowy – was a man she'd seen before. With coaching and encouragement, she would regain her confidence, it must have been believed by those for whom her evidence was essential: the prosecution case rested on this identification, on little else. But the long delay had taken a toll, the witness had been wearied by preparation and did not, in court, conceal her worries. When the first morning of the trial was about to end, the Judge calmed his anger to declare that in his opinion there was no case to answer. In the afternoon the jury was dismissed.

Katherine pulled back the curtains, settled her make-up, made the bed. Blame was there somewhere – in faulty recollection, in the carelessness of policemen, in a prosecution's ill-founded confidence – yet its attribution was hardly a source of satisfaction. Chance and circumstance had brought about a nightmare, and left it to a Judge's invective to make a nonsense of it. He did so, but words were not enough: too much was left behind. No other man was ever charged, although of course there was another man.

She banged the door behind her, as she'd been told to. They had not said good-bye, yet as she went downstairs, hearing again the muffled gabble of the racecourse commentator, she knew it was for the last time. The room was finished with. This afternoon she had felt that, even if it had not been said.

She did not have coffee and walked by the Prince and Dog without noticing it. In her kitchen she would cook the food she'd bought and they would sit together and talk about the day. She would look across the table at the husband she loved and see a shadow there. They would speak of little things.

She wandered, going nowhere, leaving the bustling street that was gracious also, walking by terraced houses, lace-curtained windows. Her afternoon lover would mend the marriage that had failed, would piece by piece repair the damage because damage was not destruction and was not meant to be. To quarrel often was not too terrible; nor, without love, to be unfaithful. They would agree that they were up to this, and friendly time would do the rest, not asked to do too much. "And she?" his wife one day might wonder, and he would say his other woman was a footnote to what had happened in their marriage. Perhaps that, no more.

Katherine came to the canal, where there were seats along the water. This evening she would lie, and they would speak again of little things. She would not say she was afraid, and nor would he. But fear was there, for her the nag of doubt, infecting him in ways she did not know about. She walked on past the seats, past children with a nurse. A barge with barrels went by, painted roses on its prow.

A wasteland, it seemed like where she walked, made so not by itself but by her mood. She felt anonymity, a solitude here where she did not belong, and something came with that which she could not identify. Oh, but it's over, she told herself, as if in answer to this mild bewilderment, bewildering herself further and asking herself how she knew what she seemed to know. Thought was no good: all this was feeling. So, walking on, she did not think.

She sensed, without a reason, the dispersal of restraint. And yes, of course, for all nine years, there'd been restraint. There'd been no asking to be told, no asking for promises that the truth was what she heard. There'd been no asking about the girl, how she'd dressed, her voice, her face, and if she only sat there talking, no more than that. There'd been no asking if there had really been the usual misery on the Northern Line, the waiting for a taxi in the rain. For all nine years, while work for both of them allowed restraint, there had been silence in their ordinary exchanges, in conversation, in making love, in weekend walks and summer trips abroad. For all nine years love had been there, and more than just a comforter, too intense for that. Was stealth an excitement still? That was not asked and Katherine, pausing to watch another barge approaching, knew it never would be now. The flat was entered and Sharon Ritchie lay suffocated on her sofa. Had she been the victim kind? That, too, was locked away.

Katherine turned to walk back the way she'd come. It wouldn't be a shock, nor even a surprise. He expected no more of her than what she'd given him, and she would choose her moment to say that she must go. He would understand; she would not have to tell him. The best that love could do was not enough, and he would know that also.

William Trevor was born in 1928 at Mitchelstown, Co Cork, spent his childhood in provincial Ireland, and attended Trinity College, Dublin. One of Ireland's most celebrated writers of fiction, he is the author of 11 collections of short stories, two novellas and 13 novels. His most recent book, A Bit on the Side *(Penguin), a collection of stories, appeared in 2005.*

TWO POEMS

Michael Coady

THREE DOWN

i.m. John Lovett, Tommy Finucane, Brian O'Keeffe

Brian, when I learn you're gone I'm once
again back there where we were all invincible.
Now three of four are down, one left to speak.
I dial Ireland and hear your wife weep
across the ocean and the years. When we
were learning things by heart we never dreamed
that this is what we'd come to know, to top off
Maths and Shakespeare, Latin, Fiannaíocht.

Last day of school the clock struck four and we
proposed to meet each year whatever happened.
But then the water deepened with the days
and now it's down to words across salt waves
until I have to plead, in truth, *there's someone*
knocking on the door and I must go.

THE MYSTERIES

Two women, neither a gazelle,
living on the south side of the river.

Every August after hairdos
at Madeline's Salon

they head off by bus on pilgrimage
to Our Lady's Island in south Wexford

where such as they have gone
at harvest time through thick and thin

since Rudolph de Lamporte of that place
was killed on the Crusades.

One of the two is fat, bad on the legs,
the other fine-boned, skinny, sallow –

not a pick on her to feed a maggot
we say, and of the other

it's a wonder she can make it
up the stairs to bed –

as though we need to highlight
and confirm the common

imperfection of the world
that we've been given.

*

In her time the fat woman married,
bore children, buried one;

her soufflés and apple tarts
won prizes at the Barony Meeting.

The other lives alone
and gets on well with solitude;

when she has time to kill
she knits to complex patterns

and is prepared to sit up with the dying,
or lay out a corpse when needed.

Each has known joy and sorrow.
They travel by whatever

light they can envision,
and are not blind

to what may darkly
stir in any garden.

*

On Sunday morning each prepares
and dresses in her best,

attending to the ordinary
hunger for the beautiful.

Come hell or high water
they show up in time for Mass,

are usually in place before the priest,
who sometimes sleeps it out

following sick calls in the night
or card games with the undertaker.

After *Lord I am not worthy*
the thin woman and the fat

drink from the chalice and receive
the Host, then each lifts a ciborium

and takes her stance at her habitual place
to share out Communion with the faithful

who come in slow procession and seem
not to be paying much attention

other than to eye
the Nigerian altar girls

and mutter unconsidered
prayers across the pews.

If hymns are sung before or after,
the thin woman's in her element,

soaring with a lush vibrato
adopted since she starred as Margot

in *The Desert Song*, live at Marian Hall
when she was young and lusted after.

*

On occasions when the priest's off to a funeral,
or at the greyhound track,

or visiting his mother, the women
fill the gap to lead the Rosary.

The fat prefers the Joyful Mysteries,
while the thin goes for the Glorious.

Of the Joyful five, the fat one's favourite is
The Finding of the Child Jesus in the Temple

while the thin woman of the Glorious loves best
The Assumption of Our Lady into Heaven.

Both leave the Sorrowful Mysteries
to the priest, and haven't yet

looked into five additional epiphanies
called Mysteries of Light

proposed by Pope John Paul as he
grew closer to the ground he often kissed,

bending day by day under
the cross of his slow dying.

*

Now and then the women find some reason
to be cool with one another

or subtly show up one another's failings.
When hasty words are said

they later make it up, exchanging
tarts and knitting, neither knowing

what the other may be thinking
in her heart of hearts.

And so they incarnate
the nights and days –

two women, neither a gazelle,
living on the south side of the river,

dealing with the wondrous
imperfection of the world,

showing how things are,
and how things hold together.

A retired primary school teacher, Michael Coady has lived all his life in Carrick-on-Suir, Co Tipperary. He is the author of four books of poetry, most recently All Souls *(1997) and* One Another *(2003), both from The Gallery Press.*

IN OTHER WORDS: FROM THE RUSSIAN AND DUTCH

I

Inna Lisnianskaya

Without you.

From the sequence FORTY DAYS

(The Russian Orthodox Church holds that for forty days the spirit of the deceased remains at home, and only after does it leave for heaven, or wherever. – The Editor)

You always said to me: "Pray and believe!"
And tempting fate, again and again:
"Everything I need, I can sense, like a beast."
Well, I found you in the garden.

Without a sound you left, like a lion,
Not wanting to stay inside.
And I found you between two trees,
Found you in the snowy yard.

Whether it was the first snow or the last,
I don't know. What does death care.
As a man, you came into this world
And you left it like a tsar.

26 April 2003

Great now is the Sabbath
And I grieve to the limit,
And tomorrow freedom will rise up –
Christ and His Power.

The departed bring to the celestial tent,
Over the living make the sign of the cross.
And forgive me, who have lived so long,
For my widow's verse,

Which mumbles, lamenting,
Mumbles as best it can,
That He is raising you,
As He raised Lazarus.

27 April 2003

Tears became a storm,
Eyes became fire.
Flame, as you know, is blind –
I shall put some wine, bread
On the table for you,
By touch, in our hut.

Maybe you'll want a drink,
Maybe you'll feel like a bite,
Or at least a chat …
How shall I manage without you,
How weave my verse,
My trusting, sagacious man?

No, I'll not weep and cry out,
Not lightning, but a candle
I lit, when I became a widow,
I spin a thread of after-life
Playing the video
On which you live forever.

28 April 2003

I let go of the last hour of your life,
And reproachfully your blue eyes

Froze, directed at the bleached sky.
How absurd everything has turned out!

For thirty days, you have not visited me
In my dreams – you do not forgive me.

But I see, with the light of this hell,
That over the trees of the garden

The cloud has dispersed. Your way
To paradise is clear.

30 April 2003

I bathed your eyelids, chest and belly
With water from the tap,
And my mouth, an open wound,
Kissed your cold mouth.

I held back my widow's wailing,
A pillar of salt now
It stands at your bed-head
In this late spring weather.

It can be seen by the Lord,
Only an angel guards it,
For strangers my day is ordinary,
As your life was ordinary.

30 April 2003

Unsteady on my pins, yet firm as a writing-stand,
I write to you by starlight over there
Where the birds are building
Their celestial nests.

And ours, wooden, with its little porch,
Where you would sit on the steps,
Is encircled by the rings of Saturn
And the little triangles of birds'

Wings, birds that made themselves nests
In our pine-needly yard.
As best they can, they share a widow's grief
Keeping a minute of silence at dawn.

1 May 2003

Colleagues, friends, neighbours enter our house,
Your two sons and two daughters,
Candles are burning in the brass candlestick,
In each glass is wine, like a tulip in the grass.

In the house a funeral banquet is laid out,
And I continue to sing your song of praise:
Unhesitatingly you answered the questions of destiny
Even if in old age you still knew how to blush.

There are blanks, but no blots, in your life,
Not the worst third of it spent with me.
So, your jacket dropped from the nail, like a winged bird,
Brandishing an empty sleeve and unable to take off?

1 May 2003

To believe the weather reports
A cyclone is approaching.
I shall not disturb your eternal dream
With my weeping, in rainy weather.

But as I recall your prognoses,
That in Russia the spirit leaps up,
I shall read your lines aloud
And shed a grateful tear.

1 May 2003

And no man's a prophet in his own land,
And you left so lonely,
As if there were not a trace of me.
Did you think of offences given in old age?
You breathed your last breath on a walk
To the as-yet leafless rowan-tree.

We shall never again feast one another,
No more will we bill and coo,
Nor gossip about other people's business.
Never again will we entertain one another
With various considerations
About the most special and the most ordinary.

And time makes its senseless way,
Breathing long-since soured oxygen
And making notches in the trees.
Of course, it has played its part
And I am divided equally in two:
In the grave, on the porch.

1 May 2003

For forty days I am your widow,
Forty days, I tremble
And seek the only words
For you, the only one.

I sing a song of praise
And the rhythm stumbles, like my feet.
You entered my besotted life
Like a king, like some god.

You were both stern and chilly,
Knowing the limitation of words and numbers,
But almost until '92
You sang me the Song of Songs.

You saw the glow of heavenly wings
Above a mound of adversities,
And in a trice completed
The journey from life to death.

Before the icon in the red corner
In the flickering candle-heat
For you I shall offer up praise
To the Almighty.

8 May 2003

I honour the silent wake,
And how, like slender rowan-trees,
The family crowds
Around me.

Where are you? In God's kingdom
Or just a few steps away?
Spirit is time, and of course
Space is our remains.

In my mind, May splits
Between spirit and mortal remains,
With me like a straight line
Between two points.

25 May 2003

Under the canopy of an immense
And dense-leaved aspen is silence;
Under it, for three months,
You, my beloved, have slept.

Here everything is lifelike;
The bench, the drizzling rain,
Through my solid flesh
An aspen tremor.

There is a yellow tomtit,
And course grass,
And the life I am living
As from a tale often told.

25 May 2003

I put on your fur-lined jacket,
Attached your glasses,
Sat on the bench where you would sit.
The dew was like fireflies,

Lighting the night, like the stars
You'd glance at so affectionately.
But now even these are omission points
In which my lament comes to rest.

The dew was like uncut diamonds,
Like the emerald of fireflies, stars
Freckly above the pond, illuminating
Your graveyard home.

27 May 2003

A chalice. Sun's honey, moon's milk.
Shadow casts a light, so distant,
The world's not lit by it.
Echo gives out a sound, so distant
I hear nothing.
Death metamorphoses into life, so distant,
The chalice cracks
And honey and milk spill out.

28 May 2003

TRANSLATOR'S NOTE

Daniel Weissbort

Inna Lisnianskaya was born in Baku, Soviet Azerbaijan, in 1928. Her first publication was in 1948 and her first poetry collection appeared in 1957. From 1979, and for many years, her books appeared only abroad. In recent years she has published several collections in Russia and has contributed regularly to all of the country's major literary periodicals. Lisnianskaya was married to the late Semyon Lipkin, also a leading Russian poet, and her most recent collection, *Without You* (2004, from which these translations are drawn), consists partly of an elegy to him. She lives in Moscow.

Joseph Brodsky wrote of her work in 1983: "Of what I have read in the last few years, Lisnianskaya's poems have impressed me most. Russian poets, poets in general, are the product of what has been written before. They start by alluding to or contradicting it. The only echo I clearly discern in Lisnianskaya's poetry is that of Akhmatova – thank goodness! She is a wonderful lyric poet, especially in the short poems. Of all Russian poets known to me today, Lisnianskaya is the most precise and immediate in her manner of writing about death, after all one of the main themes of literature ..." And in his Preface to her volume *After Everything* (1994), Alexander Solzhenitsyn also wrote of her style: "Always intensity of feeling, and a tranquillity (rare) of the most profound sort. No artificiality, no posing, total sincerity. The author's soul exposed, but the poem solid, freely breathing, and the form irreproachable. [Lisnianskaya] conveys feeling laconically, through little details, sometimes through secondary or evanescent hints, nothing crudely direct, as with so many of today's writers who seem to have to name everything. The short poems consummately embody feeling, imagistically, aphoristically. And as for metaphors, there is no deliberate pursuit of them; they are not fabricated or hunted down in the contemporary manner. After Akhmatova and Tsvetaeva, apparently it has not been easy to preserve one's independence in Russian poetry, to lend it colour and significance; but [Lisnianskaya] has managed, and clearly this is not due to some set programme, it has simply come of its own accord."

Until recently, Daniel Weissbort edited Modern Poetry in Translation, *which he co-founded with Ted Hughes in 1965. His translation of other poems by Inna Lisnianskaya,* Far From Sodom, *was published by Arc in 2005. Carcanet will be publishing his anthology,* Contemporary Russian Women's Poetry, *co-edited with his wife, Valentina Polukhina.*

See page 177 of this issue for Daniel Weissbort's essay, "Ted Hughes and Truth".

II

Esther Jansma

Crossing the Styx.

SAFE HOUSE

Snow is the felling and falling of giants.
Fells eardrums, trees that yell.
Whispers are water, rafting downriver
to Dordrecht timber market.

The market tomorrow, hull and house.
Building is fire and knowledge of stove.
The stove our city. Back then the city
slowing to an etching, soundless, old.

Etched is what you see and cannot reach:
distance, harbour, house. House is
tree-bark closing off back then, the brig
in which I live, where rain drums, here,

now, wood groans green, does not split
since I am good, my skin my god, idled
time: voice which tells us we are, no
not us, but Bosnians, but Algerians will,

and anyway they'll end up – dead
is reflections of a son gone blind
on a retina racked with thirst.
Thirst is thinking of big water.

Small is dead children, charred people, far away.
Small is press reports, hands, tears are small,
"not even the rain has such small hands." Hands
are what passing time falls through like water.

Water is big. Time is big. God as well,
and so are we in our womanless womb of wood.
Here it is cold. Cold is never being
reborn, so still enduring in this here

until all ends, the scars that burst
with scurvy, the year that burst and loosed
so much – no more thinking of back then.
Noah a hero. Barents the hero.

Heroes trail tales in their wake
like ships. So why does no-one speak?
The splintered figurehead points across
the rock-hard water, there is no rain,

we left the rain behind, and in its stead
there came this cold which gnaws our fingers to
the bone, which smokes from our mouths, this dragon
of glass that slithered inside us and smothers our words.

We are somewhere, we can stand, up there
exists but it is dark: the days are short.
Eating up our ship for forage, food,
fuel, we snap at each other like the ice

we shuffle across like shadows, we want to be
what we still know from the dream which is
back then: bread, telescopes, windows,
pigeons, children, trees. A wife.

At night I bury myself. Night is a way
back to warmth, to flesh, my homeland.
Pissing and shitting as well: a way back
to the crib, the city, lazy days behind

the house, sitting between the flies on
the privy – at least I can still sleep and shit.
I must be getting old. I think
this white plain in the night is what

old age is all about: losing count,
slowly sliding down and out of the dream
into a sort of waiting, losing all sense
of who you are, how long, or when, what

people are, what wood, hands, a place –
yes I remember a place, it's ground beneath
your feet and space overhead and being
there then, and understanding why

but this here's beyond me. I am the others
and myself, a knot of skin sweat
sound in endless white on which
I turn my back, I turn round,

I count the hairs in beards, scratch
the scabs off faces, gnaw leather, what
I want is words, to hear what I must do,
first order, second order, commands

are the arteries that feed this house,
rhythm that fills the void, tell me
how to do it, vein the white
with blood of words like hunt cook

saw mend tomorrow next week,
and god just say that god can see this,
say he knows us, that here exists
on charts we are not lost.

Talk so I may know what
people are about. I dream of wood
and rain, come hold my hand,
comfort me while I look for walls

while I fall into the womb of sleep.
Falling is being reborn,
womb is a safe house, sleep
is a coursing awareness of warmth

while I wait for the thaw.

Note: William Barents and Jacob van Heemskerck led three expeditions in the 1590s in search of a North-East Passage via the North of Russia to the Indies. On their third expedition, the leaders' ship, separated from the rest of the expedition, became trapped in the ice off Nova Zembla (Novaya Zemlya) in September 1596. The men were forced to spend nine months through the polar winter in a hut they had built themselves of driftwood trees. They took the name of their hut (Safe House) from Psalms 31:2 – "Be thou my strong rock, for an house of defence to save me." In June 1597, their ship still trapped in the ice, they set off back to the Netherlands in an open boat. Barents died while they were crossing the sea that now bears his name, but the surviving thirteen returned to a heroes' welcome.

THIS HERE

You stroll along the beach: the sea,
the skyline, sounds that fill the bowl
of all the world to the rim – no, smaller.

You press your shoes in the sand: leather
soles, hill weathered to null, they
leave a hollow – no, something other.

You are somewhere, where does not matter,
always on a rim, of land and water
this time, what it's all about is now – no,

you sprawl on your belly. Sand sings away
like water, ribbed. You pick the littlest rib.
Hill. You pick the littlest grain. Earth.

SWIFT

The way that grand
goes round grassland
and a cow lies
in its cowl of flies,
swiftwings flit with a sigh

into sight and, swifter
than the telling, a tail
ineffably
light in flight
veers out of this
verse.

Note: As wordplay almost never translates directly, as a translator I had to find equally ludic ways of reflecting Jansma's original here. The most radical change was transforming her hare *(in Dutch,* haas, *becoming* haast *– both "hurries" and "almost" – when given the tail of a t) into a swift.*

SON

He closes his eyes and
the world unfolds. He falls
while nothing hints at depth

the walls give way, the floor caves in,
air comes storming through.
Down he plunges, knowing no bounds.

Every lullaby is a prologue,
a shrill voice which sings into
his head like a drill. Sleep

billows the skirts of the house.
The nest is tossed like a ship.
He shivers, clinging on to earth

which his hands, little grapples,
sparrow-talons, knead
from the branches of the sheets.

THE FALL

We were crossing the Styx.
The ferryman lay drunk in his ship.
I gripped the tiller and we sank like stones.

Water is made like earth of layers,
transparent ribbons, glistening strata
of shrinking life, ever less warmth.

Bubbles blossomed in your hair,
the current tugged back your head
and caressed your neck.

Stones waved arms of weed and fern,
softly gurgled singing "peace".
They cut away your clothes.

Fishes licked the blood from your legs.
I held your hand. I wanted to comfort you
but we fell too fast and no words

can live without air, my love
was left up above, blue balloons,
brief beacons marking the accident site

before they floated on. Your mouth fell open.
Your face went red, your hands grasped
for balance, grasped my arms.

You tried to climb up through me. You were
a glassblower with a cloud of diamonds
at his mouth. I held you like a kitten.

I stroked your fingers.
You did not let go.
You slept and I stroked your fingers, let go.

MORNING

Had you lent someone else your face?
Briefly borrowed different eyes?
A mouth for firetalk, watertalk? You

sang to two worlds while losing this one.
You gripped us tight. Not true:
you lay still and spoke with ghosts.

Beneath your sheets emptiness opens
her shears. Longing has broken
into o's and a's on your lips. Morning light

caught in droplets clings to your
fingers, your cheeks are cool. This is
the moment when the trees unfold

with a sigh and delicate green
creatures flee behind the sparkling
defenceless hands which are spiders' webs,

leaving us behind, a brief shadow
of heel or wing on our retina,
then nothing. Oh elves

are weak, my little lad, and die like mad
and we – we are already forgetting how full
the light once fell on you, how you are lying here,

this silent now so full of you, so utterly yourself
and past, so fucking past.

Note: "elves are weak ... and die like mad" is a reference to elfin-face syndrome (Williams-Beuren Syndrome).

BELOVED

Washed ashore, he lay on reddish rocks
and dreamt her voice was calling him, sand
that scattered across him and wafted away.

The sea lay meekly by his breast.
His heart was the nesting ground
of gaudy birds. The wind returned.

One by one the birds took wing,
screeched and tumbled upwards, powerless
they were swept aside.

His heart was a wound, an empty room
when she found him, love alone
set him apart from the ground.

She lifted him up. Gently she tried
to close his mouth. In the ship
she tried to close his mouth.

She did not speak, and pressed his lips together.
She did not speak, and placed his arms around her neck.
She succeeded. His head lies on her shoulder.

He does not speak. They sail.
They mean the world to each other.

TECTONICS

Mineral existence, earthship sliding
through strata of earth: I in the hold of we.

Time foams against the ground. The egg
in which one's I trails thin layers

of longing out of the world – it is
a bridal bed, galley where one lashes

oneself as slow as stones to the mast,
stops one's ears to the sirens, those wispy

fingers of time which prise into the ground
down faults and hairline cracks,

raise the ship, lift the giant numb with I
up and away into the daylight

where everything, living and dead, is merely itself,
bleeds dry on the retina and dies.

NEW YEAR

Smoke blows into your mouth. The sun kicks
your hair. Lads in sleeveless T-shirts
rub the blood from their eyes.

Surgeons polish their instruments
and put them away. Everyone is walking
toward the quayside. You, between the cast-off

summer dresses of light, the shell
and shadow of fireworks, run behind them
and all at once, you lighter and lighter,

the speechlessness fills and lifts you up
till you break with so much emptiness
and blow all over the city which in a small

enclosed before, which is quiet, where night,
where all the people are where they want to be
and have forgotten themselves and are asleep

and all at once in that very breath
you dream: a fleet of paper birds,
a rustle, there is a way, you can return.

SMALL DREAM

open the doors
sweep the words
out of the house – amazed

up straight in the long
canoe of his sleep
he drifts into your light.

blood, heartbeat,
going open and closing
between your hands

heat-breathing
vase of ribs, in-
floresence, flight of

small round sounds,
gentle rain and a little
red *o*.

ABSENCE

As roses open, you do not notice –
a rose is a rose is, is suddenly knowing
that what was said is saying itself again,
missing is plural, keeps unfolding into now

and you do not understand how. Inside the heart
you lie and wait, while nothing seeks you, nothing
sleeps you into the light, keeps unleafing
and falling into itself.

FRACTAL

In all of her parts a rose is rose
in each of her petals she is complete

as each millimetre in this continent's outline
always equals likewise the whole of its coast

and the slightest wisp of mist
the biggest skyfilling cloud, so

a rose right down to the tiniest
outline of every single petal

and the space suffused with molecules
of scent between these petals is that rose

and does not know it.

A SORT OF EATING

What never knew anything, what painlessly
could have been not itself but, say, a chair

I can only seem to have by
naming (a sort of eating)

and so becoming it. A dead whatever
to which I give myself and meaning.

What has fallen apart till her elements here on
the table no longer remind me now in the slightest

of that rose, this is the rose I think
when I say I want her back – so, if need be:

non-rose.

LOGIC IN LOVE

"Roses" is a different set than that
of what are not called roses

just like "I" and "all roses". Reasoning
onwards in non-logical terms, this implies

this flower must be in disguise if it is
to be with me – for instance I can only

love her in a poem, which a rose is a rose is
something that has long been done

so no set theory here, though one thing is dead
certain: there is space for a simple little

rose and me.

OUTDOORS

There is space for complex simplicity
to announce itself unbidden here

since where this is no reflection exists
although so many things are mirrored:

there in the blue-black of water, say,
what is leaning across it in leaf-red

and skin-grey. Gravely by a bed of flowers
I then think: wind and pressure are moving

everywhere, but insight is missing.
How lucky that I am here.

Just look how nature needs me.

POTATOES ARE MORE IMPORTANT THAN ROSES

except in poems, where roses are more important
although it is a mistake to view tubers

those knobbly starch-packed paunches and pouches
as somehow less fit for a lyric

than the genitals of plants.
Suppose a person named after a flower is in the earth.

Dead, in other words. Not so pretty now. Disintegrating.
Give me potatoes any day: they do not stink.

And yet – suppose a person who gave her name to a potato
is in the earth. Not only her state but even her name

is against her. Better to be called rose after all.

THE WAY WE TALK

Those who most like saying names
want to know the named like themselves.

Brand-new widows and mothers
and royalists are good at this.

They cannot make themselves again
cannot be the unknown child

cannot eat their queen
but see them lap up her name.

And then there is the comfort of using of a name.
Language that points out a person

and this person exists.

REALISM

It already exists before I bite it off
lick it up from the unknown

with new positions of mouth and tongue
and an even newer feeling in my head

let it fall from my lips and know that now
I will be bigger and emptier than before.

But it does not need saying
to be what it is: absence

the many ways I miss her
but she does not exist

it is not her.

NOMINALISM

It is not here until I think of it
with a name. I name it rose

and in its wake I think unnervingly
tender eyelids, vein-patterned petals

and behind them a secret as if
in a baby's fist. This will be death.

It does not know itself.
It seems to be sleeping

and stays this way, whilst
petal after petal drops

and is gone.

FRAMEWORK

Time, I know, is a constant wind
in the sails of today, a stiff and die-straight

displacement of now. As if you are in a train,
but the view is broader and you are travelling

backwards. Okay. But how a rose can move
so gracefully pastwards, can grow so gradually balder

in question-mark curls – that I cannot grasp.
Or am I the one who framed it here this way

because I am simply missing it: the sense
of all that is suggested by

question-mark curls?

PRESENCE

No more questions from me: from now on I am going
to know things. From now on she is not rose but julia

and her sleep is not the sleep of things.
From now on she can be known, I am going to live

a long long time with her in a house and feed her,
teach her to speak and she will tell me how it is

while she is always changing. Always using different words.
Sometimes I cut her hair. Then her head changes.

As for me, I change so slowly that she will
not notice: when she is grown up

I will always have been old and happy.

Note: "Julia" is also a type of fractal.

ARCHAELOGY

If we have to dress, when all is said at last,
against the cold or in something's name, let's say,
in what remains of this or another past,
tales and aides-memoire which simply betray

the fact that we were here, and nothing more,
in time which existed before this today –
if we can only stay in this now for sure
by forever reinventing ourselves in this now,

then let it at least be easy, by means of clothes.
You sit at your table. You suddenly see a
person crossing ice, and how the cold

or some other end overcame him and you say: look,
here you have his mittens, shoes, and leather cloak.
"Where is time? Time is here."

HISTORICAL REALITY

Now is reality this: the stillness
of worn woodwork in this outworn house,
which like scorched cookware in glass cabinets
carries weight, for our ancestors made it?
Or this: living stooped over strip fields and wood fires,
losing their teeth young, their children young,
leaning on long-handled tools to leer
with toothache-twisted gobs at whatever
was different (travellers, beautiful women).

Sometimes stabbing the strange with a pitchfork.
Not smelling too nice, things if truth be known
being none too nice at all, working themselves to the bone,
believing in god and the intricacies of a myriad sins,
slaughtering pigs to eat and strangers
to set their heads at rest?

STRUCTURAL SURVEY

The dusk that I expected under the
wooden repetition, the capsized wreck
(keel upturned) which is the roof, is not this.
This is the dark of ages, centuries of cattle

breathing in and out, groaning as they shift in the night –
who thought of what back then, who knows?
We measure the rafters, copy the carpenter's marks,
drill into skylights and purlins, we work until

it is late, we are shadows who want,
no, hope to be more real than what
is here at hand: this wood, and
everyone who built in it and is not here.

ALL IS NEW

What was about to happen was already here,
spelt out precisely by a cup which shattered,
shards marked with the prints of thumbs,
the shiver-script of pinsharp twigs.

It is not a tale we have made up but what
was here and is here in the traces of ditches
and postholes and log-fires long gone cold.
It just needed finding, that was all.

Someone had to look at it and say: what is it
this is it, and there it was, a house with a hearth,
people as always and always being themselves
for the first time here and now, sitting

with warm hands which clasp a cup
by the fire and talking and the ticktock of rain
is a circle of sound and nothing matters, night,
the invisible clouds, the silence of all that

lies asleep or waits for day outside are the roof
and the walls round the roof and the corners
of the house that is already old but new
for it is newfound in this now.

THE BEGINNING

Suddenly she saw the size of the world.
Nothing was the way she had expected
things were fuller than she had thought before

and more colourful, on looking through
the glass that had now found her she saw
the inside of shells, what moved throughout it

was form and utterly itself and all
the while a rainbow of possibilities
blown into life and lost and found again,

after the ages had painted their mother-
of-pearl across it, ever so fragile
and there it lay, just like that in her hand.

TRANSLATOR'S NOTE

Francis R. Jones

Esther Jansma (born 1958) is recognised as one of the leading Dutch poets of her generation. Her debut collection, *Voice Beneath My Bed* (1988) established a set of motifs that underlie her whole oeuvre: the merging of personal experience into a poetic concern with transience and inheritance; the drive to fix or recover the traces of the personal past before they fade; and a vividness of image in which the present moment becomes timeless. In *Flower, Stone* (1990) Jansma confronts the reader with the unbearable: the death of one's child. But it also sets a tone crucial for her later works, where what counts is not so much the experienced as its poetic transmutation, not so much the nature of bereavement and survival as the existential questions they raise. In reviews of the collections which followed – particularly *Time is Here* (1998), *Skylights* (2001) and *All is New* (2005), which supply the poems translated here – critics realised that they had been reading one of the most (if not *the* most) original, compelling and poetically skilled voices in new Dutch poetry.

What is striking about Jansma's verse is the sheer variety of her themes and styles, though history (both of her own and a wider human past) is a constant leitmotiv. In a number of poems Jansma clearly draws inspiration from archaeology, her other profession. A specialist in dendrochronology, the dating of wooden artefacts from tree-rings, etc., she leads an environmental archaeology and conservation research team at the National Service for Archaeological Heritage Management in Amersfoort. But though (as with most poets) Jansma's personal and professional life form an input into her verse, in the volumes since *Flower, Stone* she has sought to distance herself from poetry as reportage. As she stresses: "In poetry, the reader tends to equate the I-figure with the writer even more than in novels, since poems often explore feelings and are personal. But it is fiction just the same." One way of fictionalising is to focus not only on the signified (events, narratives) but also on the signifier – the poem as artefact, and the language in which it is written. This means, for instance, that her poetic form is painstakingly crafted in word-sound and rhythm terms, and that language often refers to itself in the form of double meanings and allusions – thus setting a considerable but enjoyable challenge to her translator. This is not to say, however, that Jansma's poems are abstract or hermetic. The inward mind that reflects on events always draws on the inward eye that sees them. In this, her task as poet seems to reflect her task as archaeologist. Both poet and archaeologist seek to interpret, to use the visible traces of an event or artefact to construct a narrative from that is not only plausible, but is also generalisable, that reaches beyond that particular event or artefact.

The poems translated here reflect these intertwined themes. In "Safe House," an Arctic overwintering from Dutch history seems to reflect a personal overwintering. The ludic wordplay of "Swift" highlights language as poetic subject. The following poems, from "Son" to "Presence," combine two different cycles from two different books. The keystone of the poetic arch is the poem "Absence," which both ends the first cycle (embedded in *Time is Here*) and begins the second cycle ("Having," from *Skylights*). This poem marks the point at which a personal loss becomes transmuted into a Rilkesque concern with how the tiniest detail contains the universal. The rose of "Absence" and the second cycle, however, does not only echo Rilke's rose, with its petals angling outwards into infinity, but also the flowers of mathematical fractals, which remain the same no matter how many times you zoom in or out. The final set of poems ("Archaeology" to "The Beginning") reflect Jansma's passion as an archaeologist, showing how multiple strata of past lives underlie our present, and give it meaning.

Francis Redvers Jones teaches translation studies at the University of Newcastle in the North of England. He has translated extensively from Bosnian-Croatian-Serbian, Dutch, Hungarian and Russian, including the poetry of Mak Dizdar, Ivan Lalić and Vasko Popa. He is the author of 11 books of poetry translation, most recently Camp Notebook *by Miklós Radnóti (Arc, 2000, from the Hungarian) and* Against the Forgetting *by Hans Faverey (New Directions, 2004, from the Dutch).*

TWO ESSAYS

Denis Sampson

I

THE ZEALOT AND THE COUNTRY BOY

A reader's progress.

"All religions I think have the same inner conception," D.H. Lawrence wrote to an Irishman named Gordon Campbell in December 1914, "with different expressions." Campbell had given him a draft of a novel, but Lawrence, mid-way through *The Rainbow* at this time, dismissed his friend's work: "Why don't you seek out the whole of the Celtic Vision, instead of messing about talking of Ireland." I was surprised that the novelist would use an expression like "messing about"– it sounded so contemporary – but even more, I was startled by a defensive feeling that Lawrence was challenging me, for I had recently left Ireland and it was still very much the only place I knew much about.

When I read the letter, and *The Rainbow,* and *Sons and Lovers*, and everything by Lawrence, it was not so long since I had abandoned the Catholic "whole" of my childhood. "It is very beautiful," Lawrence wrote of his new religious vision, "and a very great conception which, when one feels it, satisfies one, and one is at rest." But I could not fall under the spell of his prophecies. I could not feel this "rest" in Lawrence's work, or in my own life. I was in search of my own kind of liberation, a boy from the country, adrift for some time already, trying to hold on to a tentative version of scholarship as a scaffolding for my scepticism. I was not ready for another wholistic vision, even if it was called "Celtic".

From elementary school years, we were encouraged to think of ourselves as Celts, and I knew that Yeats and other Irish writers had drawn major inspiration from the rich mythology of gods and heroes. An explicit kind of political, religious and cultural identity, a version of "de-anglicization," had been attached to this Celtic mythology since the nineteenth century, and in my schooldays, nationalist zealots had already dominated the cultural discourse for generations. They too seemed to be inspired by a vision of a "whole," not the geographical whole of the island of Ireland, necessarily, but a sense of spiritual wholeness in the pure and essential idea of Irishness. In adolescence, however, I read Joyce's portrait of an Irish Catholic lad in search of something more than orthodoxy. Disillusioned, disenchanted, I was encouraged by the protective arrogance of Stephen Dedalus.

For a time, I became active in left-wing politics. The scholar-activists were my mentors, Noam Chomsky and Conor Cruise O'Brien. I marched and demonstrated for many causes on the streets of Dublin – anti-Vietnam, anti-apartheid, better public housing – and on the streets of Belfast – against the discriminatory practices and prejudice of the Unionist establishment. These were the years when the Civil Rights Movement was transformed by reactionary thugs of a unionist persuasion, by the Provisional IRA and the British Army into an all out war. The viciousness and the lies, the confrontations orchestrated by the IRA and by some Marxist "revolutionaries," the trigger-happy reprisals by the army all frightened me. The liberation of Ireland, liberation of the world, liberation through politics were other versions of religious zeal, Lawrence's flaming Godhead, and they all lost my allegiance.

A little guiltily, I left Ireland for Canada; the study of literature seemed to be altogether more manageable than the abstractions of liberation and justice, not to mention the commitments demanded by the bloody politics of the streets. I would become a scholar. I would maintain the necessary detachment from the slippery slopes of zealotry, of which, I was inclined to think, there was too much in Ireland. Literary scholarship had its own visions of perfection, the purity of expression, the perfection of style, the exhaustive weighing of detail. Scholars left no stone unturned, but to what end? If truth was no longer revealed by oracles, scriptures and zealots, what was it? Something discovered in a library? As a professional student, I had to believe so. I did not want to be respected for the intensity and clarity of my political commitment but for the imaginative pressure of my attention to literary style.

Little did I know how out of step with the times I was in my loss of faith, how old-fashioned in my Joycean wish to be freed from all mythologies, for the sixties would live on, its promises of liberation proliferating, especially within the university, and in particular in the ways literature would come to be studied there. It would have been easier later on if I had been able to throw in my lot with early manifestations of fervent deconstruction, the progressive camp in the culture wars, as these bitter struggles would be known in the eighties, but I could not. It was in Montreal, in the seventies, that my mind became oppressed by D. H. Lawrence's mythology of "resurrection" and his mystical faith in "the whole." In a way I could not articulate or even recognize, the novelist kept open my rawest, unresolved inheritance from my formation in Ireland.

In my first year in North America, it dawned on me that the revolution I had felt a part of in Dublin was not the real revolution. The student revolution, the anti-Vietnam movement, the New Left, I had embraced enthusiastically in the late sixties, but now I discovered, to my discomfort, that sex too was part of politics, that the Revolution was against all forms of repression, and that sexual freedom was the real utopian absolute.

This revolution seemed to have been born in California, but Lawrence, formulating his doctrines of liberation in Italy with his lover Frieda, had anticipated some of this by fifty years. His mystical sensualism was expressed in the paradisal symbolism of flowers, but everyone seemed to know it was sex he was writing about. While some of Lawrence's high-minded interpreters spoke of "the priest of love" and his "love ethic," others, less sentimental, wrote of a fierce Oedipal conflict, of ingrained Puritanism, and a purgation of shame. In North America, in the sixties, the public exhibitions of sexual freedom asserted that if only sex in all its variations were no longer hidden from public view, everyone and the whole culture of materialism and militarism would be cleansed.

It was certainly a revolutionary subversion of every principle on which Catholic Ireland was founded and with which I had been indoctrinated, but this vision of "the Whole" also troubled me. The once-banned author of *Lady Chatterley's Lover* and *The Rainbow* had now become an icon not only of "free love" but of the liberation the sixties offered. Why was I holding back on D. H. Lawrence? What young man wouldn't identify with the desire for freedom from middle-class and Christian inhibitions and in favour of rehabilitating the instinctual?

The further reaches of the sexual revolution, the purgation of inhibition, the freedom from repression, the absolute of the pleasure principle, had a psychedelic glow. Revolutionary philosophies (Cuban, Maoist, anarchist), philosophies of sex, of mysticism – all the utopian impulses seemed to have trajectories that merged at infinity. The "mysteries of the organism" that had to be released seemed to me to have more to do with chemical bombardment of the brain than with a liberation that I could manage.

Without knowing it, perhaps, I had cooperated earlier in keeping even the simplest of pleasures invisible – invisible in a certain way even from myself. The most difficult part of my adolescent revolt, it had seemed to me, was a doctrinal one, focused on the claims of the Church to have the monopoly on truth; little did I realize that its ethos had already infected my emotional and sensual life, so that to declare "I do not believe in Catholicism" or "I am no longer a practicing Catholic" was only a superficial liberation, a limited, intellectual revolt.

Yet if I always was a scholar in the making, could it be that it was not Lawrence and his visions but scholarship itself that was oppressive? I had been brought up in a culture of prophets and zealots and great men through whose agency, we had believed, the Truth could be revealed. My sense of oppression may have come from that constant self-discipline required by dispassionate scholarly work, the cautious holding back, the deferred commitment to certainty that makes the future a permanent hypothesis, when it is a breakthrough into the Truth that one craves.

I was oppressed by my own anxious desire to be a scholar, and the nature of the subject I found myself trapped with, the novels of D.H. Lawrence, made that desire even more anxious. How could a reader like me who had found intense personal pleasure and a stabilizing sense of purpose in literature take the wholistic vision of Lawrence's art and measure it out with teaspoons? Either I allowed the act of reading, the pleasure of aesthetic experience in all its individual manifestations, to become an act of faith in a qualitatively different life, or I became a detached and dull scholar for whom love and appreciation were of secondary importance. I could not bring myself to betray Lawrence's fire; neither could I allow myself to be cowed into ventriloquism by a zealot.

Gordon Campbell's reaction to Lawrence's abuse is not recorded, but the messianic novelist pressed his case for not wasting one's life with local matters on another writer in the months following. He got to know E. M. Forster in January 1915. Forster knew a great deal about "the whole" of Indian religions for he had read widely in the history and culture of Islam and Hinduism, and he had lived in India for a year. He was less impressed by Lawrence's abrasive preaching about sex and politics than by the delicacy of his attention to nature and the sheer force of his visionary conviction. Although Forster had been interested in "condition of England" novels earlier in his career, he knew that the psychological and metaphysical realm Lawrence was attempting to capture in his fiction went far beyond that, and he wanted to follow him; in fact, he had already attempted to do so after his return from India. He had begun a new novel but would not be able to complete *A Passage to India* for almost a decade more.

Forster was one of the few careful readers of Lawrence in his lifetime. That attention began at the time he met the younger novelist in 1915 and endured. He was not a zealot. When Lawrence died in 1930, his life marked by widespread accusations of being a pornographer, Forster championed him as "the greatest imaginative novelist of our generation" and defended his claim against the ridicule of T. S. Eliot and others. In a talk on the BBC, Forster explained his appreciation of Lawrence: "He resembles a natural process much more nearly than do most writers, he writes from his instincts as well as preaching instinct, so that one might as well scold a flower for growing on a manure heap, or a manure heap for producing a flower … Like Blake and other mystics, he condemns the intellect with its barren chains of reasoning and its dead weights of information; he even hates self-sacrifice and love."

In his eulogies on Lawrence after his death, Forster was returning to what he had already written some years before. In his Cambridge lectures on "Aspects of the Novel," Forster had praised Lawrence as "the only living novelist in whom the song predominates, who has the rapt bardic quality, and whom it is idle to criticize … The prophet is irradiating nature from within, so that every colour has a glow and every form a distinctness which could not otherwise be obtained."

What was remarkable to me about Forster as a reader, so remarkable that he became a central part of my work on Lawrence from this point on, was that he had to overcome major resistance in himself to be able to speak out. In these same pages of *Aspects of the Novel*, there are clues about this self-transformation. "Prophetic fiction," Forster says, "seems to have definite characteristics. It demands humility and the absence of the sense of humour ... it gives us the sensation of a song or of sound." Lawrence's demand for humility is what Forster learned to respond to, and he learned it directly when he was brought face to face with the novelist.

In 1927, Forster recalled that encounter. "Nothing is more disconcerting than to sit down, so to speak, before your prophet, and then suddenly to receive his boot in the pit of your stomach. 'I'm damned if I'll be humble after that,' you cry, and so lay yourself open to further nagging. Also the subject matter of the sermon is agitating – hot denunciations or advice – so that in the end you cannot remember whether you ought or ought not to have a body, and are only sure that you are futile." This is Forster's recollection of how he had been treated by Lawrence in 1915, and this startling revelation was reassuring to me because it articulated so vividly my own feelings of being overpowered by Lawrence's words. Lawrence had indeed bullied Forster and humiliated him, and had analyzed in blunt terms the root causes of his ineffectual personality. He had urged Forster to resurrect himself, partly by becoming sexually assertive, and to join him in creating "a perfect community that would regenerate the world." The irony was not lost on Forster that Lawrence's idea of sexual regeneration was strictly heterosexual for already Forster had found such a "perfect community" among friends from Cambridge and would go on to expand his homosexual community.

In the private papers of Forster, I discovered that long before he became sexually active, in Alexandria, where he went some months after he had got to know Lawrence, his interest in painters or writers had often been focused by his discovery of their homosexuality. After *The Rainbow*, in a series of novels, Lawrence went on to explore relationships between men, Forster's central preoccupation, and when Forster began to work again on *A Passage to India*, he found inspiration in *Women in Love*. Forster read Lawrence with his own particular concerns in mind, in particular, his assumption that Lawrence had an unacknowledged homosexual side. He praised the poet-prophet for being so much in touch with his instincts, but he did not, could not, make public the reason why he had found encouragement and inspiration in Lawrence for his later life and for his greatest novel.

I discovered how Forster had read Lawrence, and also how Lawrence had read Forster, and how Lawrence's imagination had made use of that reading. I became a scholar with something new to say. In this process I did find a way out of my oppression and out of the academic hole in which I had buried myself. Although my academic work was praised for its originality and its contribution to understanding Lawrence's critical imagination, I no longer believed in it. In the end, I had grown to appreciate both writers in certain ways, but I had wearied of them. I no longer wanted to read them. My scholarship was a dead end.

Deep down, by becoming a scholar, I felt I had sidestepped the issues. I was still perhaps the country boy in awe of the accomplishments of others, lacking the fierce will of that other country boy, Lawrence, to clear the space for himself. Forster had known what he needed to take from Lawrence and how to keep the space clear for himself. I was left with this conundrum of how to read, how to surrender oneself to the pleasure of being inside someone else's world, to assent to its truth, and how at the same time to affirm one's own self, one's own separate and distinctive truth.

My first published writing in Canada was an appreciation of *The Leavetaking*, John McGahern's novel of a day in the life of a man who must leave Ireland. The novel, together with his earlier books, *The Barracks*, *The Dark*, and *Nightlines*, became, in my expatriation, the most deeply-felt books I had ever read; they were books of the farming world I had grown up in and left behind, and yet he had revealed in that small world a universe of meaning.

His four volumes of fiction, so well known in England and Ireland, were almost unknown in North America. This was the mid-seventies, before the boom in contemporary Irish culture, indirectly promoted by the slaughter in the North that won headlines worldwide and provoked a curiosity about the background to the slaughter. McGahern's work was not diagnostic in political or historical terms, but it did open up darknesses of faith and violence, of terror and fierce despair, of personal isolation and censorship, of vulnerability and mortality, of love lost and won. His images of Ireland came to me with a such visceral immediacy and poetic power that I can no longer say to what degree McGahern's fiction has coloured my whole way of seeing Ireland and seeing myself. Certainly, my admiration for his work led me to think of it as an articulation of an incontrovertible truth about life; in his books, he had found a way of using language that was beyond speech and silence; they became a new scripture for me and the man who wrote them an artist-prophet.

Unlike Seamus Heaney or Edna O'Brien or other Irish writers who participated in media events, happily gave interviews and volunteered comments to reporters, McGahern did not welcome the aura of celebrity. He refused all interviews, even when he was fired from his job back in 1965, when *The Dark* was banned and he married outside the church. He never commented on his work; the language of art was his authentic expression, and for the rest he was a private person. His silence, or his refusal to promote his work, was a way of keeping the world away from his life, but it was also a way of preserving the language of his art from dilution or paraphrase. It was a way of suggesting that the language of art is essentially different from the language of conversation or journalism; it is to be experienced through that form of meditation known as private reading, and for that there is no substitute.

I can no longer recall if I had connected such modernist ideas with my own sensation of a split between speaking and writing. My inhibitions in conversation, my shyness, my inability to make small-talk or to break into the flow of animated conversation, and my sense that the oral expression of opinions and convictions was always embarrassingly close to cliche, all this had encouraged me to think of myself as more precisely myself in writing – although to escape from cliche in writing was a goal I could not achieve; my dream of writing was a dream of control. Yet because I had placed such a high value on the poetic, I seemed to be forever stuck in silence, my only recourse to point admiringly towards the fiction of McGahern, to suggest, perhaps, why it ought to be appreciated and valued.

My "Note" on *The Leavetaking* was my first effort to find a way to do this. Fifteen years after that first note, I wrote a book about all of his fiction and attempted to map the evolution of his imaginative engagement in the sequence of novels and stories of his first thirty years as a writer. It is surely ironic that even though my book includes no biographical information and does not in any way attempt to show a connection between the fiction and his life, I did indeed learn that my insight into the fiction derived from an intense and unconscious awareness of the life that informed it – the life, that is, that is hidden in circumstances. I realized that perhaps what I had been able to trace reflected in some way an allegory of my own inner life. The most intense reading, as the most intense writing, both come out of our hidden life, and so it is that writing about reading is a form of memoir. What I really wanted to do next was to invent a kind of memoir of the inner life that would trace that curious meeting of the writer's self and the reader's self.

Some time after this, I realized that Lawrence's myths and fables reflect a desire to return to an Eden of sensual contentment and peace. He had superimposed Frieda's libertarian philosophies of sex on his happy moments with her in the first few years in their Italian exile. He returned to London in 1914, certain that his ideas could become the basis for a new social order. Later, as the slaughter and oppression of the war years drove him to the edge of madness and starvation, the idyll with Frieda seems to have fallen away to be replaced by more strident theorizing. The fictions he imagined out of that first experience were written with the desperation of memory, the fury to create in the future what was already lost.

I recognized now what I shared with him, the experiences of loss and exile. Over the years, Montreal became home for me, and in my settling, I gradually moved on from thinking of my life in those terms. And yet, even as the circumstances of life become more ordinary, the mysterious depths take on their own shape. Perhaps it was this, as middle age came quickly towards me, that allowed me to discover again how to read Lawrence. The farms of his Nottinghamshire and Derbyshire reproduced my own childhood farm in Ireland. He never did make his peace with urban ways of life, and in his hideouts off the beaten track, in Italy, Australia and America, he remained a country boy. His intimacy with the hedgerows and the meadows, the trees and the animals had nourished his descriptions of a nineteenth-century landscape that seemed familiar to me as an image of my first home in County Clare.

Ireland and my childhood on the farm moved far away as the years were added to years in this city of immigrants, in this new home. But "messing about talking of Ireland" did become a way of reading my life, as indeed messing about talking of England became Lawrence's constant inspiration as he lived elsewhere. Learning to read the fiction of John McGahern was a training in learning how to read myself, and I realized too that an English novelist like Lawrence, or Hardy, could have helped me in that reading, if I had not been intimidated by his hectoring tone. Rather than a utopian visionary whose "whole" would regenerate industrial and urban England, Lawrence was a writer of elegies for the flowers and birds of his childhood, forever a writer of memoirs.

II

ACHILL BALLAST

Countrymen.

Slievemore rose up to my left, as I strolled down to Dugort beach the first morning. From the distance, it had seemed a picture-book mountain, standing alone, boggy ground sweeping up in a regular cone to a single peak. Here at its foot, it was more perpendicular, more of a hiker's challenge, yet still somewhat domesticated, the sheep grazing on its sides, the clouds gently descending and rising on its upper reaches. I considered climbing it another day, but it did not invite me there and then, as mountains in the Adirondacks or the Rockies had, theirs an invitation to enter a decidedly separate kingdom of high plateaus and thin air.

I reached the strand and headed westward, past the rudimentary hotel, not much more than an extension to a pub. Sheltered by the mountain from the westerly winds, a few trees struggled to attain a modest height; blackthorns, gorse and brambles made efforts to reach over stone walls but were bent over and down. The salt wind ruled. I quickly realized that this side of the island was impassable, or at least I came to the end of the road, and as far as I could see, the rocky side of Slievemore, the side facing the sea, spilled down to high rugged cliffs. I could imagine that further on, towards the open sea, beyond this pastoral enclave, the rock and the ocean, the wind and the light must do battle. Soft, boggy interior; rock, ocean, impenetrable limits; had Seamus Heaney been here?

A day earlier I had driven away from the farm in Clare, my first home, through Galway and Mayo, and the spirit of Seamus Heaney drove with me, in my mind that poem of County Clare when the poet drives west to the Burren coast.

It is a perfect Heaney poem, casual and precise like so many others, and for me especially satisfying because it speaks of a place I know so well, my primal landscape. I can see that wild ocean off Liscannor or Doolin or Ballyvaughan where "the wind and the light are working off each other." I have often revisited these places since childhood. I can see too my lake on the Shannon, or Yeats's tiny pond at Coole, or one of the many slate-grey lakes of this countryside with "the earthed lightning of a flock of swans."

Suddenly, at the end of the poem, the illusion that this is simply one other drive through windswept places is shattered by buffetings that "catch the heart off guard and blow it open." And there it ends, "Postscript," the last poem in the volume. A closed book, a heart blown open, last words returning the reader to his own life in the world.

I remember the first time I read the poem in Montreal. I gasped with excitement and fear, carried off by the gust in the last line, perhaps remembering a wintry Canadian road when a storm caught my Volkswagon van and I lost control, or, more likely, carried off onto another level of being by the very notion of that open heart, the purity of it, the escape from all the conditions of aging to a renewal of feeling and perception, carried away and carried back.

"Postscript" puts into words the landscape I have known and seen, Yeats at the back of the poet's mind as he drives, just as Heaney himself is at the back of mine. Is it possible to drive anywhere in Ireland without such ghosts? I am in very familiar terrain.

I returned to the sandy beach that curved gently for a few hundred yards to a jagged point. Waves unrolled themselves slowly along its length, breaking first at the west end, spilling a milky foam that ran on and on forever along this almost level strand. I was the only person here, the sound of the breakers filling the whole space. Rainclouds, veils of rain and mist thickened and cleared overhead and out to sea. Some miles across the water I could make out land, another island, perhaps, a peninsula, I could not tell, for although I knew this island reached out into the ocean further than any other, there were many headlands competing for this honour along the fragmented Atlantic coastline. A black dog brought me a piece of driftwood and I tossed it for him into the eddying shallows.

I walked to the further end and up the steep slope to the road, over low sand-dunes. Up here was a cluster of whitewashed cottages; they were arranged in a traditional pattern of Gaelic communities known as a Clochan. There was a long view now and I could see the northern shore. I was close enough to see houses scattered along the peninsula. There were fishingboats on the sound.

The long, watercolour views were serene and sleepy in the halflight. I met nobody on my walk. It was all still, easily framed in a picture postcard, a West of Ireland scene. My heart was not blown open.

On my first morning on Achill, I opened Thomas Hardy's *The Return of the Native*. I had brought the novel with me because I thought I would write something about my own homecoming. I imagined that I had grown up in a nineteenth century ethos on that farm in Clare. I thought Hardy would take me back, not fifty but one hundred years to a small enclosed place untouched by modernity.

I had forgotten his ponderous mythologizing about Egdon Heath, the small patch of moorland near his home in Dorset that became in his imagination a place where civilization and the primitive fought epic battles. He wondered if Lear, the ancient king of Wessex, had lived there. But it is not Shakespearean versions of history that attract him; it is the landscape itself, its geological and "natural" condition: "everything around and underneath had been from prehistoric times as unaltered as the stars overhead." Even the sea, he claims, cannot offer such a symbol of "ancient permanence." This unchanging Nature comforted him, for it "gave ballast to the mind adrift on change, harassed by the irrepressible New."

This phrase "ballast to the mind" jumped out at me, not because I was drawn in by Hardy's great drama of the ancient and the New, but for some other reason; the very notion in that phrase gave me a rush of adrenalin, the possibility that such "ballast" could be found. It may have connected with Heaney's poem of the "earthed lightening" and the open heart.

My house in Montreal is one of five built as a small terrace more than a hundred years ago. The facade of the terrace is constructed of large blocks of red sandstone. When I bought the house twenty years ago, I was told that this stone had originated in the Clyde in Scotland. Ships travelling to Canada for raw materials used the stone as ballast on the westbound journey. As the hold was emptied to make way for cargo, the stone was abandoned on the docks and an enterprising builder had made good use of it. This Victorian home in the centre of Montreal has ballast for my Canadian self, and not only in its stonework. It is where my heart gradually opened, my children grew up, my marriage became an anchor.

So why have I come here, tuned by Heaney's poem in my head? What do I expect to find in this Atlantic island?

Hardy's mythical "ballast" was marked by other convictions, adherence to something "unaltered," "ancient permanence," a touchstone of value in the face of the fashionable and the urbanized. In spite of my detachment from such nineteenth century mythmaking, "ballast to the mind" did release me into a long stretch of writing about homecoming, and now I wonder why. Was it Hardy, or Achill, or my own state of mind that made this phrase echo for days as a kind of blessing on my work?

One day, as I drove from Dugort across the island and on out past Keel to Keem Bay, another poem by Heaney came back to me, a poem of a much earlier drive, around a peninsula, somewhere on this Atlantic coast. "The Peninsula" is about a time "when you have nothing to say," in other words, a time of creative block, and while the drive does not exactly provide inspiration other than for this poem, it does say how that inspiration may be found: "you will uncode all landscapes/ By this: things founded clean on their own shapes."

The central irony of Heaney is here: he is the farm boy who looks with a fresh eye and hears with a fresh ear, the boy who became educated in literary sensibilities, and in that light articulates his own original "ground". For the North of Ireland poet everything is coded, with the murderous sectarian and historical codes, yet the image of possibility, of what is free of culture, free of prior interpretation and literary influence, is inspiring: "things founded clean on their own shapes."

Rocks, mountains, foreshore are ballast for the soaring, buffeted minds of artists like Hardy and Heaney who actually go to such places, the rugged shapes carved by elemental forces that are ahistorical, "water and ground in their extremity," as Heaney puts it. And he can still experience there that pristine geological state, that solidity and authenticity, as it were, before human histories and cultural coding began.

These Western places assumed cultural meanings in the work of Yeats and others to such a degree that for someone like me, displaced early from the farm in Clare, from this West of Ireland, the ballast may not be the rocks, the landscape itself, but the poems written about it, the memorializing of the place in that literature. Hardy's "ballast" was not, to me, the landscape itself but his belief in the power of the literary imagination to make a poetic description overawe the reader, as Shakespeare's presence in the landscape had overawed him, so that the reader too would be anchored by a belief in that power.

"The Peninsula" strips away all literary and cultural allusions in its simple account of a day's drive by the sea, and yet it seems to get to the essence of that myth of the Atlantic coast. In it Heaney seems to summon up, again in his own easy way, a century of cultural mythologizing about the nature of the West of Ireland experience. From Yeats's childhood in Sligo and his visits to Lady Gregory at Coole Park as a young man, he had it in his bones, and in his spiritualisitic soul, and it was he who encouraged Synge to leave Paris and go to the Aran Islands. But earlier in the eighteen-nineties, the journey westwards had become popular for the leaders of the Gaelic revival movement and their disciples, something that deeply affected the Joyce of "The Dead," for, of course, Gretta Conroy as well as Nora Barnacle came from the West.

Donegal, Connemara, and Kerry gained a primal significance in the revivalist cultural nationalism that dominated Irish life for almost a century, and in that myth of authenticity, Achill had a special place. It provided the visual imagery of that movement in the landscape paintings of Paul Henry and his heroic iconography of fishermen, for, somewhat like Synge, he left Paris and had a conversion experience on Achill in 1910; he stayed almost ten years, and his whole life as a painter from this time on is rooted in the images he found on this island. The largest ever retrospective of Henry's work was about to open at the National Gallery. "For generations of viewers, Paul Henry's work has been synonymous with notions of the essence of Ireland," the brochures say, "particularly the rural west of Ireland and a way of life that has almost vanished." The only equivocation here is in "notions of" and that is a hint of recent revisionism, for just as the Russian revolution or Nazi Germany had their own brand of iconography, so did the revivalist movement in Ireland. Paul Henry may not have been promoted as the official painter of the spirit of the independent nation, but his critical and commercial success gave him and his style that status.

For a hundred years, city and town dwellers have made pilgrimages to places like Aran and Achill, and parts of the West have now become oversettled with chalets and commodified by the tourist business. As natural wonders, they are not always as awe-inspiring as the Rockies, for instance, or the Alps, or the Pacific off Vancouver Island, yet for many people these are beautiful, wild, places where the heart can be blown open.

I did not grow up on this island, or on any of the celebrated Gaelic-speaking islands along the ocean. The farm overlooked Lough Derg, not far from Yeats's tower and the lake at Coole Park. I had to leave the farm to attend high school and then, after university years in Dublin, left for Canada. Montreal became home, and thirty years went by, during which time I had often returned to Ireland. This was not really a homecoming in any dramatic sense. When I decided to stay in Achill in the middle of winter, I had simply wanted a landscape with sea, a wild and quiet place to write, but for years homecoming has presented itself insistently as an experience that must be written about.

I realized that I had left Ireland partly because I could not feel that kind of attachment to the place, the country, the nation that the great mythologizers had made mandatory in their revivalist project. That project was simple, in their vision of it: to "de-anglicize" Ireland. It was to become a political and military project eventually, but during the period of promoting Home Rule, the political agenda was often promoted by other means. Although I had learned the Irish language, and had felt a real fervour during two summers on the Aran Islands, during my later adolescence, the Gaelic League project, the de-anglicization of Ireland, had failed to hold my fervour.

It did not provide the ballast I needed for my sense of myself; by the sixties, that post-colonial chauvinism carried little weight. There was the

Vietnam War to think about, apartheid in South Africa, homeless people in Dublin; there was another kind of politics that engaged me. And so notions of the essential spirit of Ireland felt claustrophobic to me. After all, I had become a student of English literature. I was reading Emily Dickinson and Henry James and T.S. Eliot; what did any of this have to do with Ireland? Yeats and Joyce wrote of Ireland, but the reason they were great writers was not that. They were respected and honoured for their internationalism.

If the nationalist mythologizers found in the West of Ireland a symbol of a pre-colonial condition that they aspired to revive, an idea of Ireland that was elemental and authentic, the writers found there material that would free them from the pressures of artistic trends and fashions of the metropolitan centres; they were freed from the contemporary and the commercial. This place provided artistic material that was away from literary society, that could enable them to write literature that could be classic. They found a way of life there that could easily be imagined in classic forms, in Greek tragedy, in Homeric and Celtic epic, in ballads and lovesongs.

Seamus Heaney has extended into another generation that same impulse to find in the local place the images and the style that carry him beyond Ireland and into a world culture. He lives in our time of deconstruction and demythologizing, yet it is not these cleansing operations that offer him conviction. He lives with the words of Yeats and Wordsworth and Milosz and Dante in his head, yet he tries to believe that the wind and the light of the Atlantic open his heart to a knowledge of things that are simply themselves.

He travels the Atlantic coast to turn over another page of the country book he has been reading and rereading since the earliest poems of Mossbawn and Anahorish: "bedding the locale/ in the utterance". He has found many ways to read the farms and lakes and their topography, yet there is a conviction in the return of the farmboy that he has found there and will find there a ballast that is forever his.

Who can separate the ballast from the fine-tuned eloquence that articulates it? Are the lines of Heaney that are most memorable, classic, a reflection of his superior powers of observation, of his deep attachment to his earliest place, or of his ability to breathe in the words of classic literary utterances so that they are faint echoes in his own utterances? When Seamus Heaney's heart is blown open on the west coast of Clare, is it possible that what he feels is elemental, free of all mythologies, or is the wind from the Atlantic freighted with voices that have also been free to articulate clean forms?

Although I am at home in my house in Montreal and in the city, and I have awe-inspiring landscapes within driving distance – the Adirondacks and the Atlantic coast in Maine – I have discovered that the ballast my imagination needs is in the literature of a local place. Like Hardy and Wessex, I am drawn back to an Ireland of the mind, believing, in spite of the new thoughts that have occupied me in my decades in North America, that there is something permanent that I can turn to, a place to begin.

One morning as I sat at my desk, looking out at the sheep grazing on the brown slope of Krinnuck, a retired schoolteacher of the island knocked on my window. This local historian wanted to show me the real Achill. I was to be his guest for a morning so he could drive me to all those places that made Achill special to him.

He pointed out prehistoric markers across fields grown wild with yellowing gorse, speculated about the reasons why a stone village of the nineteenth century was abandoned, showed me the exact Atlantic headland where Paul Henry's conversion took place in 1910, and the house of Captain Boycott which the American painter Robert Henri had lived in for a decade of summers in the nineteen twenties. He took me to the Mission Setttlement where a Protestant community was established at the time of the Famine, and to Keem Bay to tell me about the Basking Shark Fisheries; he had worked there in summers in the canteen when he was a schoolboy and recalled the tragedy of the photographers who were swept into the ocean as they filmed the netting of the sharks. He told me of the declining population on the island over the decades of his lifetime, of the disappearance of the Irish language there, and of his efforts to find work for the community which now survived precariously on tourist earnings. There were clusters of new cottages and bungalows everywhere, all unoccupied for most of the year. These investments were all about tax incentives for urban dwellers; locked-up cottages didn't help the people. Here a potter had tried to make a go of it, here a French painter; there a woman from Dublin had retired.

Every stone and bay had a story, every hill and lake a history, every turn of the road merited a commentary. The delight which animated him was the conviction that the spirit of this place was unique. Even in its decline and transformations, Achill made him proud. He was absolutely anchored in his place, and the stream of words that came from this old man was a tribute of love.

As we passed through Dooagh village, he pointed out the cottage that John McGahern had lived in thirty years before when he was writing *The Leavetaking*. He and the novelist often sat for a pint in the nearby pub while McGahern continued to live on the island. My interest came alive, for my first publication in Canada was a review of that novel, a first hymn of praise for the novelist whose earlier work I had begun to read and reread after I left for Canada.

McGahern's work is set in the farms and villages of the Shannon valley and his language breathes that local air. He has never been to the farm of my birth in Clare, but he knows it like the palm of his hand. More than anyone, McGahern has offered me ballast for my years in Canada, ballast to the mind as I learned how to read him and then through his eyes how to read so much of European literature. He, more than my years of university studies, taught me how to read and after that how to write. He, more than any other mentor, or favourite author, has taught me what ballast is and how necessary it is. More than Hardy, a favourite author of his, or more than Yeats, another favourite author, McGahern himself has taught me how to value the literature of place.

As a young man, McGahern left Ireland, had to leave it for his second novel, *The Dark*, was banned by the Censorship Board and he was fired from his job as a teacher. His spare autobiographical novel of adolescence in Roscommon captured forever the psychological scars inflicted on a sensitive boy by a repressive Catholic culture. The raw alienation dramatized in that novel speaks of an honesty and a depth of feeling that are almost surreal in their intimacy. Reading it, and rereading it, my heart was blown open, but it was a pained and painful wonder that I felt. The novel and a volume of stories of the late sixties, *Nightlines*, are the most eloquent evidence I know for why leaving that Ireland was necessary for psychic survival, for me as for him.

But after some years, the author quietly returned, to Achill, where he wrote his next novel, an account of a young teacher who must leave Ireland because he has married in a registry office in London. He returned to write *The Leavetaking*, almost a decade after *The Dark* was written. He had been unable to write in the aftermath of the banning and his departure. That return to the landscape of the west of Ireland, and then to the place of his childhood in Leitrim, renewed his writing in ways which have led on to his most recent novel, *That They May Face the Rising Sun*. It renders immortal the place he lives in, has lived in for more than thirty years, a quiet place by a lake where nothing happens and yet the essential events of a life are present and are placed in a luminous landscape. It is a novel without a story in the conventional sense for it simply records the life of a small group of neighbours during the round of one year. The precision of its poetic observation of people and their routines in a given place has made it a classic example of how a heightened vision of mundane experience may confer on it an aura of the sacred and the transcendent.

This novel is the culmination of the art he has been practicing for decades. It has the stillness of a Vermeer or a Rembrandt. His American publisher renamed it *By the Lake*, but the original title captures his intention: *That They May Face the Rising Sun*. As all things pass away, McGahern seems to say, this record of this time and place remains, this dream of permanence, this ballast.

Denis Sampson, a critic and essayist, teaches at Vanier College in Montreal. He has published a critical study of John McGahern (Outstaring Nature's Eye: The Fiction of John McGahern, *Lilliput, 1993) and a biography of Brian Moore (*Brian Moore: The Chameleon Novelist, *Marino Books, 1998).*

THREE POEMS

Richard Tillinghast

BIG DOORS

I have seen with my own eyes doors so massive
that two men would have been required
to push open just one of them.
Bronze, grating over stone sills, or made of wood
from trees now nearly extinct.

Many things never to be seen again!
The fury of cavalry attacking at full gallop.
Little clouds of steam rising
from horse droppings
on most of the world's streets once.

Rooms amber with lamplight
perched above those streets.
Pilgrimage routes smoky with torchlight
from barony to principality through forests
which stood as a dark uncut authority.

A story that begins "Once upon a time."
Messengers, brigands, heralds
in a world unmapped from village to village.
Legends and dark misinformation,
graveyards crowded with ghosts.

And when the rider from that story at last arrives,
gates open at midnight to receive him.
Two men, two men we will never know,
lean into the effort of
pushing open each big door.

HOW THE DAY BEGAN

Step by step the muezzin climbed
the hundred-and-one steps of his minaret
and assaulted the dark streets with the majesty of God.
His notes floated like jellyfish of the voice,
like the breasts of a woman
as she rides above a man,

then hardened when they struck the city's stone facades.
The street dogs roused. They took it into their heads
to rival the call to prayer with their howling.
That woke the crows, who grumbled in their leathery language
and flapped their wings like an ancient grudge
and woke the seagulls, who flocked and glided,
bringing whiteness to the city grey with dawn.

So now there were three colors:
Black of crows' wings stretching back to a time
before there was such a thing as time.
Grey of dawn and limestone and the lungs of old men
as they crept down city streets to pray in the mosque.
White of seabreeze and seagulls' ascension,
and white of the sheets where we woke.

Down in the mosque the old men had washed
away the night's blackness and were bending to their prayers,
stroking their grey beards and mumbling over their beads.
The dogs trotted along the pavement
and woke the sparrows, who told the air it was truly day.
A white tomcat named Nero curled around a juniper bush
in a flowerpot, then grumped and stretched and yawned,
and watched with sleepy eyes the sparrows' doings.

And then what happened, darling?
You sidled alongside the length of my body
and we went back to sleep for awhile.
From down in the street I heard two clangs of a trolley bell
and the aluminum surge of shopfront shutters yanked open,
and the steamy rush of a coffee machine.
You backed up onto me and warmed my hand on your breast.
What country were we in? Who was God? I couldn't remember.
The air smelled of everything.

ARS POETICA

Brush from my heart
the fine particulate matter of the World
Trade Center,
what's left of it now that floats
still in the air we breathe
and keeps us from thinking straight.

Revive me now
with anything low-tech, homemade,
handwoven from living fibers,
written with a fountain pen.

Show me lacquered Chinese red
of a box with three lucky coins in it,
thumbed turquoise of Tibetan
prayer beads hidden from soldiers –
even the powder-blue, tragic, compromised star,
six-pointed on a field of white,
flying over a tank that grinds down on Bethlehem.

Lift my eyes to the disk of the midday sun
seen through clouds
where our towers stood.

Slow me down for once in my life
to the gait of a camel crossing from Peshwar to Khandahar
with bags of rice strapped to its saddle,
while the camel driver cranes up
over his shoulder at the
vapor trails of a B52.

Show me struck flint of the North Star,
big splayed kite-frame of the Southern Cross,
and ask me to imagine how they look
from the Southern hemisphere –
while the beggar-man with his load of kindling
crosses the moon people see from China.

Write your words out Yankee-plain and iconic
as the Roman numerals
printed on the face of the clock

that kept time in my mother's kitchen.
Maybe that hand-wound pulse
will stop me thinking about
the NASDAQ, smiley faces, CEOs,
television, and Global Positioning Systems

guiding democracy bombs
into wars where people on the ground
shelter in tarpaper
shacks under roofs of corrugated tin
or pick their way maimed through mine-fields
trying to reach their olive groves.

I too love the primary colors of the flag –
its classic red and white stripes,
its machine-sewn stars
spangled over a field of blue
breezing in the September sky
this day of days.

But I've had it with "God Bless America."
Let blessings fall wherever there is need for them.
My country, it's not just
'tis of thee I sing.

When the "inevitable clash
of civilizations" crowd gets cranked up,
help me contemplate harmony.
Play me the world's music.
Let human fingers pluck the strings of
instruments fashioned from living forests.

Speak to me
in the wavery melismas of the call to prayer
that a billion people hear
this morning from a minaret before dawn,

while I feel in my bones
the bronze reverberations
of a bell that memorializes all we have lost.

A frequent visitor to Ireland, Richard Tillinghast lives in Ann Arbor, Michigan and is the author seven volumes of poetry. His most recent book is a collection of essays, Poetry and What is Real *(University of Michigan Press, 2004).*

From THE RANNAFAST SUMMER

Patricia Craig

Jeuking the edicts.

From Part I, "Corrupting Influence"

Joyce Cary begins his novel of 1941, *A House of Children*, by citing the effect on him of a swaying branch of fuchsia, glimpsed through the open window of a house in an inland town: suddenly, there's a tang of salt on the breeze, and some acute sensations of a childhood in Innishowen are returned to him in an all but tangible form. "I was waiting for a sail, probably my first sail into the Atlantic. Somebody or something must have fixed that moment upon my dreaming senses, so that I still possess it." Well, from Proust's *madeleine* on, literature is full of such mnemonic triggers, agents of all kinds of creative retrogression – and for most people too, in everyday life, the experience is fairly common. For example, it's virtually impossible, I would think, for any Irish person to get a whiff of turf smoke, in any circumstances whatever, without being instantly transported to an archetypal, agrarian-Irish domain. Sometimes, though, the movement backwards is precipitated by something more deliberate or mundane. We might be asked to recall an event from the past, or find ourselves in a backward-looking reverie, as a consequence of some chance reference or encounter. For myself – the act of "thinking back" to the summer of 1959 and its aftermath: this is a periodic occurrence, sparked off whenever I bump into one-time acquaintances (there seem to be a lot of them) who have the whole fiasco fixed in their heads.

In the autumn of 1992 I was at the BBC in Belfast to record a programme, in front of an invited audience, about the editing of anthologies. How do you go about editing an anthology? It wasn't a very exacting brief, but for someone who, like me, isn't a polished performer, any public appearance is apt to induce a state of the heebie-jeebies. Due to some unfathomable inadequacy, in these situations I lose control of my voice or my wits. A terrible tickle afflicts my throat, turning the whole thing into a coughing marathon. Fluster is not the word. Sometimes it's not so bad, when I've chivvied myself into a proper frame of mind beforehand, or when some contentious comment acts as a spur to loquaciousness. On this particular occasion in Belfast I manage not to cover myself in ignominy, though signally failing to match the fluency of my fellow panellists, poets Tom Paulin and Frank Ormsby, and chairman (the actor James

Ellis). We sit at a table on a raised platform, microphones in front of us, facing the audience who don't give us too hard a time – well, they're there, presumably, either as friends of the speakers, or because of some professional or personal interest in how a compilation such as *A Rage for Order* or *The Faber Book of Vernacular Verse* is put together. My role is to stick up for the prose anthology, my *Rattle of the North* having come out earlier in the year. A collection of excerpts from prominent Northern Irish works of fiction and non-fiction, this includes a passage from *Call My Brother Back* describing the removal of the MacNeill family from Rathlin Island to a street in Beechmount off the Falls Road. The new house, two-up two-down, is situated halfway along a run-down row; and beyond it are a brickyard and brickfields, with further "fields straggling up to the foot of a mountain". Michael McLaverty was a young schoolmaster when he wrote this partly autobiographical novel in the late 1930s, and he never again wrote anything that equalled its delicacy of expression and lucid proletarian innocence (though his second novel, *Lost Fields*, and a few of his stories come close).

"It's your fault I never learned to speak Irish." This bewildering accusation, addressed to me after the anthologies broadcast, with everyone milling about the lecture hall, comes (it turns out) from one of McLaverty's daughters, a Dominican past pupil of my vintage, who is fully *au fait* with the Rannafast crisis and its repercussions on the school. What does she mean? The explanation is pretty simple. Thirty-odd years earlier, our paltry delinquency had got itself blown up to such proportions that the Gaedhaltacht itself, the scene of our disgrace, was classed as forbidden territory for St Dominic's girls over the next couple of years. Encouraging senior pupils to spend a part of the summer in Donegal putting a gloss on their Irish was a thing of the past, at least for the time being. "Rannafast" had become synonymous with "fast" (well, there'd always been a tinge of that about the place, contributing to its fascination; but it was only now that it was out in the open, now the great scandal had broken and shame and infamy covered the school, the summer colleges, the insufficiently vigilant teaching staff and worst of all, us three expellees). Our unholy conduct was something no young pupil coming up behind us was going to get a chance to emulate. For some would-be *gaedhalegoirs*, and others in search of extracurricular skylarking, this deprivation rankled – and we, idiotic enough to get caught out, were the authors of it.

Three old ladies attending the 1992 broadcast in Belfast are also keen to speak to me. While the programme was being recorded I'd dimly registered their presence as they sat sedately on their upright chairs and made no contribution to the debate. They'd seemed as much out of place as nuns at a hooley, among the teachers and BBC personnel and council representatives and literary social workers who made up the bulk of the audience. And, indeed, they disclaim all knowledge of literary matters. They have come along out of loyalty to a dear friend, recently dead, who took a keen interest in books and writing, and, moreover, had been an admirer of mine: she had all my books, and used to cut out and place in a file every newspaper article by or about me that came her way. A Miss May Brannigan. I'm naturally gratified by this information, since it brings the number of fans I'm aware of up to two – the other being an elderly (male) eccentric and self-taught painter from Greenwich in South-East London. It isn't totally disinterested admiration, though. Local patriotism is at the bottom of it. It seems Miss Brannigan lived only a few doors away from us on the Donegall Road, just across from where her friends in the audience still live. Nevertheless, I applaud her instinct to approve of someone's progress (however limited), rather than judging them incapable of anything simply because you knew them in their pram.

I am at a loss to recall any of these ladies, spinsters all, though I do remember others from the front of the road: Mrs McNamara who gave me Edwardian postcards to add to my collection, Mr and Mrs Clark whose daughter married a Belgian soldier, the Armstrongs, Lily Beattie. While I stand there in the lecture hall at the BBC, with people commenting on various aspects of the programme, and friends trying to shepherd me across the road for a drink with the producer and contributors, part of my attention is focused on the Donegall Road in the 1950s – the far end of the road before the construction of the M1, with the Bog Meadows in one direction and the Black Mountain in the other: from my bedroom window, if you look to the right, you can see the mountain with its distinctive landmark, a field shaped like a hatchet, with a clump of trees and a barely distinguishable white house in the corner.

It was from this vantage point that Colm MacNeill, the young protagonist of *Call My Brother Back*, sat with his brothers looking down on dingy, pre-war Belfast: the patches of waste ground, the mill chimneys and dishevelled terraces. They can nearly make out their own street, down there among the homely architecture of Beechmount. Turn towards the Park, from the bottom of this street, and you soon reach the roads sloping up towards the mountain: the Giant's Foot, Rockville, Rockmount Streets and then the Whiterock Road with its comprehensive boys' school where Michael McLaverty held the post of headmaster for a good many years. Beyond the top of the Whiterock Road comes the Mountain Loney, at that time a country lane with an old tin church halfway along it, and a well of pure spring water at the end to refresh you before you tackled the mountain proper. I think the whole area is now built over – while the streets which McLaverty evoked in the novel *Lost Fields* are now lost streets.

Michael McLaverty is very thick with the nuns of the Dominican Convent on the Falls Road, my old school. It is also the old school of my friend Patricia Mallon, whom – although we are almost exact contemporaries – I don't remember from those days of the late 1950s. It wasn't until 1985 that we met at an IASAIL Conference at Queen's University, at which I was reading a paper on the treatment of women in Northern Irish fiction (McLaverty's included), and struck up a friendship. She remembers me from our schooldays for the usual reason: the notoriety that was thrust upon me back in the past. ("Má's mor do chliu, ni maith": if your fame is great, it is not good.) Her opening words – "Does the name of Rannafast make you want to laugh or gnash your teeth?" – make me laugh, but ruefully. As I've said, whenever I go into any social gathering in Belfast, up comes an ex-Dominican pupil to remind me of the episode, which seems to have loomed very large in the lore of the school – though at the time, and for a long period afterwards, I was not aware of its impact. Indeed, I had thought my exit from the school went relatively unnoticed.

I can't imagine why I believed this: it was, after all, nearly a mass expulsion – three of us cast out at the same time – and clearly caused a scandal of sufficient intensity to mesmerise the school. How they must have lapped it up – I'd have done the same, if it had happened to someone else – and how our misdoings must have gained in exorbitance! What scope for the envisaging of lurid antics! I now know that we were held up as an awful warning for years to come. According to more than one teacher, signs of insufficient tractability were apparent in the three of us nearly from the minute we set foot in the school. We were blamed for holding far too good an opinion of ourselves, for being unamenable to discipline of any kind, whispering in class and eating ice-lollipops in the street, and forever carrying on insubordinately. Inter-house competition, games and other innocuous activities were supposed to have left us cold. (All this was conveyed to me, bit by bit, over many years.) We refused to pull our weight on netball field or hockey pitch, though perfectly robust in constitution, preferring to idle around making fun of those who exerted themselves in a proper spirit. The games mistress, in particular, claimed to have predicted our bad end. She was a Mrs Cumberledge, very bleak and bony, and infamous herself for being separated from her husband, for going to the Dogs (but only literally), and for turning up at the school every now and then wearing a fearfully moth-eaten old fur coat, which gave her the look of a shaggy snake. (I can still see that coat.) I detested her, with the kind of whole-hearted detestation that's rarely available to anyone over the age of seventeen.

Rumour had all three of us expecting babies, at the very least, after midnight orgies with Donegal turf-cutters, to account for the extremes of censure and innuendo surrounding our departure – and neither the games mistress, who certainly knew better, nor anyone else in authority went out of her way to contradict such misapprehensions. If the school, believing them, could be kept suitably cowed as a result, so much the better. (Some pupils, in shocked whispers, discussed the actual presence of *boys in our bedrooms*; while others, more admiring, wondered how we had pulled it off.) As for us – good riddance to the lot of us. At that juncture in my life, the future career that so engrossed Miss Brannigan from the Donegall Road very nearly remained as much a figment as the non-existent teenage pregnancies.

Every now and then there occurs a moment when events from the past assume a striking configuration – when accumulated connections and coincidences enrich the original occurrence, or begin to impose a pattern on top of it. You can suddenly see aspects of the thing that weren't apparent at the time, as well as marvelling at the way it all holds together. It ceases to be amorphous and acquires an outline – or at least, you're handed on a plate the means of achieving an outline. It makes a proper story, complete with plot and sub-plots. And more. "We had the experience but missed the meaning," T.S. Eliot wrote in "Little Gidding". "And approach to the meaning restores the experience/In a different form ..." I'm all for having a pungent experience restored, though it's not so much *meaning* I'm after – futile to attempt so highfalutin an exercise – not so much meaning, as implications: the implications of what went on in Rannafast and Belfast at a particular period, and in distinctive circumstances, with myself and my friends at the centre of it.

It's that moment at the BBC in Ormeau Avenue in 1992, with the combination of Michael McLaverty, his one-time St Dominic's daughter and the late Miss Brannigan, that gets me thinking about the Falls Road and Rannafast, social history and convent benightedness, and the endless emphasis on chastity that marked our upbringing; all you've taken on board, as it were, merely by virtue of having lived through it. ("She was a middle-aged woman who had led a certain, not very varied but perceptive life, who had lived through enough time to write a narrative of it ..." – thus the heroine of A.S. Byatt's story, "On the Day that E.M. Forster Died".) It's true that that occasion at the BBC might have furnished a starting-point for other stories – if we're going to view the past as a succession of stories, carrying a particular import and with a beginning, a middle and an end; the Cobbles story, for example, or the Derby Street story, both capable of elaboration. However, it is Rannafast and its associations that suggest themselves most insistently – that are going to nag at me, I know, until I get them off my chest.

There's already been a slight rehearsal for this undertaking. In 1982 I was asked by *The Observer* to contribute to a series of articles it was running on the subject of being expelled from school. The piece I wrote was very short and frivolous – short enough to reproduce here in full. It was printed under the title "Corrupting Influence":

I was expelled from school for having once possessed a copy of *Peyton Place* and for having lent it to a classmate who thought it was the *Kama Sutra*. In fact, it served her purpose just as well. After years of good conduct, this girl – stocky and bespectacled – suddenly developed an enthusiasm for the pleasures of the flesh (in a mild form).

What she learnt from Grace Metallious's helpful novel she put to good use in the course of a holiday we spent in Donegal, and ended by depriving the school of three of its most hopeful pupils (herself included). Our expulsion had a profound effect on us. Of the other two, one became a terrorist in later life and one married a policeman. I lost the taste for reading American bestsellers.

It happened the summer before we were due to go into the sixth form. Our school, a Belfast convent, was run on old-fashioned lines – no eating or going bare-headed in the street, no leaning out of classroom windows to wave at workmen building the new wing, light reading supposed to be confined to picturesque Catholic pamphlets with titles like *The Devil at Dances*.

Seniors, however – those who could be trusted to uphold the standard of behaviour required by the school – were encouraged to attend an Irish-language course which was held each summer in a Gaelic-speaking part of Donegal. Pupils from schools all over the province converged on this spot at the beginning of August, were allocated to various homes in the district and set about acquiring fluency in Gaelic. (Since this was the object, you were sent home if you were caught speaking English.)

The college authorities here, we discovered, were nearly as strict as the nuns we had left behind in Belfast. Ceilis – Irish dances – were organised for our benefit three times a week; but if you were observed dancing with the same partner more than twice, you were reprimanded. Pairing-off was frowned upon.

You had to be careful, too, how you dressed: one girl was taken to task for appearing in a blouse with the top two buttons undone. According to one rumour, priests and teachers attached to the college patrolled the roads at night shining torches behind turf-stacks and into ditches in search of concupiscent couples – making killjoys of themselves, it seemed to us, on the scale of Yeats's Father Rosicross.

Other rumours, however, had reached us before we left the city. We all looked forward to fulfilment, or at least entertainment, in the arms of some Donegal turfcutters; and we weren't disappointed. Groups of these local boys, home for the summer from part-time jobs in Scotland, used to roam the district between one and three in the morning, rapping the bedroom windows of girls who, they

> thought, might be game for a little hanky-panky behind a cow-byre. We quickly acquired the habit of scrambling out in the middle of the night (priests and teachers all safely in bed by this time – or so we hoped), wearing more clothes than we did in the daytime to discourage excesses of passion, and of scrambling in again at every intimation of danger. A dog barking or the glimmer of a torch in the distance was enough to send us scuttling for the windowsill.
>
> So much hilarity was bound to be followed by sobriety: this nursery maxim proved well-founded in our case. Things began to go wrong. Our landlady at last realised what we were up to and nailed up the windows to stop us getting out. Worse, at a ceili on the last night of our holiday, we – pupils belonging to our school only – were summoned to the secretary's office and told that a letter, written by one of us and describing our activities in ribald detail, had reached our headmistress via the parents of the girl to whom it was addressed. As a consequence it was probable that we were all going to be expelled.
>
> As soon as we were released, we headed for the girls' cloakroom where a state of extreme agitation soon prevailed. Who was to blame for this misfortune? We narrowed it down to two girls, both staying at a cottage at some distance from mine. I concluded, rightly at this stage, that I wasn't too seriously implicated in the business.
>
> However, the fateful letter now in our Mother Superior's hands – all exclamation marks and knowing innuendoes, I believe – turned out to be the work of a girl whose supposed naivety had been a byword in the school. Clearly, some corrupting agent had been at work. What was it, the headmistress wanted to know.
>
> It might have been a book she read. A book? What book? A terrible immoral novel called *Peyton Place*. And where had she got it? ... That was when my far-from-brilliant school career went bung.

There is nothing fearfully askew about this as far as accuracy of recollection goes (though I've presented some things as facts when they're only suppositions). But it is most unwarrantably simplified. It was wrong of me, for example, to apply the word "terrorist" to my one-time best friend, who later went on to carve out a doughty career for herself in the South: her "Irishness" took a different form from mine, or than mine would have taken if I'd stayed in Belfast, that was all. Living where she did (in West Belfast), at a particular time (the early 1970s), and as a crusader against social injustice, she didn't have the option of remaining neutral or disinterested as things fell to pieces around her, of observing excruciating occurrences from afar and forming judicious opinions on them. She was there in the thick of it, having her political consciousness raised along with her hackles: night raids, sectarian aggression, violence in the streets, vehement partisanship, an atmosphere of anarchy – anarchy tempered by a local republican camaraderie. What could she do but get involved – and once that had happened, a sequence of events including all the horrors associated with a clandestine affiliation was set in motion. This old friend, whom I shall call Olivia McAloon (more about her later), became famous, or infamous, for more than being expelled from school. Recently, yet another St Dominic's old girl, of a humorous disposition, bounced over to me in a public place to assure me that I was only the second most scandalous past pupil in the history of the school. In the notoriety stakes, our republican classmate had beaten me hands down.

As for the other delinquent (a most unlikely delinquent) specified in my *Observer* article, who was never a kindred spirit or even a close school friend – I don't know if it's appropriate to attribute to her as much of the blame for my downfall as I do, or even if it is true that she married a policeman (I seem to remember hearing something to this effect, but I can't be sure about this: I've chosen to assert it merely in the interests of symmetry). I've also conflated her character and that of a couple of lesser-known, more childish girls who were minimal participants in the dramas of that summer. And yes, *Peyton Place* did come into the picture; but it was not the only, or even the main, reason why I was expelled. There's a lot more to the story than that, and several aspects of the business only became known to me after a considerable lapse of time. In the weeks after the verdict was delivered, I think I latched on to *Peyton Place* because I had owned a copy of this deplorable novel and it had gone the rounds of Form 5A; this provided an explanation of sorts when I was badly in need of one. I must have pieced it together from things said, or intimated, by some of the girls concerned; no one ever alluded directly to *Peyton Place* and its indecency, as far as I am aware. But I was not in a state to make much sense of anything. The whole episode was devastating and bewildering. Like Sean O'Faolain after hearing that his novel *Bird Alone* had been banned by the Irish Censorship Board, I felt that "Somebody had thrown me out of an accepted club without my knowing what I'd done." First I was told that I might resume my place in the school at the start of the new term, then – after a reversal of opinion – that I was, instead, to be ejected (the second, I was given to understand, as evidence of my depravity came to light). These successive edicts were conveyed to my mother. It seemed I was too depraved to be actually summoned to the school, confronted with my supposed transgression and given a chance to defend myself. Nuns were very autocratic in those days. At the same time, they were under the thumb of priests. More than twenty years went by before I gained an inkling of the part played in the whole sorry affair by an extraneous character, a priest attached to Clonard Monastery in Belfast, a total stranger to me. ("Is maith an scéalaí an aimsir", time is a good historian.) I learnt of his existence, eventually, through the novelist Michael McLaverty.

It was after the publication of the *Observer* article. I've said that I wasn't acquainted with McLaverty's daughter, but the same was not true of her father, whom I did get to know, very slightly. In 1976, my parents had moved to a spot in County Down between Strangford and Ballyhornan, saying goodbye without regret to the Donegall Road and the sight of a burning bus forming part of a barricade every time they stepped out of the door. The owner of a weekend house just down the road, along the shores of the Lough, was known in the district as the author of several novels. One day my father was accosted while mowing the lawn by an elderly, gnomish gentleman wearing a black beret, and demanding to be told if a writer lived there. He was a writer himself, by the name of McLaverty. It was explained to him that the writer – me – was based in London, but came over to stay in Co Down fairly frequently. (How had he heard of me? My "writing" at the time consisted of a study of girls' fiction, written jointly with Mary Cadogan, and a handful of magazine articles.) It wasn't long before I met Mr McLaverty myself, some years before his astonishing loquacity and story-telling gifts were eroded by old age. (He ended his life being cared for in a nursing home.) We were all intrigued by him and his fund of anecdotes about Ballymurphy and the Strangford/Portaferry districts of Co Down. It's true that after a certain point we noticed a degree of repetitiveness and forgetfulness, or misremembering, beginning to afflict him. He sometimes mistook me for one of his past pupils (I think – or were they all boys?) and complimented me on having grown into a lovely big girl. (I was over thirty at the time.)

While he still had full command of his faculties, though, McLaverty read my *Observer* article and promptly paid a visit to his pal Mother Helena of the Dominican Order, the nun at whose hands my prospects for a university education came unstuck. To go by what he told me later, he found her in a penitent frame of mind. If she'd had the thing to do over again, she said, she'd have acted differently. At the time – well, drastic measures needed to be taken, to restore (as far as possible) normality and a high moral tone to the school. Mother Helena wasn't to know that the world was on the verge of change – that 1960s freedoms would soon extend even to the corridors and classrooms of St Dominic's High School on the Falls Road. The truth was, in the weeks following the discovery of our Gaedhaltacht goings-on, she came under tremendous pressure to make an example of me, me in particular, even though my relative innocence with regard to the Rannafast imbroglio had been more-or-less accepted. Father So-and-So of Clonard Monastery (if McLaverty ever mentioned this person's name to me, I quickly forgot it), in his full rage and indignation, was insisting on my removal from the school forthwith. Why, when he had no more personal knowledge of me than he had of Mata Hari – indeed had never set eyes on me in his life? An aunt now comes into the picture, the aunt of one of the other girls involved, my best friend Olivia McAloon.

This aunt – Aunt Ita – was a gaunt woman, a cripple, who was often seen propelling herself about the town in an invalid carriage. Her great purpose in life was to carry out auxiliary work for the church, supplying flowers for the altar, organising collections on behalf of the Foreign Missions, that sort of thing. She was off to some non-essential church service every minute of the day. The Clonard priest was an acquaintance of hers, and it was to him that she went with the terrible story of her niece's expulsion. It was no skin off Aunt Ita's nose to cast me as the prime mover in the affair. She had never considered me a suitable chum for her niece. Something about me didn't commend itself to her. It may have been nothing more radical than my current hairstyle, which – by accident – produced an "arty" impression. Up until the age of fifteen, I'd been subjected by my mother to a nightly ritual involving rags or curlers, the effect of which was to make me look a bit like a sheepish Young Christian or an exceptionally gauche barn dancer. (The look she was aiming at, sort of Margaret Lockwood-cum-Doris Day, was unfortunately not available to me: I didn't have the face or the personality to carry it off.) Then, the summer before Rannafast, I went to stay with the McAloons in a cottage in the Mourne Mountains, where my hair reverted to a natural state: straight. It was a revelation to me how much better it looked, and I resolved to hold fast to the inadvertent improvement. But, in those days, to have straight shoulder-length hair, and a fringe to boot, proclaimed a deficiency of moral fibre, as far as women like Aunt Ita could judge. At the very least, it indicated a wish to attract attention. Whatever. There was disapproval there to begin with, and I imagine the tale Aunt Ita carried to the priest went something like this: I'd led the others astray, out of sheer badness, and then contrived to get off scot-free. God knows what evidence she produced to back up her story. Whatever it was, it sent him off in a jiffy on his mission of ill will. ("Is fearr eolas an oilc na an tolc gan eolas", better is knowledge of evil than evil without knowledge.)

When Michael McLaverty recounted to me his conversation with Mother Helena, in the early 1980s, he alluded to this priest as if I'd always known all about him and his impact on my life; but in fact I'd lived all those years in utter ignorance of his existence.

(I have to try to be fair here: it is possible that Aunt Ita and the nuns and the priest were perfectly correct in their assessment of my character – that they all perceived, long before I did, my inability to subscribe to the system they revered; that they saw me, rightly, as a disruptive influence and opponent of Catholicism – or, for that matter, any other dogmatic religion. But if this is so, it was on my future, not my present, behaviour that I was being judged.)

Father So-and-So: once his name came up, his role in the affair made perfect sense. This was one of the pieces that finally slotted into place, backed up by passing comments from my London friend and closest neighbour at the time, Rory McAloon (the brother of Olivia), with whom, for various reasons, I hardly discussed the matter at all. (I'm aware that the McAloons' version of the events described below will not coincide with mine.) In those days, I lived with my husband Jeffrey Morgan in the top half of a graceful Georgian house in south-east London, while Rory and his wife and daughters had the other half – and it was because of Rory, whom I bumped into in Blackheath in 1976, that this joint ownership came about. He and his family were installed in the basement of the house when it came on the market (it was in such a shocking state that it was under threat of compulsory purchase and demolition by Greenwich Council), and he went to considerable lengths to secure the property, finally bringing us in on the deal. As architectural enthusiasts, we were intrigued. Along with the house next door, ours had functioned as a hostel for the employees of a local drapery firm, Hinds (many of whom were Irish shop girls, some from Donegal). In an earlier incarnation, under a Miss Mary Tatlock, the house had been a boarding school – and then a Miss Jane Caroline Corbett and her heirs lived there between 1873 and 1940, after which began the long decline from London suburban respectability. Forty-odd years later, we moved in – after a full-scale renovation had been carried out.

It was a lovely and unusual place to live. (This is true also of our present home, a stone-built one-time manse in Co. Antrim.) And our occupation of it was due to a set of circumstances arising from a link with the past, my past – a link so tenuous it was down to a spider-web thinness, though about to be solidly reinforced.

How it came about was this. For some reason, I was sitting on a bench at the end of Vicarage Walk in Blackheath, between a great friend in the area, a shrewd and incorrigible old lady from the north of England who concealed her formidable intelligence, but displayed her humour, by opting to look like an old clothes woman, and an elderly black gentleman – idly sitting there, when Rory McAloon rode past on a bicycle, looked, stopped, looked again and rode back. It's an occurrence that calls to mind Anthony Powell's famous sequence of novels, *A Dance to the Music of Time*, in which the vagaries of social intercourse are likened to a dance whose complicated movements keep bringing you face-to-face with a particular person, and then out of their orbit for a time.

This fortuitous meeting, then, had consequences which none of us could possibly have foreseen. (To begin with, it's unlikely that I'd be sitting here, looking out at a pair of 200-year-old yew trees, in a house with a hidden garden and mysterious attics, if it hadn't taken place.) It nearly didn't happen. It was a wonder that Rory had recognised me, after a lapse of twenty-odd years, and given the fact that we'd only known one another slightly, between the ages of eleven or twelve and sixteen, while I knocked around with his sister. We arranged to meet, that day in Blackheath, and one thing led to another … Our joint occupancy of No 2 Cresswell Park proved to be quite a tempestuous business at times, Rory being volatile, maddening and moody, as well as amusing, generous and gregarious. As our friendship progressed, I became aware that his view of me was coloured ineradicably by the atmosphere in his home around the time of the Rannafast debacle. He envisaged me as a naughtier and more dashing schoolgirl than I ever was, cocking a snook at the Church and merrily getting up to all kinds of licentiousness.

He also had me down – rightly – as a poetry-lover, like himself, and would sometimes curb his wilder instincts if I was about. Once, when he didn't, I remember him charging at full steam after a crowd of juvenile intruders in the garden next door, yelling at the top of his voice; then coming back to where I was standing witnessing this performance, and declaring humorously, defiantly and apologetically all at once, "It's the Falls Road coming out in me."

Rory moved out of our Blackheath house a couple of years before his premature death in 1998 when he was fifty-three. An excess of drink on top of such perennial complaints as asthma, stomach trouble, migraine, insomnia, did for him in the end. We still find his absence upsetting and perplexing.

Long before I ran across Rory in Blackheath, my friendship with his sister had all-but evaporated. It really didn't survive the Rannafast summer, though intermittent attempts were made to prolong it. By the mid-1970s, Olivia's life had taken a few dramatic turns. On top of being imprisoned for republican activities, she'd been shot in the head and stomach and was lucky to be alive. The expulsion from school, in Olivia's case, was only the prelude to a much larger expulsion – or exclusion: from the whole of Great Britain and Northern Ireland. Though her home was in Belfast she was exiled to Dublin, unable to cross the border without fear of arrest.

In the face of these exorbitant occurrences, Olivia's capacity for insouciance was somewhat diminished. When she read my *Observer* article in 1982 (it was reported back to me) she was affronted by the word "terrorist" and consequently took a "scunner" at me. Well, as I've said, it's understandable that she should resent the attempt of a one-time friend to blacken her deepest convictions, merely in the interests of obtaining an effect of smartness. But it was a sorry end to an old school friendship. *Allies in the Fourth*, you might have dubbed us; and the Third, and the Fifth, while those early days threw up unimportant dramas, trivial school contretemps, around us. One of us might have to defend the other during a brief campaign of putting worms and spiders in her schoolbag, to see her lose her rag; or exercise her wits to concoct a plausible explanation for some bit of rule-breaking threatening to bring down ire on the other's head. The great topics of the day, to which we were devoted, included the question of who would get off with whose brother at a classmate's Hallowe'en party, whose end-of-term results were not up to standard, what teacher had it in for whom. We were acting out in our own lives the substance of a thousand girls' stories, immersed as we were in classroom politics, the forming and reforming of alliances and cliques, the modish contingent versus the hard workers, the good sports and their opposite, the affected brats. Some among us (only a very few, alas) were admired for their beauty, their ostentatious cleverness, or their ability to make things hum. Where we departed from the standard school of fiction, Springdale, St Madern's or the picturesque Gulls' Haunt, was in the religious conditioning that permeated everything, down the pain in your thumb. If you complained of a pain in the thumb, you were told to offer it up for the souls in Purgatory – who thereby got themselves associated with so many minor discomforts that they were eventually thought of themselves as a pain in the neck.

The scarcity of contiguous role models may have been a factor in the allure, for us, of more or less daring, American teenage films including "Peyton Place" – shown, I think, at the old Imperial Cinema in Corn Market – whose delectable atmosphere was *not* reproduced in the book. When I read the book, I found it sickly and shoddy beyond anything I could have anticipated, and I couldn't wait to get it off my hands (with the consequences adumbrated above). No, throughout the fifties, the figure most assiduously presented to us as a role model was that of Maria Goretti, an obscure Italian peasant girl who fought off a would-be rapist and literally died to stay chaste. (She'd achieved the status of "Blessed" by the time we became aware of her – I think she was canonised later.) The fate worse than death, in this instance, really was, in her mind, worse than death. Not that we understand, for some years, what Maria Goretti's virtue consisted *in*, being insufficiently knowing to grasp the nature of the "sin" she resisted so exorbitantly. When we were only eleven or twelve, the nuns' version of the story – a "man" had tried to persuade the devout young girl to commit "a sin," but even the prospect of dying bloodily couldn't erode her aversion to wrongdoing – meant little to us. Was it a thieving enterprise he'd tried to coerce her into, or did he want her to tell lies on his behalf? Requests for enlightenment were met with evasion. Of course, before too long, we knew exactly what was entailed during the lethal confrontation in some backward part of Italy – by which point, I think, most of us were sufficiently pragmatic to reject the slant imposed by the Church over the pathetic occurrence. Better deflowered than defunct, in our opinion: or, what was the point in retaining an intact hymen if the rest of you was ripped to pieces? Nevertheless, the temporary popularity of "Goretti" as a Christian name among Irish Catholic parents testifies to the impact of the little Italian's insensate heroism.

Those girls (there were a few) among us who aspired to a similar invincibility were ripe for admission to a society called The Children of Mary (a Catholic coterie whose *raison d'etre* is a blank to me, if I ever understood it); while the rest of us were judged of insufficient piety to merit the broad blue ribbon, with holy medal attached, which denoted membership of this Mariolatrous, senior-school group. Entitlement to wear this ribbon on top of my wine-coloured gym-tunic was a status I never craved. I was more interested in acquiring a *fainne*, or ring, to pin on my blazer: a silver *fainne* to begin with and then a gold one, indicating degrees of proficiency in Irish.

My Irish was coming on, but it was still very much at the lesson book stage; it wasn't yet a medium of communication with peers. I was fairly good at languages, though never outstanding – by languages I mean the two on offer, Irish and French. Among the fearsome grudges I've been harbouring against my old school, all these years, is its failure to provide for us, the A-stream, a grounding in Latin – an advantage you might have assumed to be inseparable from a Catholic education. But no: by some unfathomable quirk on the part of the curriculum-arranger, Latin was available to the B-stream in our year, but not to us – or not, at least, without an impossible jiggling of the timetable to fit it in. All the Latin I ever picked up was the word "veritas" – "Our noble motto," as the school song had it, "blazoned on the shield we wear,/Truth in thought and word and deed,/The heritage we bear" and so on – the phrase "Per ardua ad astra", our house motto, and as much of the Mass as stuck in my head. This was supposed to be an efficient school, a school it did your reputation no harm to attend (unlike the supposedly inferior establishments for Eleven-Plus failures); but I remember it as a place where I was badly taught (with one or two exceptions) and badly treated (though I'd never want to play the "poor me" card). I'm astounded whenever I read friendly references to nuns in general, and to those of my Dominican convent in particular – as, for example, in Mary Beckett's novel *Give Them Stones* (1987). In this novel, the heroine's sister wins a scholarship to the place – "the school on the Falls Road" is all the identification it gets, but it's enough – and comes home enthusing about the quiet nuns in their long white habits and big rosary beads, "the lessons and the kindness and the singing in the white chapel". She's writing about the 1940s, it's true, but I can't believe that things were so different then. Kindness is not a quality I associate with nuns. My nuns didn't have it in them. They were nearly all ordinary, not very intelligent women driven to irascibility or worse by the artificiality of their situation. One or two, I am sure, were certifiably insane, like the physical-punishment addict of Aquinas Hall, or the uncontrollable hysteric I met at Ballynahinch. Nuns at the time were stuck with the veil for life – except in very extraordinary circumstances – and some of them must have regretted the virtual imprisonment they had set up for themselves. We were always hearing about this nun or that nun who'd suffered a nervous breakdown. Once professed, they didn't have the option of changing their minds – probably the last intake of convent fodder in that stymied position. Soon, you'd get the cut-and-run syndrome which pulverized the whole idea of cloistered constancy. Starting as a drizzle, the I-leapt-over-the-wall brigade became a cloudburst, with nuns in droves ducking out of their vows as the life of holiness proved more than they could take. By the 1960s, even the Dominican Order was failing to hang on to its less-than-dedicated recruits. And when they resumed their laity, they went the whole hog. One contemporary recalls bumping into a young ex-nun at a railway station, and being slightly shocked by the extreme shortness of her skirt, the redness of her lipstick and breeziness of her manner.

The old perception of nuns as holy and good and the convent as a haven of stability was due for an overhaul, and, along with many ingredients of Irish myths and truisms, it was about to get it. Revisionism would soon come into its own. But, as yet, we had no intimations of upheavals in the political or the moral sphere. We thought we inhabited a world in which Catholic values were unchangeable, in which the church hierarchy would continue to lay down the law, a law transgressable only by those already brimful of badness. All forces for change were regarded with suspicion by elders with mitres and elaborate headgear, and their stern views filtered right down to the lowest of their flock. At school debating contests, for example, those of us who upheld the mildest form of socialism were warned we were on a slippery slope: the merest push, we were told, would tip us over into a godless Communism. (An alarmist attitude to a possible Communist takeover was widespread at the time.) Communism, divorce and popular entertainment were the greatest evils of the modern world, and they were all tied up together. But Catholicism had its own, unassailable, resources, including the resource of domestic praying.

A few years earlier, our seven-, eight-, and nine-year-old heads had come under considerable liturgical pressure, as rosary dementia got the country into its grip. This craze, like a good deal of popular entertainment, was imported from America, and it smacked of a Catholic transatlantic smarminess which – even then – one or two of us found unpalatable. Well, I can only speak for myself, of course. At school (Aquinas Hall) we were urged to go around proselytising on behalf of the rosary, and in particular to persuade our parents to hold rosary sessions in their living-rooms in the evenings, if they weren't already doing so. Even at that age I had read enough, and was scornful enough of the "ministering children" strain in Victorian fiction, to resent any attempt to cast me, me with my self-professed affinity with anarchic William Brown, and Jane Turpin of the tearaway ingenuity – to cast me as one of those goody-goody, obnoxious softeners of obdurate adult hearts. I'd no more have suggested praying to my parents than nude bathing in the Falls Park "Cooler". I couldn't imagine anything more preposterous than the four of us (grandmother included) down on our knees going "Hail Mary/Holy Mary".

There wasn't a chance of it: we were not that kind of family. But, to my consternation, it looked as though I was unique in this respect, as the whole school immersed itself in the devotional brouhaha. My family's cheerful impiety – well, relative impiety – seemed perfectly natural to me. But I hesitated to disclose our aversion to communal praying, since I could tell it ran counter to the stirred-up sanctity enkindling our classroom. I though if I just kept quiet I could pass as a rosary devotee along with everybody else. But then a nun, in a further access of zeal, came in one morning bearing a chart which she proceeded to pin up on the classroom wall. Across the top of this chart ran the names of every child in the class, with the days of the week down the left-hand side. The idea was that each of us should tick every day on which the family rosary was said in her home. As soon as this was explained to us, I was filled with anxiety and agitation. If I were to be honest, my column would remain a total blank, week after week, and there I'd be, exposed as the pitiable and freakish child of an insufficiently dedicated household. There was nothing for it but to grit my teeth and produce a row of deceitful ticks. It wasn't a complete row, as many people's were; but I simply had to pretend that we occasionally knelt down, beads in hand, to say the rosary in common with everyone else. I hated doing it, it made me feel uneasy and grubby, and even though I kept my ticks to a minimum, each one jarred as I filled it in. I thought I was committing some kind of terrible sin, a sin peculiar to myself, and endangering my entree into eternal bliss. I also worried that I'd be caught out. I wasn't, of course; no one ever questioned my claims to conformity in the matter of the family rosary. The only comment on the subject I remember was the observation that I should try to make it happen more often, to which I probably responded with a bashful smirk. I wasn't a natural liar, but common sense and expediency were turning me into one. *Is fusa tuitim ná éirígh*, it is easier to fall than to rise.

In 1920, the Archbishop of Armagh had decreed that the only acceptable form of Catholic education was the school in which Catholic children were "educated as faithful Catholics in a Catholic atmosphere, and under the care and direction of their pastors, whose strict right and leading duty it is to watch over, direct and safeguard the religious education of the lambs of their flocks". Blah, blah, blah. Such pronouncements boded ill for the prospect of integration. But integration as a concept carried very little weight at the time, or indeed later. Catholic bishops were still crowing over their exclusivity twenty-five years on, when they averred, "We have had control of our Catholic schools for over one hundred years, and whatever the action we are driven to take we are determined to maintain it." No surrender. They represented the church as being in a state of siege, even when things in the North were relatively tranquil, harking back to the early days of the Northern Irish state, when "the very existence of Catholicity [sic] in Down & Connor, and in Belfast in particular, was menaced, and [when His Grace the Most Revd.] Dr MacRory, by an appeal to the Catholics of the world, was instrumental in procuring relief for his imperilled people."

His imperilled people. The period in question, it's true, was a particularly fraught and traumatic era in Irish history, with a partial autonomy conferred on roughly four-fifths of the country, and the remainder sticking like glue to the UK connection. It was an awkward resolution of the Irish problem and bound to cause chaos and virulence; and chaos and virulence weren't long in coming. "The outlook is desperate," reported *The Times* newspaper in August 1920, while in the streets of Belfast newsboys bawled out the latest casualty figures: "Twelve shot dead! Two hundred wounded!" The Northern government, once it came into being, didn't know what to do with the unruly minority it was saddled with; while those of the minority left high and dry by the terms of the Treaty, seethed with disaffection and a sense of betrayal. Ambush, riots, machine-gun fire and pogroms were the order of the day. When District-Inspector Swanzy was shot dead in Lisburn, the ferocity of Orange reprisals caused a mass exodus out of nationalist quarters in the town, with whole families tramping by night across the Black Mountain towards the (comparative) safety of Belfast.

There was misery for many, but the Catholic Church went out of its way to appropriate all the suffering and uprightness going. It was all "his imperilled people", the highlighted image of "bishop, priests and people [standing] together in unbroken and … unbreakable solidarity," and Catholic integrity lording it over Protestant iniquity. You'd have thought that what was going on was a religious war, not the hoary old clash of ideologies, the struggle on the part of some political activists to obtain social justice and a chance of betterment for those who lacked these graces, the determination of others to preserve a way of life agreeable to themselves and to their followers. It was sometimes hard to tell where principle ended and pigheadedness began. Bigotry on one side was naturally answered by bigotry on the other, and when it came right down to fisticuffs and jeering at street level, the Catholic/nationalist contingent gave as good as it got. There were people in Catholic Belfast for whom it was a matter of principle not to buy a "Protestant" loaf of bread (i.e., one manufactured by the Ormeau Bakery rather than Hughes's). And there were other people, in other parts of the city, who knew absolutely nothing about the tradition of Protestant support for the Irish language, and couldn't have cared less if they had known. They knew where they stood on the language issue, that was all, and it wasn't the position occupied by Robert McAdam, Sir Samuel Ferguson, Douglas Hyde, Francis Joseph Bigger, and many, many others. "If parents want their children to learn Irish or any other useless language, they should pay for it out of their own pockets," snorted the opposition to state subsidies for voluntary schools, speaking in the infant Northern Irish parliament. Well, they weren't alone in this opinion. Daniel O'Connell, the great Liberator himself, in the nineteenth century was also convinced of the uselessness of Irish. It was, he believed, a hindrance to social progress and a millstone round the necks of those, mainly the rural poor, bogged down in its benightedness. The sooner it became extinct the better. If it had to survive, the best place for it was in the heads and hands of those with sufficient leisure and money to cultivate it – i.e., the (mainly) Protestant middle and upper classes. It is by way of suchlike ironies, paradoxes and complexities, that the fortunes of the Irish language may be traced.

As for native Irish-speakers themselves – socially they were the lowest of the low, despised as ignoramuses by those among their peers who'd mastered English and begun the upward scramble out of poverty and muck; or they were the last custodians of an ancient and endangered civilisation, and best approached as one might approach an unfathomable tribe discovered in the remotest corner of the earth. We may be certain that neither attitude was much to their liking.

If Catholic hyperbole is detectable in Cardinal MacRory and his imperilled people, it surfaces again in a comment made about MacRory's successor as Bishop of Down and Connor, the Very Rev. Daniel Mageean. Dr Mageean was praised in 1941 as a pastor "who has guided and defended the Catholics of Belfast through the fires of persecution," which makes him sound like a Gandhi or a Nelson Mandela. In truth, the fires of persecution added up to a moderately low-key affair in Belfast during the 1930s. Catholics on the whole remained unreconciled to the system they were living under, and the system itself certainly didn't have their interests at heart. Some cultivated subversion, and some went in for the kind of congregational freemasonry mentioned above. Most complained about the Unionist regime from time to time. And the chronic debility of the body politic erupted occasionally in serious sectarian disturbances, like those of 1935. But, for the most part, Catholics in the North got on with their lives like everyone else, aspiring to middle-class respectability if their origins were lower, consolidating whatever degree of comfort they'd attained. They bought summer outfits and other goods at enticing department stores like Robb's and Robinson Cleaver's, and enjoyed the camaraderie of St Malachy's Old Boys' Club or the bustle of Campbell's Cafe filled with shoppers and dripping umbrellas on a wet morning in December.

My sense of the atmosphere in Belfast during those pre-war days comes partly from books, and partly from the recollections of people alive to its nuances, such as my mother. My mother, Nora Brady, was a student at Queen's University where – among other things – she received a grounding in Scholastic Philosophy under the tutelage of Father Arthur Ryan (later Monsignor Ryan), a course of study unavailable to non-Catholics. As Marianne Elliott remarks in her magisterial history, *The Catholics of Ulster*, this course came into being "in response to a successful campaign to create separate Catholic teaching programmes in controversial subjects" – in other words, as part of the Church's endeavour to safeguard the faith of impressionable young Catholics exposed to the heady non-conformity of Queen's. It was no big deal, however, though probably it contributed to the undergraduate predilection for religiously-differentiated alliances (a predilection more pronounced at that time, I think, than it was a generation later – at least in my experience as a student at the Belfast College of Art). Overt sectarian prejudice didn't stand a chance in the (more-or-less) liberal ambience of Queen's, *circa* 1936, where my lively-minded mother had the time of her life. She never suffered personally on account of her (temperate) Catholicism, though she was well aware of the disabilities Catholics in general had to contend with, and deplored the subjugation of "the nationalist people" – Cardinal MacRory's people – as much as anyone.

She was also in thrall to the nationalist version of history with its torments and triumphs (respectively inflicted by the English and achieved by the invincible Irish), though this didn't preclude an enthusiasm for everything to do with the First World War, and in particular its poetry – her father, whom she never knew, having died in that war. But, for the moment, tremendously exhilarated at having got to Queen's against the odds, she concentrated on enjoying as many undergraduate activities as she could handle. These included travelling on the train to Bangor with her friend Celia Lenaghan, and heading for a prominent street corner where the two of them would stand flogging copies of the student magazine *PTQ* (*Pro Tanto Quid*, after the city motto of Belfast). This magazine was famous for the innocence of its dirty jokes – or the dirtiness of its innocent jokes, whichever way round you preferred – jokes along the lines of, "If I told you that I admired your bosom, would you hold it against me?" These ex-convent girls liked to be mildly shocked, as long as the shock didn't arise from anything seriously objectionable, such as blasphemy.

My mother at the time lived with *her* mother and sisters in a terrace house off the Stranmillis Road, from which she'd set out every morning, jaunty though myopic (and far too vain to wear her glasses), to walk the short distance down to Queen's and the day's lectures, past exclusive Friars' Bush Cemetery, once a magnet for grave-robbers, the new Ulster Museum and the delightful small gate lodge at the entrance to the Botanic Gardens, which always made her think of Hansel and Gretel. English and History were her principal subjects, and she was and remained under the spell of these compelling pursuits for the rest of her life. She had her Palgrave's *Golden Treasury*, her Bradley's *Shakespearian Tragedy*, and copious notes taken down from Professor Savery (I think his name was Savery) to bolster her against inevitable ill hap. She was a scholarship girl, duty-bound to do well. Her anxiety to please, though, was tempered by a good-humoured, quizzical wilfulness which might have landed her in the soup with her tutors if the course she was taking hadn't proved to her liking. There were bits of it, indeed, such as maths, which represented an obstacle for her. But English and History, always a pleasure and never a grind, saw her through. These things really mattered to her: the Romantic Poets, the English Civil War, and the escape of Red Hugh O'Donnell from the English stronghold of Dublin Castle on a snowy night in 1591.

Selectively studious, she was nevertheless disposed to gaiety and enjoyed being voted the best-dressed girl at Queen's in 1937 (quite an achievement for someone with absolutely no money to spend on clothes). She relished the attentions of male fellow-students, some of whom spent a large part of the summer break theatrically pining for her, and expressing their desolation in breezy, flirtatious letters, letters beginning, "Nora, my dove". (It was around this time that Nora's paternal grandmother died and left her and her sisters five pounds each. She and her closest sister, Kathleen, blued this windfall on a week's blissful holiday in Rannafast where they inhaled the ethnically and ethically pure air of the Gaedhaltacht and grew familiar with its salient features.)

My mother's educational luck had begun when she was twelve or thirteen, and the nuns of her primary school in Lurgan had recommended her for a scholarship to a recently re-housed Sisters of Mercy convent, Our Lady's Secondary School, which quickly became known as Mount St Michael's after its new setting. It was located within walking distance of hilly North Street, Lurgan, where Nora lived at the time: you went down the hill, up an incline, over a railway crossing, round a bend, and there in front of you was the convent perched on top of its own hill, a grand Victorian mansion known as Irishtown Hill House in earlier days, surrounded by trees, firs, pines and beech trees, and complete with gardens, tennis courts and hockey pitch, for all the world like something out of *Septima, Schoolgirl*. From its upper windows you could see Lough Neagh, with the occasional fisherman's boat or a tug guiding lighters to the Rivers Bann and Blackwater, and far away the mountains of Tyrone and Antrim contributing a suggestion of wildness – but only a distant wildness – to the scene. No mere school of fiction could hold a candle to Mount St Michael's, my mother thought; to be a pupil here was the summit of happiness, and a near-miracle in her case, in those days of deprivation and social stratifying. She was the youngest of five daughters of a strong-minded war widow who fully supported her brightest child's claims to be educated; but it wasn't easy, even with the scholarship.

There was no snobbery at St Michael's, yet Nora dreaded kneeling down for prayers and exposing the soles of her shoes to public scrutiny. This was because there was no money in the house to pay for mending: if a hole appeared, it just got bigger and bigger and you had to go on wearing the shoe regardless, until the sole fell off. To show herself in this condition was a torment for a sensitive girl with a horror of slovenliness. But the shame she felt was all in her head: no one ever taxed her with being ill-bred on account of her shocking footwear. (Money was very scarce, but she nevertheless managed to scrape up 4d a week to buy *The Magnet* and *The Gem*, essential items of juvenile reading, and had founded her own "Famous Five" at school, in honour of Frank Richards's Greyfriars characters.)

In the novel *Call My Brother Back* by Michael McLaverty the hero's education at St Malachy's College is sponsored by a priest who has spotted the boy's intellectual gifts. This is fine – but then a moment arrives at the end of Colm McNeill's first term when bills for the school fees are about to be handed out. The diffident fourteen-year-old is overcome by trepidation at the prospect of being conspicuously omitted from this ritual. When he receives an envelope along with everyone else, it's a relief at first, but then he is terrified that some awful mistake has been made, and an unpayable demand issued to his mother. In fact, inside the envelope is a slip of paper saying, "Father So-and-So's pupil". Exactly the same thing happened to Nora at Mount St Michael's. She was only aware of one other girl at the school in a similar position to herself, and both of them, like the McLaverty protagonist, were included in the bill-distributing at the end of term to spare them embarrassment in front of their friends. The slip of paper inside the envelope addressed to Nora's mother bore the reassuring words, "No charge".

It's hard for me to reconcile this solicitude for their pupils' peace-of-mind (I am taking the McLaverty account to be a true one) with the attitudes of those in Religious Orders known personally to me. My nuns would have been more likely to taunt a pupil for coming from a less than socially desirable area of the town, such as the Pound, Ballymurphy or Rodney Parade. During my first year at St Dominic's, one twelve-year-old, the oldest in a family of nine from the Lower Falls, was found crying in the cloakroom because a nun, in front of the class, had commented sneeringly on the less than pristine condition of her white viyella blouse. (Such were the trivial barbs often directed at us.) This, mark you, was during the supposedly more democratic fifties when almost everyone was a scholarship pupil and the few exceptions, those whose fees were shouldered by their parents rather than the state, were looked down on on account of their supposed intellectual incapacity. There was no winning with these nuns unless you had average brains, were exceptionally docile and could boast a rich, turf-accountant or solicitor father. (I am talking about the general run of things: exceptions here would be the odd girl taken under the wing of a particular nun and encouraged in whatever aspirations she might have. But this was rare.)

My mother rejoiced in her schooling and fitted in with her teachers' expectations in a way that I did not. She became a prized past pupil who'd conformed to an unspoken school code and ended by reflecting credit on the place, getting her graduation photo into the first issue of the school magazine, *The Michaelonian*, in 1938, and contributing to the same issue an appreciation of "The School on the Hill" – an establishment which, she claimed, "...had grown into one of the finest Convent Secondary and Boarding Schools in a country famous all over the world for the excellence of the education and training imparted by its Religious Orders to the young". Whew! Despite the punctiliousness of that assertion, however, I don't believe that my mother was inherently more tractable than I was, or any more committed to academic success. (Though she had, indeed, a lot of gratitude to express, and this was one way of expressing it.) But between her schooldays and mine some vast changes seemed to have come about, social and psychological and in the reciprocal commerce of activity between church and community. At the same time, superficially, things went on in much the same way: Sunday church-going and other rituals were conscientiously observed, education continued in the hands of the clergy, sexual morality was still firmly in place. We were not aware of a general change in outlook, either present or impending; or if we were, it was only at a subliminal level. But something, other than my own incorrigibility (I think), brought about an extreme divergence in our respective school careers, my mother's and mine.

Of course it was a different world back there in Co Armagh in the late 1920s, slower and steadier and a lot more sedate (or so we like to think). You were not exposed to unsettling furores via magazines, cinema and television, and fewer channels altogether existed to put ideas in your head. The concept of self-expression had not reached Lurgan. In Catholic circles at any rate, its opposite, self-suppression, was fostered in accordance with church teaching. In practice, this could not work, or could work only partially, but it was kept to the fore as an idea, and incessantly enjoined on those in subordinate positions, such as schoolchildren. You were supposed to put others before yourself, and to curb the instinct to go all out to achieve your own ends. If you happened to be exceptionally talented in any area, the credit for this was due to God in the first place, not yourself; and your gift, whatever it was, was meant to be employed in the service of the school, not the individual. This was not peculiar to the Catholic education, of course; as a ploy to quash self-conceit it was axiomatic, a defining feature (in its "team spirit" version) of innumerable girls' and boys' school stories, though generally without overt reference to God. And it was all very well, most sensible children would have thought, though not especially to be applied to themselves. Still, the habit of obedience would have caused them to pay attention to this and other recipes for achieving a state of grace.

It was perfectly possible, even for an intelligent pupil like my mother, to regard nuns and their way of life uncritically – even to admire them for their piety and unworldliness. Convents, nuns, priests, the Mass, indeed everything to do with Catholicism, were part of the social fabric of that time and utterly taken for granted. They didn't stick out like a top hat at a football match. It wasn't until after the Second World War that convent life began to acquire an increasingly anomalous relation to ordinary life, and even then the winding-up of nunnish sequestration was a long-drawn-out process, and tied up with the secularisation of society as a whole. Eventually, the idea of a religious vocation for Catholic women would seem so mad and outlandish that it has virtually ceased to exist (in the last decade or so). But it wasn't like that in the past, not for my generation and certainly not for my mother's generation. And Nora in particular accepted the package of nuns and education without the smallest dissenting qualm. She was a Michaelonian, a hilltop girl; it wasn't in her to jeopardise that status. For her it was the school that distilled a magnetising glamour, not the wider world which contained such things as unemployment or lowly employment, scruffy corner shops, back-yard toilets, overcrowding, wet pavements and doors opening straight on to the street.

The nearest my mother came to my Rannafast experience (without coming to grief) was a joyous occasion when she and four or five of her classmates (the brainiest girls in the school) were sent up to a convent at Ballycastle, on the north coast (The School on the Cliff), during the summer term, in order to sit some examination or other. They all failed the examination, but no one minded this very much; it wasn't important. This was a hiatus in ordinary school life: what was important was to make the most of the beach, the sea bathing, the country lanes, the girlish high jinks, the fizzy lemonade, the proximity of someone's male cousins who happened to live nearby. And they did make the most of all these delights. There are snapshots to prove it, showing my gamine mother looking pensive and self-possessed. Out of school hours, the girls loll about, picnicking under dry-stone walls and briar hedges, or stand on rocks accompanied by grinning schoolboys. They are out of sight of the Convent and free, for the moment, to gad about to their hearts' content, in their silky flapper tops loosely belted around the waist, and flowing skirts à la Jeanette McDonald. What larks!

Cardinal MacRory's successor Dr Mageean was Bishop of Down and Connor between 1929 and 1962. Dr Mageean presided over my schooldays as well as my mother's, setting the tone for Catholic life in the North during the long years of his reign. Catholics had to dance – if at all – to the tune of Dr Mageean, which boomed out as dreary and solemn as he could make it. He spent a lot of time ensuring that Catholic schools would not be contaminated by the smallest measure of "Protestant" liberalism. No "Inst" inclusiveness for him. There's an Ulster-Scots word "jeuk" or "juke", meaning to dodge or evade: to have any kind of a jolly time during those years you had to jeuk Dr Mageean's prescriptions for piety, such as shunning "Protestant" entertainments and immersing yourself in the Rosary Crusade. And his doctrinaire assertions didn't stop with church affairs. During the mid-1950s, as a young teenager, I held Dr Mageean personally responsible for the meagreness of my wardrobe and the cobbled-together nature of our summer holidays (a week here or there, usually with relatives in Coventry, Essex or

Dublin). We had no money to spend on luxuries because of the ban imposed by Dr Mageean on married women teachers who were ousted from their posts the minute they left the church and had picked the confetti out of their hair. Henceforth their skills, whatever they were, would be devoted to household management and the rearing of children. They were expected to stay put. "Somehow a girl was meant for one spot," observed Michael McLaverty in one of his later, inferior works of fiction. "When she starts the roaming she's like a dog that goes after sheep – never contented." Well! This striking pronouncement indicates the persistence of antiquated attitudes in the Catholic North of Ireland, while the rest of the world was moving on. And indeed, there was no jeuking the Bishop's edict. So my mother, with one child – me – and her mother on the spot to act as willing baby-minder, was stuck restlessly at home until wartime marshalling of resources got her into the Censorship Office at Stormont. Post-war, it was back to the Donegall Road to sit looking out at the plane trees in St James's Avenue, or reading – and rereading – the works of Graham Greene. This state of affairs went on until 1956 or 7, when the pressures of modern life, not to mention the shortage of teachers as a vast new school-building-programme got under way, caused the Bishop's ban to pass into history.

A few years later, it looked as though other malpractices, sectarian malpractices, might also pass into history, as voices of reason began to make themselves heard and egalitarian possibilities were bandied about. It was the mid-1960s, with its sense of new beginnings. Such a feeling of exhilaration hadn't flourished so strongly in the North since the last decade of the eighteenth century and the United Irish movement – about which Tom Paulin lamented, "Hardly a classroom remembers/Their obstinate rebellion." Alas, the twentieth-century revival of that democratic spirit wasn't destined, any more than that of the Lagan Jacobins, to come to fruition. Equally, it came up against intransigence, in the form of an awful atavistic figure popping up like an evangelical Jack-in-the-Box to rant about the Pope of Rome and the threat to Ulster's Protestantism, and causing sectarianism to be re-ignited.

One shocking image from those years is the Burntollet marchers, those remaining on their feet after an ambush by loyalists in the Ulster countryside had left half their number unconscious, clutching their heads where batons had landed or streaming with blood, staggering on towards Derry in support of civil rights. No one at that moment could have failed to regard these people as heroes. They had looked at the society they inhabited, disliked what they saw, and tried to take some action to promote long-overdue reforms. The attack on them simply demonstrated to the world at large the justice of their position. But what was their position? As you find with almost everything to do with

Ireland and its enormities, tangles and complications quickly enter in.

A book like Bob Purdie's sterling study of the Civil Rights movement, for example (*Politics in the Streets*, 1990), goes a considerable way towards indicating what the social reformer was up against. In the first place, the movement was never homogenous, but consisted of many small groups and sub-groups, all with slightly differing biases and objectives. They all, indeed, promised a better deal for those in the North enduring social disabilities; but some just wanted to knock humanity and a sense of justice into the existing state, while others were holding out for an entirely new system – Irish republicanism, socialism, Marxism or whatever. If some issues – principally, the issue of discrimination – caused sufficient outrage to bring them all, briefly, under the Civil Rights banner, there were still too many factions involved for anything approaching unity to be sustained. Looked at closely, the NICRA dissolves into the CSJ, CDU, NILP, CPNI, PD, NCCL, NDG, NDP, DCAC, RLP, RSSF … the abounding acronyms tell their own tale. It wasn't a pattern peculiar to the decade; ever since the establishment of the Northern Irish state in 1921, opposition to Unionism had been marshalled under a whole spectrum of headings, from Catholic nationalism to communism.

It was, indeed, a place where it was easy to get into the grip of a grievance, and at moments it seemed as though everyone, everyone in the province was advocating some form of remedy for its discords. You had the nationalist remedy, the republican remedy, the reformist remedy, the conciliation remedy, the socialist remedy, the republican-labour remedy, the liberal-unionist remedy, the hard-line remedy, the Gaelic remedy, the priestly remedy, the cultural-nationalist remedy, the middle-of-the-road remedy, the atheist remedy, the anti-segregation remedy, the pro-segregation, or ghetto, remedy, the repatriation remedy, the Kilkenny cats remedy. In the face of all this, it's possible to feel some sympathy with a body like Saor Uladh (Free Ulster) which once opted out of the whole business by proclaiming a republic in the centre of a Co Tyrone village.

However, it is probably true to say that the North, for all its unruliness, has never lacked a civilising spirit to interpose itself between competing prejudices. And this liberal spirit sometimes surfaces in unexpected places – I am thinking, for example, of the Irish-speaking club mentioned above, Cluan Ard, located in a street not far from St Dominic's High School, on which my social life was centred between the ages of seventeen (the year after I was expelled from school) and twenty. This club enriched the lives of a good many people, not all of them Catholic, and fostered wrong-headed aggression in no one. Even though English was never spoken on the premises, it held fast to the anti-sectarianism of the republican tradition. (This unfortunately could not be kept up. By the 1970s, with the "Troubles" raging, no Protestant, however liberal-minded, would have dared to set foot in West Belfast.) Whatever fluency in Irish I once had, it was acquired in this spot, or in the Gaedhaltacht, not at school; and here, as well, I gained a smattering of insight into the erotic, or bawdy, element in Gaelic literature, and began to understand that Ireland's literary heritage wasn't confined to the pious unrealities of a novel like *Mo Dha Roisin* (*My Two Roses*) or Charles Kickham's *Knocknagow*. The eighteenth-century Co Louth poet Cathal Buidhe Mac Giolla Gunna, for example, has quite a bit about the delights of seduction, even if in the end it all boils down to a heart-rending renunciation: "Ach anois, faraor, tá mo saoghal-sa caithte, / Is is mian liom stad agus leigean dóibh" ("Now, alas, my life is spent, / And I must stop and leave them to it.")

At the same time, at twenty or thereabouts, I was reading Brian Moore and relishing the cogency of his case against Belfast and against provincialism, including the provincialism of an Irish-speaking Ireland – not that I went along with it entirely, indeed, but it appealed to me at various levels. He made disgruntlement invigorating – the disgruntlement of someone whose birthplace is a backwater. Belfast, in the view of Brian Moore, does nothing for its citizens beyond stupefying and hamstringing them at every turn, lumbering them with deadly ideologies, dulling their perceptions and soaking them with its perpetual downpours. In the background to his writings of the fifties and sixties, though it isn't singled out for special attention, is the Unionist misrule which overshadowed all the other indigenous forms of oppression (church, economy or whatever). It's a place, he implies, from which anyone in his proper senses will remove himself as soon as possible. "A dull, dead town", he calls Belfast, in *The Emperor of Ice-Cream*. And *Judith Hearne* positively bristles with the stifling effects of suburban Catholicism. But it was the sexual failure – indeed the sexual shipwreck – of Diarmuid Devine in Moore's *The Feast of Lupercal* that most strongly alerted me to the horrors attendant on a puritanical education. Poor Devine, after an episode of excruciating ineptness, bitterly envisages the words of penitence he will offer the priest in confession: "... do not worry about that sin, Father. Tried it once and didn't like it."

Tried it once and didn't like it. There's a powerful indictment of Catholic puritanism for you. Moore's point is that the school Devine went through, and to which he returned as a teacher, did for him in this important respect ("It was a matter of ignorance, pure and simple"). He has neither a natural talent, nor the skill acquired through practice, to see him right – and when, at thirty-seven, he takes a fancy to a silly young girl from Dublin and tries, very tentatively, to involve her in a sexual relationship, an appalling evening ensues.

Moore has presented the schoolmaster Devine as a casualty of the Catholic education, a person in whom a natural modesty and primness interact with churchly inflexibility and the mood of the time (the book was published in 1958), to devastating effect. He is, indeed, an extreme case. Others, more pragmatic, would have sidestepped unacceptable embargoes, such as the embargo on "company-keeping," or manoeuvred themselves into some kind of principled opposition to the religiose conditioning of the era. The years between fourteen and eighteen – say – are indeed a time when all kinds of passions are rampant, including the passion to purge society of its ills. When I edited *The Oxford Book of Schooldays* some years ago (yes, there's a joke about my own educational experience) I called one section "At Odds with the System" and into it I put the rebels, the dissenters, the social critics, the scoffers, the outsiders, the outraged – all those whose temperaments weren't in step with the schooling they received. My own temperament – it is now clear to me – clashed with Catholicism, though I certainly hadn't articulated any such unorthodoxy before the age of sixteen. I swallowed what I was told, and acted accordingly, going to mass on Sundays, confession once a fortnight, and so on – though never in any spirit other than that of performing a chore. (Given the choice, I'd rather have tackled the back yard with scrubbing-brush and soap.) It was possibly a question of heredity: I didn't have a religious temperament, neither of my parents had a religious temperament, I don't think my grandmother had a religious temperament (though in her case it was harder to be sure, since the trappings of Catholicism, holy water, saints' statues and so forth, meant more to her). A secular, academic school would have suited me down to the ground. But there I was, pitched by circumstances into a convent, and – as yet – only moderately receptive to intimations of oncoming scepticism.

Of course I'd like to align myself with that intrepid group, those at odds with the system, but I fear I am not entitled to do so. I was one of the herd, never a leader or an innovator. I can't claim to have suffered for my principles; principles were not conspicuous as a motivating factor among my classmates of Form 5A. Such defiance of authority as we engaged in tended to be somewhat underhand (inventing excuses for not having done your homework; passing notes in class). It would have been a different matter if I had repudiated the nuns of St Dominic's and their restrictive ordinances, instead of sticking to their wretched code as far as I was able. I wish I had, but I lacked the gumption, or the insight, or the courage to be openly insubordinate. I was far from being an apostle for sexual liberation.

Still, the majority of us weren't as ignorant or inexperienced as Mr Devine, in our seventeenth year; for some of us, sexual intercourse existed as an intoxicating prospect. What would it be like? Wonderful, we thought, having gained an inkling – the merest inkling – of what might be in store for us, with the help of the more knowing boys of St Mary's or St Malachy's, at the back of the City Cemetery, in the Falls Park, up an alleyway, in a garden shed, on the slopes of the Cave Hill or up against our own back gates. It was always, at the very least, a pungent topic. When I read a poem like Tony Harrison's enticing "Allotments" – imbued with a *frisson* of the wayward and demotic – I find it strikes so many chords that it's hard to approach it in a proper spirit of detachment. "And young, we cuddled by the abattoir, / Faffing with fastenings, never getting far ...". Smoke, cobbles, brick, alluring darkness, industrial grime, frustrated lust … all that comes back with a full force of recollection. In Leeds, though, they weren't inhibited into the bargain by a moral prohibition enforced so strongly that it nearly got absorbed into one's system. The poem's allusion to the River Aire,

> The old canal that ran to Liverpool
> Made hot trickles in the knickers cool
> As soon as flow …

prompts me to reflect that it wasn't a cold canal, but a cold doctrine of sin and damnation, that produced the same effect on us. It made us behave like prissy Sally Shannon, the bane of Gavin Burke in Brian Moore's *The Emperor of Ice-Cream*. "We can't," she tells him, as he reaches for the waistband of her knickers. "It's a mortal sin." The phrase "It's a mortal sin" was uttered frequently, in those days. It's true that for many girls, some of my own friends among them (the hormonally challenged), the embargo on fornication wasn't especially irksome; for myself, at that age, it was manageable, as long as the sexual instinct had at least a partial outlet, and as long as I remained pretty confident that I wasn't going to end up like Elizabeth North's headmistress in the novel *Dames*, who only gained a vital bit of carnal knowledge in late middle age. "So that is an erection, thought Miss Bedford." Deferred fulfilment was all very well, but I didn't want it to be deferred as long as all that.

Ten years later, the authority of the Catholic Church in Ireland was beginning to subside, even if Catholic attitudes didn't necessarily follow suit. An inexorable flexibility was in the offing, meaning in practice that you'd be able to call yourself Catholic, while picking and choosing among the tenets of church teaching. It was an advance on utter authoritarianism, I suppose, but it came too late to be of any benefit to me, since my natural atheism had asserted itself once and for all as soon as I got to London and the Central School of Art at the age of twenty. I don't have any hankerings after a spiritual framework for my day-to-day activities. I'm also a bit bewildered by incomplete apostasy, believing, I suppose, that it makes more sense to be one thing or the other. But now the definitions have changed. You can be divorced and call yourself Catholic; you can be an unwed mother six times over and remain within the flock. Good heavens, you can be a Catholic bishop and go about fathering offspring if the fancy takes you. This is a newfangled church. It is also a disintegrating church, one that can't afford to alienate any of its adherents, whatever "sins" they come laden down with. Well, all along, this church showed an instinct for expediency.

I know the Catholic Church wasn't all bad. I know it performed many useful, indeed indispensable, functions. It acted as a curb on would-be violence and hooliganism. It knocked obstreperousness out of some of those harbouring anti-social inclinations. It provided a badge of identity, a stake in the community, for people who need some guiding system they can fit into, to make sense of their lives. But some of its behaviour was very bad indeed. For example – during the 1950s and 60s, as I remember it – the onus on poor parishioners to subscribe to various Church Building Funds was completely over-the-top. The Church Building Fund and its needs was really dunned into us. One diabolical scheme to drum up money involved a solemnly touted bit of moonshine designated "The Golden Book". A donation of £5 or more entitled you to have your name inscribed in this metaphysical ledger; and once you were in, your place in heaven was assured. If your name was *not* in The Golden Book, due to parsimony or carelessness, you had to take your chance; but payment of the entrance fee would guarantee salvation. So we were told, and it may have given some of us an idea of heaven as a vaunted football match or celebrity concert for which tickets were at a premium.

On top of the cynical manipulation of the credulous suggested by this and other expedients for drumming up support, you have to consider into the bargain all this putative church building and what it entailed. What it entailed in many cases was the destruction of historic churches which distilled as much of a sense of the numinous as it was possible to attain; and what you got instead was a series of replacements in sixties concrete-and-crassness. This may be read as a visible sign that the church was relinquishing its role as custodian of anything at all in the way of spirituality.

"Puritan Ireland's dead and gone," wrote John Montague; but it didn't go quickly enough to decontaminate our escapade. Indeed, it never died out completely; the puritan ethic is not a spent force even yet, though it's no longer backed up by social usage or an unassailable religious system. It survives as a caste of mind, not necessarily an unattractive caste of mind. A puritan note is sounded in Tom Paulin's "dream of grace and reason," "the sweet equal republic" that came to nothing. There are old Ulster churches, small, whitewashed, with polished pews, in which you can nearly see the point of puritanism, with its high regard for propriety, calm and order. And plainness and sobriety, those Planter virtues which reached some kind of epitome in the poet John Hewitt, whom I used to visit in Belfast between the late 1970s and his death in 1987. His Ulster puritanism was carried with grace and vigour. There he sat, in his tweed armchair, looking upright and sturdy, with his pipe, his books and his strong liberal views, an old-fashioned latitudinarian secure in his humanism, while Belfast blew itself to pieces around him. Offered the Freedom of the City – or what was left of it – in eventual recognition of his importance as a poet, and as a conduit for civilising views, his comment was, "I thought I already had it."

Perhaps it's only when puritanism is tied up with sexual prudery that it turns disabling.

Unlike many people possessed by the urge to explore some aspect of their lives, or unfold a narrative to show themselves and their times in a particular light, I have very little to complain about. I didn't undergo an unsatisfactory upbringing. I was not deprived, abused, accident-prone, made little of, precipitated into awful circumstances or forced to grow up too quickly (some might say, I've never managed to grow up at all). Of course, like everyone's, my childhood contained long stretches of boredom, doldrums interspersed with dolours. Sometimes a dreadful action was imposed on me, like having to appear as a flower in a silly school play. "It'll all be the same in a hundred years," my mother would say encouragingly, to put the thing in perspective.

I loved my wayward father and sometimes at night I couldn't fall asleep until the sound of his key in the front door announced his safe return from wherever he'd been out on the spree; and I loved my sharp-tongued grandmother whose hard life hadn't completely knocked out of her a capacity for fun. But the centre of my universe was my clever and affectionate mother, who ensured – among other things – that my infancy was enlivened by copious recitations of verses which she had by heart. Among these was one which I found particularly diverting. (I've never come across it in any other context.) It concerned a pair of namby-pamby mice ("Now Horace and Willy were stupid and silly,/And couldn't say boo to a goose"); then there's a bit about "tears", "Which only made Daddy/Fly into a paddy/ And give them a whacking, poor dears." The two mice muffs are sent away to be educated at Rat College ("College" rhymed with "knowledge"), where they do so badly that they are promptly returned to their doting parent with a letter of explanation. If he'd had them much longer, the headmaster tells her quite frankly, "... I'd have given them both to the CAT./I remain, yours respectfully, Rat."

I am two, three at most, and already able to distinguish between ruthless humour, which is bracing, and some ruthless threat creeping out of the night, which is disturbing. There's another story, in an old lesson book, about a wolf in sheep's clothing slinking in the dark towards a flock of unwary lambs, which I don't like at all. But my mother is always there to cushion me against upsets. It is also her role to adjust the dodgier bits of information I pick up at school. One day (I am five) I come home smugly repeating something I've just heard, about how it must be so awful to be a Protestant and banned from heaven, and how lucky we are that it doesn't apply to us. "But your Grandma and Grandpa, your Auntie Ruby and all the rest of them are Protestants," she says, matter-of-factly. This gives me something to ponder.

A Protestant, then, was never as alien to me as a Muslim; my experience to that extent didn't parallel Denis Donoghue's. Indeed, his remark to that effect made me jump when I read it. It occurs in his memoir *Warrenpoint*: a mostly engaging, occasionally exasperating and wholly idiosyncratic account of an unrefractory boyhood in that Co Down resort. What does he mean by it? As a boy growing up in an RUC barracks where his father was a sergeant, he must have been in daily contact with Protestants - but perhaps it's a Protestant particularity of outlook he has in mind. Whatever it is, it's an alarming admission. Clearly, for Ulster Catholics, there were degrees of circumscription.

"I could never understand," Donoghue writes, "how William Empson, a critic I revere, could hate Christians and especially Catholics, thinking their religion nothing but a sordid cult of blood and sacrifice." I can't understand how Denis Donoghue, a critic I revere, could have submitted so readily to the Catholicism of his upbringing, using his tremendous intellectual powers to rationalise the tenets of the church, rather than employing a more undermining strategy ... For myself, I always preferred the spirited to the spiritual, protesters to accepters, intrigue to indifference. I relished the sense of things going on – though not, I think, to the point of upholding disruption. A tiny incident from the late 1960s illustrates that avowal. It was the time when civic disturbance was just beginning to get off the ground – or on to the ground – and I remember the affront I felt when an acquaintance described to me how she'd recently enjoyed a good night's rioting. A crowd of them, she went on, returned to the same trouble spot on the following evening, and were terribly disappointed when a similar outbreak failed to occur. Of the first occasion, when a policeman hit her over the head with a baton, she remarked that she had never enjoyed anything so much in her life. I think of Caroline Blackwood's jaded question in her "Memories of Ulster". Can there be, she wonders, "a boredom so powerful that it finally acts like an explosive?" If there is, indeed, it's not a sound basis for political action – though it makes a vivid impression: all the wrongs and repressions and afflictions of Ulster simmering away for a couple of centuries and finally reaching bursting point.

The Blackwood essay enumerates a few of Northern Ireland's ills – bigotry, inertia, "an industrialised provinciality", a philistine mentality and so on. It harks back to MacNeice's

> ... the voodoo of the Orange bands,
> Drawing an iron net through darkest Ulster,
> Flailing the limbo lands.
> The linen mills, the long wet grass, the ragged hawthorn,
> And one read black where the other read white, his hope
> The other man's damnation. Up the rebels, to hell with the Pope...

and forward to Derek Mahon's "Pale light of that provincial town ...[punishing] nature in the name of God", while obliquely endorsing Brian Moore's critique. These authors are all forceful commentators on a very flawed society, homing straight in on the causes of disaffection, and turning them, in their writings, to richness and stimulation. If it's tackled with sufficient energy, the whole bad business of Northern Ireland's awful heritage can gain an effect of pungency rather than desolation. All these writers, though, approach the topic from a point-of-view of dislike, or at best ambivalence; they're not enamoured of the place. I have to record that I never hated Belfast, never hated the North, never even hated the school that so readily washed its hands of me. On the contrary, I enjoyed the sense – however illusory – of living in a more interesting, more diverse, more complex society than anything available to an *English* contemporary, an inhabitant – say – of boring Slough or Crawley (I had no knowledge of these places, but they *sounded* pretty dull). The look of Belfast, even my part of Belfast, didn't have a lowering effect on me. I couldn't get enough of rain, back streets, waste ground, the back ends of laundries and cinemas, bleak playgrounds with bonneted toddlers going round and round on wooden carousels. And as for the Dominican Convent – well, although most of the lessons I learnt there are now, in Philip Larkin's phrase, "a forgotten boredom," the place afforded an outlet for the gregarious side of my nature. It was large and forever astir and I had lots of friends; and something of interest was happening every day, a row in prospect over some misdemeanour, a glorious piece of gossip to recount, some unpredictable moment of elation. All the usual madcap enterprises. I rarely left the house with reluctance in the mornings, anticipating, rightly, some highlight of the day. "Fourteen-year-old, why do you giggle and dote?" Stevie Smith wondered, before answering her own question: "I'm fourteen years old, that's the reason." At fourteen, a teacher's unbecoming hat was enough to set us off, and keep us entertained for days.

Now, when middle-aged women come up to me at literary parties, full of the half-remembered events of forty years ago, my strongest reaction is to amplify or correct what they have to say. It seems to matter, God knows why, that they should get the facts right – not mislay or muddle any detail of that shady business in the past. Yes, I suppose it makes the episode more colourful to lumber us all with illegitimate pregnancies when we came home from the Gaedhaltacht – that is one persistent chimera which I'm obliged to contradict. And when Rathmore is cited, as it frequently is, as the school I attended during my final year: this produces in me an agitated response, since it misses the significance of that part of the affair. No, I have to keep insisting, no, it wasn't Rathmore, it was a different school entirely; and *that* ties up with my brief perception of myself – to borrow Karl Miller's motif in his engrossing memoir of his early days, *Rebecca's Vest* – as "disastered me". I wasn't, I believed, a natural magnet for disasters, but suddenly they seemed to be proliferating; and one could only meet them in a spirit of humorous lugubriousness, if such a thing were at all attainable. As for Rannafast itself and what went on there: well, indeed, as I've said, that afforded enormous scope for speculation. And no, I find myself repeating obsessively, no, it wasn't like that at all, that didn't happen, this is what actually happened, this is the way it was.

from Part III, "Tuilleadh Salachar"

"…raised in a northern land of rain and murk …"
Derek Mahon, "Death and the Sun"

It is wonderfully amusing and amazing to consider the pronouncements which issued, in the early part of the last century, from the mouths of especially zealous priests such as Father James Cullen S.J. Cullen's biographer, a fellow cleric, laments at one point in his narrative: "In his efforts to start a Campaign for Modesty in Dress, he did not achieve much success." Father Cullen, it seems, spent a lot of his time looking askance at contemporary fashion, or pagan apparel, as he dubbed it; what really got his goat was the spectacle of Irish women having the gall to approach the Altar for Holy Communion wearing all kinds of "repulsive attire". Since he died in 1921, the year of the founding of the Legion of Mary, it's hard to envisage exactly what caused him so much agitation: hobble skirts? Tea-rose tea gowns? Arts and Crafts dresses of the type worn by Lily and Lolly Yeats at the Cuala Press? Land girls' breeches imported from England? The sight of ankles? Whatever it was that got his dander up, you might have thought – with the country in an uproar, as the Land War was followed by illicit drilling of Volunteers in the North and the South – you might have thought he'd have better things to do than interfere with people's freedom to dress as they pleased. But no. It gets worse. What's likely to instil the greatest alarm in present-day readers of Father Cullen's life story is his strictures on the practice of putting insufficient clothing on *little girls* (his italics): the short skirts and bare legs of little – and worse, big – girls are an abomination to him.

The Irish Messenger of the Sacred Heart, founded by Father Cullen himself back in 1888, along with other periodicals such as the Irish Catholic, kept the subject well to the fore in devout readers' minds as the flighty twenties, with their plentiful temptations for the clothes-conscious, got under way. The onus was on true Irishwomen "to stem the tide of immoral fashions". Failure to go about buttoned up to the chin was tantamount to proclaiming an indifference to Irishness – at any rate, in the eyes of priests and nuns and their followers. It was, indeed, a fairly futile proscription: these people were up against an instinct more fundamental than erotophobia, the instinct to achieve an appearance as pleasing as possible. But the fear of fashion and its implications for immorality: this force, by dint of incessant trumpeting, did work an effect on Irish social life of the mid-century. Its more egregious outlets are pretty well documented. Frank O'Connor, in his travel book of 1947, *Irish Miles*, is rendered speechless by the tendency of Catholic activists to go about pasting strips of brown paper over images of women's chests on advertisement hoardings in cities and towns. And then you got odd members of the laity appointing themselves a scourge of the bedizened. Women and girls in the streets of Dublin, according to Austin Clarke in his autobiography *A Penny in the Clouds*, used to take to their heels – their high heels – in droves, at the approach of an eccentric person named Philip Francis Little, whose mission it was to denounce in a loud voice any shortcomings he spotted with regard to neck – or hemlines. There's a priest in Brian Moore's novel Fergus, a master at St Michan's College in Belfast (a fictionalised St Malachy's), who, the rumour goes, marches off every now and then to the school dentist's office bearing a pair of scissors to excise certain advertisements from magazines distributed about the waiting room. It's to spare the boys exposure to corsets and brassieres, or anything else likely to have an inflaming effect. (Things have changed. On a recent – 1998 – visit to St Malachy's, I was amused to spot in the reception area an *Ulster Tatler* with a picture of "Christmas Lingerie" all over the cover.)

The scissors as an emblem of expurgators crops up again in a real-life anecdote about Brian Moore. When his first novel *Judith Hearne* was published in 1955, his mother in Belfast sent a copy of the book to her youngest daughter Eilis, a nun in a convent in England. But first she took a pair of scissors and went through the book cutting out anything overtly sexual or blasphemous, leaving Eilis – Sister Anne – with a severely mutilated text. Like the mother of the Leeds poet Tony Harrison, Mrs Moore must have had the thought go sorrowfully through her head, "You weren't brought up to write such mucky books."

It was a different world. Of course it's unfair to apply the standards of the present to enormities of the past; change is a built-in factor of the human condition, and attitudes taken for granted at one moment are apt to be strongly repudiated the next. We are all enlightened now – or so it seems, until the next exposure of current misbeliefs comes into being. However, the Ireland of the mid-twentieth century, de Valera's Ireland, presents such an extreme case of backwardness that it seems fair game. At the height of its churchly monomania, it was out of kilter with the rest of the world, especially the post-war world. Where else but in Ireland would you find an edict going out from an Archbishop ordering members of a Girl Pipers Band to lengthen the hems of their kilts, lest the sight of knees marching smartly in unison should induce affront, or arousal, in spectators in the streets?

Poking their nose into girls' bare legs is only a sample of the ways in which the Archbishop of Dublin, Father Cullen and their ilk assert an unassailable power over their congregations. There is more to their scope for outrage than the cut of their flocks' frocks. No aspect of life goes unregulated by them. "In Ireland," notes the American Paul Blanshard, in his 1953 account of the conflict between Catholic policy and modern democracy – *The Irish and Catholic Power* – "In Ireland, … courtship is the business of the Irish priest, and petting is the business of the Irish priest, and even the etiquette of the marriage bed is the business of the Irish priest" – along with birth control, mixed marriage, illegitimacy, sodomy, masturbation, divorce, separation, sex education, the kind of sanitary protection permitted to women, and "keeping company". Well! To get the population into a tractable state with regard to all this it's necessary to catch them early – and indeed, the guideline for teachers is set out unambiguously. Their aim should be to foster in every pupil "a true Catholic outlook on human life as planned by God". Dissenters from full-blown religiosity need not apply. As the case of the novelist John McGahern illustrates, church control over the employment of teachers extended until well into the 1960s. In the mid-century, fearsome Catholic groups came into being to sabotage "Protestant" or liberal influences in the professions. In 1944, the edict placing Trinity College out of bounds for Catholic students was reinforced by Archbishop McQuaid in his Lenten Regulations. Catholics were segregated at University College Dublin where their doings could be monitored by the Archbishop and his henchmen. All this was vastly over the top. No one can reasonably disagree with Paul Blanchard when he deplores the Church's "tendency ... to represent all modern, non-Catholic progress as decadence".

Blanchard finds himself at a loss to explain the docility of Irish people in the face of all this priestly coercion and interference in their daily lives. It's not a new perception. Around the turn of the twentieth century, you get George Moore attributing the malaise of the West to the strong-arm tactics of fanatical priests – priests whose moral development is often in excess of their intellects. And for a rational commentator like Michael J. McCarthy (author of *Priests and People in Ireland*, 1902) acceptance of the Church's "perplexing and interfering with our adult population in every sphere of secular affairs" is a cause of surprised dismay. Why was it that scant attention was paid to these voices of reason, while the ludicrous pronouncements of bishops and archbishops were swallowed without a qualm? To even begin to answer that question, you'd need to take historical circumstances, ideas of national identity and other large matters into consideration. For certain critics of Catholic submissiveness, though, it was pretty simple: the people had had the spirit bludgeoned out of them by a barrage of spirituality. Or at least, they'd allowed themselves to be deprived of some vital impulse: as Blanchard has it, "the total sexual expression of the Irish people is much less than it is in other countries .... The Catholic crusade against normal sexual life has actually created a nation of men and women who try to drown their fundamental instincts". It's wrong, he says, to blame the moist damp climate for eroding Irish ardour, as some have tried to do. Rain is not the primary constraining factor here.

Elizabeth Bowen puts her finger on something fundamental about Irish writing before the 1950s, when she alludes to its sexlessness: by implication, the point she is making about Sheridan le Fanu's *Uncle Silas* – that "no force from any one of the main characters runs into the channel of sexual feeling" – this point may be extended to apply to the whole genre of Irish writing, traditional Irish writing. In its pages, the sexual act is simply edited out altogether (the more usual course), or presented as a feat, as in one of Benedict Kiely's stories when he has someone applaud a pair of lovers in a field who ruin a half acre of turnips in their enthusiasm.

Though it wasn't peculiar to Ireland, of course, censorship operated here a long time before it was officially imposed. In a book which sets out, as far as possible, to defend the Catholic Church and its achievements (*Goodbye to Catholic Ireland*, 1997), Mary Kenny mentions George Orwell's singling out of 1917 as the year in which literature took an unbridled turn. Before that date (she agrees) "mainstream literature maintained a certain decorum. It did not describe sexual acts in detail, and it seldom challenged established religion or morality." This is true as far as it goes. However, there's a difference between those English classics of the nineteenth century, in which an erotic dimension is palpable, if subterranean, and equivalent Irish works, in which the point made by Elizabeth Bowen (above) is amply borne out. There are, of course, many reasons why the Irish novel, for all its liveliness, failed to reach a level of sophistication displayed by its counterparts elsewhere – not least, the abandonment of the native language, allied to poverty and instability. But an endemic prudery seems to have marked it from the start, a prudery that escalated as the Ireland of Cardinal Cullen (another Cullen) gained its defining – Catholic – characteristics. (Paul Cullen, 1803-78, one-time Rector of the Irish College in Rome, set out to impose a definite – a Roman – shape over Irish church affairs, thereby opening the way for the eventual constitutional alignment of church and state, as well as fostering illiberalism in every area: interdenominational relations, policies of education, sexual morality and what-have-you.)

The Gaelic League, though its aims were different, was at one with the Catholic Church in putting up a stiff resistance to any moral contagion spreading in from England. In fact the church took over the League's stern views about the worthlessness and vulgarity of English commercial culture. It's rather ironic, then, to find a priest in Portarlington (in 1905) getting into his pulpit to rant against the Gaelic League's Irish-language classes for mixed students (i.e., male and female). Such classes, he claimed, "were not conducive to the good morals of his flock" (quoted by Mary Kenny). It was feared – and indeed the same fear persisted right down to our day – that enthusiasm for the language among the young was only a pretext for try-out dissipation. I'm not suggesting that this fear was ill-founded – only that a disproportionate importance was attached to it.

There were good reasons why the Gaelic League came into being when it did (in 1893). By the end of the Victorian era, a demoralised populace was badly in need of something to reinforce the sense of national worth and distinctiveness. Misgovernment, famine, emigration, poverty, land wars, evictions ... every imaginable abuse had been inflicted on the Irish, and to cap it all they were fed up with being portrayed, in the pages of *Punch* and elsewhere, as assassins or buffoons. The Gaelic League, and subsequent "Irish-Ireland" movement, offered a means of retrieving dignity and cultural respectability. "Not only Gaelic, but free as well; not only free, but Gaelic as well": this dictum became its watchword – a stance, as many social historians have pointed out, underpinning 1916 and its aftermath. The thing was to cry up every particular in which Irishness differed from Englishness – and religion, and by extension a specific type of spiritual soundness, loomed large here, and got itself grafted on to the language movement (notwithstanding the Protestantism of the Gaelic League's founder, along with a good many of its adherents).

The whole field of Irish-Irishness is fraught with anomalies and complications. Everyone is familiar (to cite a famous example) with the "Playboy" riots of 1907, which saw *Gaeilgeoirí* up in arms over the supposed aspersion cast by Synge on the morals of Mayowomen. "It's Pegeen I'm seeking only," Christy Mahon declares at one moment in the play, "and what'd I care if you brought me a drift of chosen females, standing in their shifts itself, maybe, from this place to the Eastern world?" "Shifts" was the last straw; perhaps this is the only occasion when Irish belligerence erupted over an issue concerning bodice and soul. Gaelic League members who took part in the protest did so, presumably, in ignorance of the fact that the national language had produced a literature in which references to this particular item of underclothing weren't unknown; as an example, we have the folk song, "Eadar Caiseal agus Ur-Choill" ("Between Cashel and the Greenwood"), in which a girl rejected by one man announces that there are plenty of others who would be happy to take her in her shift (*leine*) if that was all she had. Synge, understandably annoyed by the whole furore – "Did you hear that we had to have 57 peelers in to keep the stage from being rushed, and that for four nights not a word could be heard for booing?" – got off to his friend Stephen McKenna an entertaining account of Lady Gregory's first action in the crisis. She went backstage to consult the Abbey Theatre charwoman about whether or not a breach of decorum had been committed. The verdict was that "chemise" was the only acceptable word for the garment.

The outcry provoked by Synge's plays was modulated gradually until it had turned into an ovation; by 1910 the Gaelic League, or one of its representatives, had proclaimed a reversal of opinion in a magazine article which included the work of Synge, along with the *Tain Bo Cuailgne* (*Cattle Raid of Cooley*) and the anonymous ballad, "Slan le Padraig Sairseal" ("Farewell to Patrick Sarsfield"), among the glories of the Gaelic tradition. The recantation came too late to gratify the playwright, who'd been dead for a year. It's also, you might argue, an assessment scarcely more judicious than the earlier nationalist denunciations. There are those who believe that Synge's literary impulse was satiric, reading into his creation of Christy Mahon, for example, an intention to deflate the heroic Cuchulain figure of Irish romance. This is a plausible and illuminating speculation. What's certain, though, is that Synge's own writings provide for the satirist or parodist a target even more conspicuous than anything contained in the Irish sagas. Here is Flann O'Brien: "I have personally met in the streets of Ireland persons who are clearly out of Synge's plays. They talk and dress like that, and damn the drink they'll swally but the mug of porter in the long nights after Samhain."

The sagas and other Irish writings were not at all mealy-mouthed, but it's true that translators of Gaelic material, from Charlotte Brooke on, had tended to tamper with any robustness of expression they found therein. It wasn't until the middle of the twentieth century that a few – a very few – collectors had the gumption to take down the bawdier portions of songs and recitations along with the rest. Pádraigín Ní Uallacháin, in her monumental study of the song tradition of South Armagh (taking in parts of Louth and Monaghan), *A Hidden Ulster* (2003) mentions her father Pádraigín Ní Uallacháin's familiarity with the Rabelaisian aspect of Rannafast culture which quietly flourished alongside more seemly features. Some previously censored lines were retrieved by him and passed on to his daughters, including those in which you get a sexual braggart alluding unabashedly to his *seanbhríste mór*, his "big old trousers," and the maidens' delight they're concealing. Among the friends and acquaintances of Ó hUallachaín, his daughter tells us, were many of the older women singers of Rannafast between the 1920s and 40s, and he used to take great pleasure in the hearty laughter they broke into during the singing of such risqué songs. Pádraig Ó hUallacháin, incidentally, was the *rúnaí* – secretary – of Coláiste Bhridhge in Rannafast between 1937 and 1947, a role filled in our day by a George McAdam who was present during the diatribe delivered to us caught-out debauchees on the last night of our Rannafast stay.

This is not the place to go into the vicissitudes of the Irish language – but, in brief, it was all but obliterated as a living tongue before Douglas Hyde's call for "de-anglicisation," in 1892, brought about a measure of resuscitation. Throughout the nineteenth century, at least in the more accessible parts of the country, the language had been mainly in the keeping of scholars and antiquarians like Robert MacAdam (see above): safe enough, as far as it went, but not exactly alive and burgeoning. And most of the fragments of Gaelic literature that reached the public (in translation) had already been through the hands of bowdlerisers. (Breandan Breathnach, in his authoritative, 1989 study of Irish music and dancing, *Ceol agus Rinnce na hÉireann* – mentions George Petrie's reaction to certain words and phrases in Gaelic manuscripts which struck him unpleasantly. "Of such a nature as will not allow even a specimen of it to be translated," was his outraged attitude.) This bowdlerising had something to do with the sedateness of the age – but more, I think, with a wish to present antique Gaelic culture as unimpeachable in every respect. Whatever required prettifying or purifying was heartily attended to. No one was going to get the chance to say that those old Gaels, Fionn, Oisin, Goll Mac Morna and the rest of them, were a lecherous lot. And the more Gaeldom and Catholicism converged, the more it seemed the people should be kept well away from any circumstance or conjecture at odds with the church, for all the world like a crowd of unruly infants denied access to a dangerous play area. Irish grown-ups – i.e, the Church Fathers – reserved to themselves the right to make judgements about what was, or was not, suitable fodder for their dependents. So it was inevitable that censorship should become an expedient of the Free State government, after the State came into being in 1923 and entered into an unspoken competition with its counterpart in the North to produce a society as rebarbative as possible. If you'd wanted to award the palm for bigotry, it would have been hard to decide which of the two – North or South – to fix it on.

Those of us enrolled at Catholic primary and secondary schools in the North in the1950s were at the mercy of educators who'd inherited the church's whole package of pietistic hogwash. What was clear to Michael F.J. McCarthy in 1902 – that "we have allowed the education of our children to become a branch of theological administration" – still held true over half a century later. Most Six-Counties Catholics felt themselves to be adrift, politically; but as far as religion was concerned, the same structures and devices operated throughout the whole of Ireland. As for the liberal ethic – it is difficult to judge whether we in the North were in a worse position, with a clashing form of bigotry constantly before us to reinforce our own; or whether the proximity of a different system of values and beliefs actually worked, willy-nilly, to lighten the moral air. Ghettoes or religious enclaves certainly existed, but it was impossible to ensure that segregation would be total. Some of us had non-Catholic friends, despite the Church's disapproval.

The Church's – or the Churches' – disapproval. Given such an attitude, any movement towards integration was suspect. Integration equalled adulteration, or at least dilution: dilution of faith and morals which could only be safeguarded in a (selectively) devotional atmosphere. So we underwent our separate forms of spoon-feeding. Of course, while our education was in progress, we were hardly aware of its larger implications: we just enjoyed, or chafed at, appropriate parts of it. We were fortunate, getting a kick out of companionship and juvenile intrigues, doing our best to re-enact the experiences of our favourite story-book characters, mystery girls brought up by gypsies, *School Friend* crusaders against colourful breaches of justice. We had summer meadows to lie around in in our white cotton blouses, chewing blades of grass and gossiping; and the thrill of fog-bound classrooms with the lights full on at midday and the prospect of having to grope our way home.

Our school is strict, but in the battles between pupils and nuns we sometimes come out on top, evade punishment, "get away" with things. And strictness is relative, anyway. I hear tales of children at Catholic schools being made to crawl on bare knees along gravel paths, having mutton or semolina pudding – whatever nauseates them – forced down their throats, of getting their hair whacked off. "Charitable institution" tales, like those concerning the now infamous Magdalen Homes, those supposed refuges which embody the dark Satanic side of Irish provincial Catholicism. To undergo a normal convent education, even at a school such as Ballynahinch – this was, by comparison, a bracing and congenial business, especially if you enjoyed being one of a crowd, immersed yourself in school activities and avoided a reputation for misbehaviour, as some found easy to do. Some pupils took so enthusiastically to school life that they left their alma mater only for the length of time it took to gain a teaching qualification, whereupon they were back again and involved in the reassuring routine of classrooms, timetables, school lore, inter-house competitiveness, rallying one's charges, apportioning encouragement and censure, upholding and enlarging the school tradition. These are the ones who have the history of the school at their fingertips, who can name the prominent members of any class in any year going back to 1926, who applaud the achievement of distinguished old girls, such as Mary McAleese. For them, the school is a community in itself, a haven, and a source of emotional sustenance – never a place where harm is done.

A couple of years ago I went back to St Dominic's. I took a taxi from Rugby Road in Belfast, where I was staying; down Botanic Avenue, along Great Victoria Street, up the Grosvenor Road – or what remains of it; and then I had to direct the driver. Turn left, I said; then right – into the school grounds. It's a winter's day towards the end of term. The drive is crammed with teachers' cars. Otherwise, it's just as I remember it – the enormous twin brick buildings joined at ground level by a passageway; the imposing entrance to the convent part; the modified gothic detail. Good heavens, there is even a nun, in proper Dominican habit, standing in the opened doorway – or am I seeing things? I thought the habit was a thing of the past. The scene in front of me – the red of the brickwork, the green, nearly oval-shaped patch of grass with flower beds in the middle, the bare trees, the lull during lessons, the little gateway I know to be let into the school wall round to the right – all this strikes deep into my seven senses. I was four when I first came here. The school had a kindergarten department in those days, in which I spent a year before being transferred to

Aquinas Hall on the Malone Road, as a shake-up of the system occurred with the implementation of the 1947 Education Act (the start of the Eleven-Plus). I was four, and desperate to get to school, as an only child with a yearning for playmates. However, I hadn't quite understood that the new experience would entail parting from my mother and taking my place among a crowd of strangers, in a strange setting. In the event, I was dragged kicking and bawling into St Dominic's on my first day there, hauled and pulled along by a hefty nun in a habit, while I tried my hardest to keep a hold of my mother, my anchor. Coercion seems to have marked both my coming and my going. The nun won, as was inevitable, and I was left to my fate: parked in a room full of toddlers doing peculiar things with chalk and plasticine. I made the best of it, having no alternative. I ceased to snivel – though I met with no particular kindness or understanding – took a scornful line about some contemporary wetting the floor and having to be hustled out of the classroom by a tut-tutting teacher, and gained a bit of credit for being able to write my name. Soon there were tears in the morning if I couldn't go to school, through running a temperature or some such. Like everyone else, I wore a small box-pleated maroon-coloured tunic and sash, with the school crest emblazoned on the left-hand side, and regulation white viyella blouse. These garments were purchased from a school outfitters' near Dunville Park on the Falls Road. In the classroom, we learned things by rote – "Four ones are four, four twos are eight"; "Who made the world? God made the world". This led to some misunderstandings. One child for years declaimed the line from the "Apostles' Creed", "Suffered under Pontius Pilate", as "Suffered under a bunch of violets." To her, one version made as much sense as the other. (Years later, I remember hearing about a similar misapprehension on the part of a non-comprehending pupil. The Secondary Intermediate school where my mother taught, St Louise's, has a school song in praise of its patron saint, which goes something like, "Hail, St Louise, something, something/ Captain and guardian of our school...". This stuck in one person's head as, "Kept in the garden of our school," which actually did make sense, since the school grounds contained a statue of St Louise.) Some of the big girls about the place made a pet of me and brought me sweets and did up my shoe laces for me, while others – teasers – went in for pinching and hair-pulling. Once, when I turned on one of the latter and bit her, I was put to sit on a high stool in a corner to contemplate my wickedness. I was prepared for my First Holy Communion in this place – the first important ritual of the Catholic church. Photographs show a group of us smirking for the camera, our parents standing proudly behind us wearing their choicest suits and hats. We communicants are dressed up to the nines in nasty little fussy white art silk frocks and veils, clutching mother-of-pearl-backed missals in our kid-gloved hands: Margaret Dornan, Margot Farrell, Fiona Devlin, Sally Smith.

My first return to St Dominic's is at the age of eleven, happy to be a grammar-school pupil, an eleven-plusser. Since leaving it five years later under that fearsome Gaedhaltacht cloud, I'd tended to look the other way while passing the place on the top deck of a Falls Road bus. Certainly the time has come to quell any residual antipathy I may still be harbouring. The first thing is to learn whatever I can about the history of the school – hence my current visit, to pick up a hundred-and-twenty-fifth anniversary booklet. Dominican nuns, I find, existed in Ireland seven hundred years ago; Penal Laws in the seventeenth century drove them into exile in Spain and Portugal, before a motherhouse was established at Cabra, Co Dublin, in 1818. Fifty years after that date, a communication went out from the Bishop of Down and Connor to these Cabra nuns, inviting them to Belfast to found a school. This is it. Opened on the Falls Road in 1870, with four day pupils and a boarder, the convent, according to a contemporary report in *The Ulster Examiner*, "occupies an elevated and agreeable position in the environs of Belfast and commands an extensive view of the surrounding country ... Unremitting attention is given to the health and comfort of the Young Ladies ... No efforts are spared to train the Pupils in habits of obedience, industry and neatness ... During the summer months the pupils are permitted to take long walks in the country." We're in L.T. Meade territory here, accompanied by a whiff of peculiarly Irish Catholic innocence and decorum. Whatever the realities of the situation for these early Belfast convent girls, they are now irretrievable, absorbed into an idealised, holy haze. However, judging by the numbers of them who went on to become nuns themselves, there can't have been too much insubordination. Early photographs show small girls in pinafores, strolling arm-in-arm through the extensive grounds, or sitting in the long grass making daisy-chains. You get no sense of things being fraught or disagreeable – though no doubt they sometimes were. Reminiscences of St Dominic's earlier days, mostly written by nuns, are uniformly jolly in tone, as though to suggest that eventual assumption of the veil needn't entail a goody-goody girlhood.

By 1914, St Dominic's had 161 pupils, all of whom would have come from well-to-do families; most children at the time didn't receive secondary education at all, and in the Falls Road area you would have had "half-timers" (i.e. those whose days were divided between the classroom and the mill) learning the rudiments of English, Arithmetic and so forth, in a school such as St Vincent's, run by the Sisters of Charity and accommodating up to five hundred pupils in four classrooms. We're all appalled nowadays by enormities of the past, insupportable living conditions, hair-raising ills, unimaginable deprivations. In compensation, though, we might note the tendency to applaud the spirit of people who tholed all these, and more, and more – and the Falls district, in particular, entertains the strongest possible sense of its industrial and political past, charged with culturally assertive energies. The cluster of red-brick streets, some named topically after battles of the Crimean War (Sevastapol, Omar, Balaclava) nurtured all kinds of insurrectionary affiliations. There was more to the Falls than men in duncher caps discussing greyhound racing at street corners, shawlies scurrying towards the local pawn shop, exuberant young mill-workers taunting stodgy looking passers-by, street games involving lamp posts and paving stones, garrulous grandmothers and brazen youngsters hitching dangerous rides on the back ends of lorries, or defrauding the management of the Clonard Cinema – though these fragments of Falls Road life were far from being figments. Parts of the road were semi-suburban, though its core was anything but; it was rich in local lore and indigenous repartee, and harboured a fraternity of the self-taught whose spiritual home was the fusty public library on the corner of Sevastapol Street. Catholicism and nationalism pervaded the air it generated – with the odd gust of socialism just to keep things polemical. Religion and its rituals shaped the life of the area: Sunday masses, Holidays of Obligation, evening devotions, weekly confessions, Men's Confraternity meetings, Children of Mary, May altars, Corpus Christi processions, the family rosary and what-have-you. The Dominican convent was only one of a score of religious buildings dotted along the road, though its elevated position – pace *The Ulster Examiner* – enabled it to take a haughty view of itself.

The further you penetrated into the Falls's hinterland, the narrower the streets became, the rougher the brickwork; flat paving stones gave way to cobbles, with ruts in the roadway where the wheels of tradesmen's handcarts trundled through. Front doors were dingier and windows constructed to let in only the smallest shafts of light. Families living here either clung with desperation to the remnants of an imagined respectability, or had given up altogether and thought nothing of sticking their knickers and petticoats out through a front-room window to dry in the tainted air. Photographs from the early part of the last century suggest that about half the children from these areas went barefoot.

I think of the Falls as distilling its strongest backstreet flavour between the 1890s (say) and the late 1940s: sixty-odd years of fearsome privations, raucousness, clan-solidarity and disaffection. It would be an interesting cinematic exercise to show its built-up areas dwindling bit by bit as you go backwards in time, until nothing was left but the original fields and ponds. *Bothar na bhFal*: the road of the hedges. Before 1840, indeed, as we've seen, the buildings beyond Townsend Street could nearly be counted on the fingers of one hand: a linen factory, a flax mill, a bleach works, two houses and a pub. Closer to the town centre, however, there were plenty of built-up, run-down localities to outrage the sensibilities of a social commentator such as the Minister of the Congregationalist Church in Upper Donegall Street, the Rev. W.M. O'Hanlon, whose *Walks Among the Poor of Belfast* was published in 1853. "We advanced along Durham Street," writes O'Hanlon in his study of Belfast's nineteenth-century riff-raff, "peering ... into all manner of courts and entries." You get the sense that he and his companions, in this rough area, advanced very gingerly indeed. Possibly its inhabitants weren't beguiled by the clergyman's shock-horror expose of their living conditions. O'Hanlon made no bones about telling them what was what. As far as he was concerned, poverty and debauchery went hand-in-hand; and he'd have liked nothing better than to affect a cleaning-up of morals along with living quarters. Drunkenness is O'Hanlon's chief horror; counting no fewer than twenty-two public houses in the vicinity of North Queen Street, he succumbs to an appalled disbelief. Prostitution, sodomy, incest, not to mention feckless procreation ... all these, and worse, he believes, can be laid at the door of drink. No wonder the strains of a lewd song issuing from a slum makes his hair stand on end.

It's hard not to poke fun at O'Hanlon – however, as a would-be reformer, he was more in the Mayhew than the temperance-propaganda tradition. What he recommended as a lower-class modus operandi was simply an industrious, orderly, sober, well-scrubbed routine. It's just that the practice of obtruding his sniffy clerical nose into all manner of hovels makes him a target for moderate ridicule. He's not at all akin to MacNeice's mad preacher (for example) who embodies the sour, black, rebarbative, life-withering aspect of Ulster religious practice:

> Among old ashes, cinders, sizzling dumps,
> A world castrated, amputated, trepanned,
> He walked in the lost acres crying, "Repent
> For the kingdom of death is at hand."

We Catholics, secure in the rationality of our own brands of denial, don't scruple to point the finger at such potty forms of Protestantism; but in truth – as we've seen – there are pleasure-quashers of equal intensity on both sides of the religious split, who together add up to a demented fraction on the edge of normal life. And how you react in the end to the restrictions of your upbringing is as much a matter of temperament as indoctrination. Most sensible grown-up people, all along, would have worked out some personal compromise between churchly obligation and worldly inclination.

It's only in the last decade or so that we have really grasped the extent to which the religious edifice in Ireland was a superstructure imposed over a basis of ordinary laxity. Even priests, it seems, were never as holy *en masse* as we once assumed. Some church dignitaries allowed themselves more leeway than they meted out to their flocks – or so the spate of scandals flummoxing Irish ecclesiasticism would suggest. One lurid misdemeanour after another has come to light: we've had bonking bishops popping up all over the place, clerical brothel-haunters, priests and nuns running off in droves, and revelations of the sexual abuse of children by clerics on such a scale that the thing has become a commonplace. The randy Christian Brother has all but succeeded the Scout Master as a joke sexual predator.

I suppose all these, and other transgressions, have been going on all the time, only kept very carefully under wraps. (Even Paul Blanchard, for all his investigator's nose, accepted that Church Fathers practised what they preached, and that their parishioners gave them credit for their abstinence.) They can't be peculiar to the present – though no doubt the current moral climate makes it easier for religieuses to step out of line. Well, you've only to take the name Taggart, or McTaggart, to understand that priests didn't always stick to celibacy. But it still seems strange to me to envisage those in religious orders as sexual beings in any sense. In my experience, they'd so surrounded themselves with an aura of fortitude and holiness and ascetic segregation, that it seemed an impertinence to suspect them of bodily functions at all. They were a group apart, and in a self-elected monitoring relation to the rest of us.

Possibly the most brutal, rancorous and disagreeable of the nuns I remember were actually taking their sexual frustrations out on us, their charges; but fortunately no overt sexual molestation was ever inflicted on us alongside the other vexations of the school day. Indeed, such a thing is utterly unimaginable. No lesbian or lecherous nuns ever crossed our paths to scare the wits out of us. The aim of our Dominicans was to keep their nubile pupils out of men's clutches, never to get them into their own. (A ludicrous and revolting thought.) As for priests – they celebrated Mass and heard confessions, and that was all I knew of them. I didn't come from one of those church-besotted families who had them constantly in the house. No priest whatever had any personal contact with me. In fact, I never met a priest socially until 1998, when the Jesuit brother of a friend came to visit us at Blackheath. I only saw them in their full regalia performing some ritual or other. Of course, like everyone else above the age of fourteen, I was cross-questioned in the confession box about minor sexual delinquencies; but if my embarrassed disclosures were having an arousing effect on the pastor in question, I'd never have noticed. I wasn't very observant. Indeed, extremes of self-abuse could have been going on under my nose; and if I'd been aware of anything out-of-the-way at all, I'd have attributed it to some innocuous cause such as trouble with undergarments or a flea in the cassock.

"It must be tough on a priest who, while trying to abstain from fleshly pleasures himself, has to sit in a darkened confessional, hand cupped to his ear, as half his congregation sorrowfully parades its fumblings, erections and ejaculations before him." This observation comes from Cal McCrystal's spirited memoir of 1997, *Reflections on a Quiet Rebel* – one of the recent autobiographies which alert us to the fact that Catholic schoolboys in the middle part of the last century actually had it worse than girls, when it came to a confrontation with unbefitting sexual conduct (well, unless you were a Magdalen inmate and consequently fair game for any rapacious priest). They do, however, seem better equipped to make light of these matters. For the memoirists at least, sexual eccentricities were hardly more alarming than other teachers' foibles. It was almost *de rigueur* for boys' establishments to include a weird bod or two among the teaching staff. Pupils soon grasped the identities of those it was best to steer clear of, outside lessons:

> He was in his early thirties and affable enough, but the boys tended to give him a wide berth, fearing a call to his room ... This was the priest who seemed to enjoy thrashing boys with a cane while in their pyjamas, and had strange nocturnal wanderings. ...One night I was awakened by a slight movement of my bed....He seemed to have trouble with his breathing. What appeared to be a white handkerchief fluttered in the vicinity of his waistband. I squeezed my eyes shut, pretending to be asleep.

Cal McCrystal, at the time, was a boarder with the Marist Fathers of Dundalk; this, *circa* 1950, was the school from which a boy named Daly was expelled "for climbing a wall to kiss a town girl". I have a lot of sympathy for this unknown boy called Daly. And for Tom Campbell, who, some years earlier, left St Patrick's College, Armagh, in similar circumstances. Campbell's innocent jingle,

> I have a dainty girlfriend
> And this you'll comprehend,
> Every time she bends her knee
> I see the Promised Land

transcribed in a friend's album and spotted by a ravening Dean, got him expelled from the school for indecency. This incident is recalled in John Montague's biting sequence of poems about his years at the college – "a harsh, boorish, ignorant" regime – pointedly called *Time in Armagh*:

> Endless games designed to keep us pure –
> "Keep your hands out of your pockets, boys" –
> We wore togs even in the showers.

Daly, Campbell: I wonder how many of us, thirty, forty, fifty-odd years ago, were given the boot at the behest of some puritanical maniac?

By the 1960s, things were changing; or perhaps it was just that some boys' schools accommodated an unusual degree of oddness in their employees. An unabashed sexual enthusiast, for example, slaked his lusts quite openly at the Christian Brothers school attended by the novelist and short-story writer, Dermot Healy. (Again, recalling our decorous classrooms, I find it hard to envisage such smutty goings-on.) Healy's illuminating memoir, *The Bend for Home* (1996), saddles the town of Cavan with a merry sexual ferment. Joining in, with his own mode of hanky-panky, is a Brother Felim who turns his roll-calling duties to his own ends:

> ... he brought you in behind his desk and felt your mickey as you called out the names ... He undid a button, then another, and curled a finger round your member ... You could feel through his dress the hump of his erection against your thigh ... He suddenly let you go like a bad thing. Did your buttons up ...

The cheery tone suggests that no lasting damage was done to the objects of this lewd quirk. It was only a minor annoyance of school life. And yet – one can't help wondering if clerics all along, while upholding chastity with one hand, were actually undermining it with the other. It is possible that a schizophrenic approach to life, either overtly or subliminally, has been bred in those of us exposed to such contradictions.

While many of us dithered for years over the rights and wrongs of church teaching, some people knew exactly where they stood, from the word go. "Once I discovered sex," confides the poet Pearse Hutchinson (in his introduction to *New and Selected Poems*, 1990), "I began to chafe at the almost incessant killjoy barrage that came at us from all sides: school, pulpit, confession box, home." There was nothing for it but to reject the whole caboodle and its summation, Ireland. Ireland and puritanism went hand-in-hand. This was the 1940s, a dusty decade. It requires gumption and clear-sightedness to identify an unreasonable pressure, before you're out of your teens, and consequently to take evasive action. Independence of outlook is the prime mover here – and those who possess this quality usually attract, and deserve, our admiration. With hindsight, you can only applaud anyone courageous enough to repudiate that overwhelming institution, the Catholic church in Ireland, in the mid-twentieth century. At that time, Catholic Ireland was, or seemed to be, invincible, and there was no escaping the malaise it generated. But, as we've seen, other religious systems weren't behindhand in enforcing equivalent constraints; and it wasn't always easy for recusants to get the form of their rebellion right. I've already alluded to the Louis MacNeice poem about the raging preacher:

And in the city at night where drunken song
Climbed the air like tendrils of vine
He bared a knife and slashed the roots and laid
Another curse on Cain. The sign
Of the cross between his eyes, his mouth drawn down,
He passed the flower-sellers and all
The roses reeked of an abattoir, the gardenias
Became the decor of a funeral.

I am now about to cite the peculiar case of the novelist Anthony C. West (1910-198?), whose repugnance for the anti-erotic atmosphere of Protestant Cavan led him into a succession of bloomers. Some of these may not have seemed like bloomers at the time, but they certainly do from a perspective in the present. Casting himself as a free spirit, West in fact has severely blinkered himself as far as his partners in sexual emancipation are concerned. His fiction presents one of the most egregious instances of anti-feminism in literature that I have ever encountered. And the really extraordinary thing is the reputation it gathered to itself. It's not, thank goodness, that West is widely known – but he does have, or has had, a small band of admirers which includes people who should know better, such as Sean O'Faolain and Seamus Heaney. You don't expect wrong-headed judgement from these – or, for that matter, from John Hewitt, John Wilson Foster or John Cronin. But what do you find? "A tremblingly sensitive imagination", according to Sean O'Faolain, is among West's assets. "Lyrically evocative," writes John Cronin. The words "brilliance" and "genius" are bruited about. Have I missed something? I turn to page 15 of West's collection of stories, *All the King's Men*, and encounter the following: "a great bosom straining the seams of a frock". On the same page, "a fine-skinned white breast," "a round plump bottom," and "a flat chest without a breast-valley, as Anne's full breasts were valleyed, their secret hollow starting almost under her chin." Some "young breasts" promptly appear, followed by "low, leathery breasts"; and then, most bizarre of the lot, "tomato-red breasts". The possessor of the last is clearly in need of medical attention.

From the novels and stories of Anthony C. West you derive an impression that women's breasts and bottoms are constantly being thrust in his face. These parts, at any rate, are all he sees. Here is his description of a Land Girl glimpsed in passing by the hero of the novel *As Towns With Fire*: "Knickerbockers full of behind and green pullover overstuffed with breast." (The protagonist of this novel, incidentally, is a Co Monaghan RAF pilot whose mind is so deranged by the war that he plans to set up home with his wife and children in a barrel in the woods.)

West persuaded himself, and some of his readers, that he was casting off cant and repression, while actually displaying a kind of indigenous misogyny which is fearfully disheartening. It's among the forms of blight afflicting Northern Irish society – a society, you might conclude, spectacularly lacking in resources for tranquillity or civility. It's one way of looking at it, but not the only way. There are others who've portrayed things differently. The province has never been short of verses (for example) to keep the spirits up. "I take my stand by the Ulster names," wrote John Hewitt,

> each clean hard name like a weathered stone;
> Tyrella, Rostrevor, are flickering flames:
> the names I mean are the Moy, Malone,
> Strabane, Slieve Gullion and Portglenone.

And there are other ways of naming names in order to strike an affirmative note. There's Tom Paulin: "I lay claim to those marshes,/The Lagan, the shipyards,/The Ormeau Road in winter." Heaney's Toome and Moyola, Mahon's north coast, Longley's Lisburn Road or Portavogie with its prawn fishermen, Ciaran Carson's obliterated Falls: all these, and more, add up to a kind of communal exercise in re-creation, or appreciation, betokening the strongest understanding of a community about which there is more, much more, to be singled out than its savageries and miseries.

> Most people of Healy's [Dermot Healy: see above] generation will remember summer trips to colleges in the Gaedhaltachta, the Irish-speaking regions of the country, which were supposed to inculcate a reverence for the Irish language and the rural way of life, the twin obsessions of Eamonn de Valera. Of course, they became occasions for explosions of adolescent hormones and doomed love affairs with people otherwise impossible to meet. In a strange way they probably achieved a connection between the Irish language and sexuality, which could only be good for the language.

The above passage, from Catriona Crowe's review of Dermot Healy's *The Bend for Home* in *The London Review of Books* neatly sums up both the ideological colouring of these extramural courses, and the actual subtext. Of course the Irish-language summer school goes back some way before de Valera. The practice was initiated under the auspices of the Gaelic League, and to begin with, the schools were attended by adults; it was only after Padraig Pearse and St Enda's had identified the potential benefits to a younger contingent that senior pupils got in on the act.

Ballinageary, Co Cork, started the whole thing going back in 1904: a time when convent schools still taught deportment to their girls, when "patriotic dress," complete with embroidery copied from the Book of Kells, drew jeers from Dublin fishwives in the streets ("Them Irishers are going daft"), when Springfield in Belfast was described as an old, old, stone-built hamlet and optimists in the North believed that bigotry was on its last, though still strongly kicking, legs. Tourmakeady, Co Mayo, Spiddal, Co Galway, Cloughaneeley, Co Donegal, and Omeath near Carlingford in Co Louth were other early venues for summer-school high-mindedness and conviviality. Rannafast was a late addition to these prestigious localities, with its Colaiste Bhridhge coming into existence in 1926 as a replacement for Omeath, whose Irish-speaking populace had dwindled to the point where the place could hardly be termed a Gaedhaltacht at all. One of Omeath's directors, Father Lorcan O Muiri (Larry Murray), decided to move the enterprise to Donegal's Atlantic coast, where the language continued eloquent and undiminished. O Muiri, priest, folklorist and indefatigable song-collector, could count among his attributes the distinction of having been expelled from Maynooth, after his superiors took it on themselves to brand him as a bad influence. (He was subsequently ordained in America.) The Rannafast undertaking did not get off to a painless start. Funding was obtained – after prodigious efforts on the part of O Muiri – a site was chosen and the college buildings slowly went up. Colaiste Bhridhge was about to open its doors to students when a huge wind suddenly blew up and swept the whole thing out into the Atlantic Ocean, as an eagle might have carried off a baby in a blanket. Father Murray's second brainchild must have had stronger foundations for it is still there (as far as I know), dispensing Irish and amusement to those enrolled in its courses, though perhaps not so enticingly as in the past.

Not every commentator, though, is attuned to that bygone Gaedhaltacht ambience. According to Michael Tierney, biographer of one of the Gaelic League's founders, Eoin MacNeill, "it is difficult now to recapture even in imagination the spirit of the summer schools with their plain living amid beautiful surroundings, their open-air classes, their students living in Irish-speaking homes, their ceilis, their excursions, often by the sea, to visit historic monuments and places of antiquarian interest, their endless discussions and the deep and lasting friendships to which they so readily gave rise ..." Well, he makes it all sound fearfully decorous and antiquated: it wasn't like that in our day, and even in the distant past it's unlikely to have been so staid – though you can't quarrel with his list of Gaedhaltacht pursuits. Tierney's po-faced prose is simply not equipped to communicate the uniquely exhilarating atmosphere he touches on. To get a real sense of summer-school bedazzlement you have to turn to a writer like Sean O'`Faolain, to whom the act of evocation comes as naturally as sneezing:

> In groups we spent the livelong days together. We spent half the day down in the village studying the language in the corrugated tin shed grandiosely called the College. The rest of the day we spent swimming in the rock pools, or climbing the mountains, or cycling to the farther glens, or dancing informally by the roadside at night, or more formally in the College, or boating on the lake if the moon was up, or simply sitting in the kitchen listening to some local boy or girl singing a traditional Irish song or playing old tunes on the fiddle, or we merely sat and conversed. Late hours were the common rule. I was always so pleasantly tired, so full of oxygen, that I could have slept soundly under a hedge or on a stone floor. On hot nights I often slept, in the clothes in which I stood, high up in the hay of the outdoor hay barn, waking only when I heard a horse's hooves on the road or somebody working in the stone byre below. Nowadays, the learning of Irish has lost this magical power to bind hearts together....

Well, maybe; but something of that first buoyant spirit persisted, though – as O'Faolain implies – compulsory Irish did a lot to stifle it. Irish was never compulsory for us in the North – indeed, its powerful connections with defiance and dissent were a part of its allure.

The group I belonged to in the early 1960s, Cumann Cluan Ard, was fuelled by a wish to reinstate Irish as a medium of everyday communication. Its ambitions were unprecedented but not unattainable. By the middle of the decade, a lot of its members had paired off, moved into newly-built houses all close together, and established the nucleus of what became known as Belfast's Gaelic colony. The next, inevitable, step was the setting up of nursery schools to accommodate their Irish-speaking infants. Then, as required, middle schools and grammar schools came into being, followed by radio programmes in Irish, shops selling Irish books and magazines, and other amenities to boost the undertaking.

I was not personally involved in any of this. Shortly before these remarkable developments got under way, myself and my friend Maire, once keen members of Cluan Ard, had scarpered to England, respectively to London and Manchester, to further our own ambitions which had gradually diverged from *fíor*-Gaeldom. Nevertheless, the achievements of our one-time associates impressed us strongly. They had brought Irish out of the private, and into the public, domain. Their polite determination to speak their own language in all possible circumstances had tremendous implications for the future of the language, as a cultural survival wrested out of complexity and deadlock. Though the Shaw's Road Gaedhaltacht was a place apart, its singularity had to do with conservation, not exclusiveness. Its inhabitants didn't proselytise on the whole, but liked to show by their own example the relevance of Irish to contemporary life. They were, and are, idealists, but none the less practical for that.

The setting up of this urban Gaedhaltacht coincided with the arrival of agitation in other parts of West Belfast, and the two in conjunction gave rise to a new version of an old question: were these Gaelic-speakers more, or less, Irish than their daredevil contemporaries who carried on the tradition of fighting, killing and dying for Ireland and never letting ordinary humanitarian reservations affect that grandiose resolve? No one ever came up with an adequate answer (all answers were partisan), but at the same time, terms like "cultural identity" began to be bandied about, with emphasis (in liberal circles anyway) placed on the need to accord esteem to as many varieties of "cultural identity" as could be pinpointed. It wasn't long before the Irish language got itself counted among the resources of militant republicanism – a circumstance to which the Shaw's Road *Gaeligoiri* and others reacted with a measure of wryness. This wryness could hardly be contained following the appearance of political slogans framed in a version of Irish guaranteed to raise the ire of an old linguistic purist such as Flann O'Brien (say). "Tiochfaidh ar la," *mar shampla*.

The summer after the Rannafast debacle – as I've said – I am back for a month in the Donegal Gaedhaltacht, in Loughanure on the other side of Annaghry, where I keep out of harm's way and engage in no momentous misbehaviour. I am seventeen, and happy to have done with school (since the school is miserable Ballynahinch). I remember visiting a local house at Loughanure where one of the daughters sings "Buachaill ó'n Éirne" in an enthralling manner. I remember, too, that my roommates here are all demure girls with shiny hair and great proficiency in needlework. It is clear from the start that Loughanure is not quite so lively a centre of Irish studies as Rannafast. Further visits to Irish-speaking districts, over the next five years or so, take place in the company of delegates from an inter-University Gaelic Society which I have joined; or, more frequently, on excursions with friends from Cumann Cluan Ard. The spiritual home of Cluan Ard is Rannafast, and so my association with this wild place continues for a time, though on freer terms than those prevailing during the first disastrous summer. It isn't at all the same. We Irish enthusiasts tend to go there at odd times of the year – April, October – travelling from Belfast in a hired minibus, or hitch-hiking whenever we can get away for a couple of days and are feeling energetic. And even during the months of July and August, when the College is functioning and the place awash in schoolchildren, there are houses set aside for club members who've established relationships with many of the local families. You can stay in these houses and not be answerable to any extraneous authority. Of course, by now we are old enough to accept the rules of behaviour governing the visit to someone else's home, and to take a tolerantly exasperated view of schoolchildren's antics. There is no call for our later landladies to nail up the windows to keep us in our beds at night. Oddly, I don't remember, in these later years, running across any of the Rannafast boys who so preoccupied us during our first heady days in the Gaedhaltacht – or wanting to, for that matter, newer infatuations having supervened, to be fostered in their turn by the intoxicating locality.

Once I'd ceased to live in Ireland these excursions tailed off, then stopped altogether. I haven't set foot in the Donegal Gaedhaltacht for a good many years. But the sense of a kind of Atlantic idyll remains implanted in my consciousness. The outcome of that first visit didn't destroy the place for me. Rannafast and its goings-on may have landed us in a pickle, a pickle with weighty consequences; but the place itself never ceased to embody the spirit of a vibrant and pristine Ireland.

Patricia Craig is a critic, essayist and anthologist. Her most recent books are The Belfast Anthology *(The Blackstaff Press, 1999) and* Brian Moore: A Biography *(Bloomsbury, 2002). Her sequel,* The Ulster Anthology, *also from Blackstaff, is forthcoming. She now lives in Antrim.*

DÁN

Liam Ó Muirthile

ÁÉÍÓÚ

Ní rabhas i rang na feadóige níos mó
is dheineas scála ceoil de na gutaí fada
i rang pléascach Dermo.

N'fheadar an bí an pléasc
a bhlosc le slat ar aibíd
nó an riast a d'at ar bhois
ba mheasa d'aicíd,
ach ghabh lascfhórsa rois
an aeir trínn ar luas aibítreach.
ÁÉÍÓÚ
dár n-imeaglú.

Á! na mianta a phléasc inár gcroí
do chuair Mhurascaill Mheicsiceo
pé acu anfa nó cúbtha chucu,
d'fhuasclaíodar sinn ó phlúchadh
comhchosach na dtriantán
is rinceamar le lúba Chúba.

ÁÉÍÓÚ
dár bhfuascailt.

Lá dar chaitheamar
bailte na Mumhan
a chur isteach de láimh
ar léarscáil bhán ar an gclárdubh,
d'fhógair an Bráthair ar Fielder
Trá Lí a mharcáil is bheith amuigh.
D'fhan ina staic, balbh.
Fuair sé greadadh ó thalamh
nuair a chuir sé an baile siar
beagán ó dheas ar chuar an Bhá,
is an Bráthair ag rá
idir buillí de liú:

"Ní hea ansan ach ansan"
á aistriú soir an chuid is lú.
Chonac Bá Thrá Lí ina chruth
mar chíoch is sine le diúl
is neadaigh an Bráthair
baile cailce ar an sine
go brúidiúil.

ÁÉÍÓÚ
brúidiúil.

Chaitheamar fanacht
inár gcolgsheasamh sa chlós
gan oiread is lámh ná cos
a chorraí nuair a shéid sé
an fheadóg ag an sos,
is dá mbeadh éinne fós
ag rás gan í a chlos
ghlaofaí air as a shloinne
leis an ordú pionóis:
"Go dtí an Oifig. Rith."
Chleachtaíos dul i bhfolach
im chorp féin ón bhfead chaol,
is phléasc neascóidí ar mo dhrom
is ceann nimhneach im ghabhal
is ba nimhní fós an neascóid
a d'fhan na blianta im cheann,
comhdhéanta de ghutaí oifigiúla.

ÁÉÍÓÚ
oifigiúla.

Lá dar chaitheas féin
Locha Móra Mheiriceá
a tharraingt ar an gclárdubh
thosnaíos le Superior amuigh
i gcruth chloigeann gadhair
mar a dheinimis le scáileanna
ar fhalla istoíche sa leaba,
is anuas ansin le Michigan
ina leadhb fhada teanga,
is ar aghaidh arís le Huron
nó gur bhagair sé orm stopadh;

"Taispeáin anois cá bhfuil Duluth."
Is nuair a dheineas go hinstinniúil
chreideas gur fíor í míorúilt.

ÁÉÍÓÚ
instinniúil.

Thugas bosca *Cadbury's Roses*
abhaile ar chúl mo rothair

mar dhuais sna cora cainte
a d'fhoghlaimíos sna leabhair,
Maidhc Bleachtaire is *Maidhc Abú*
is *Geronimo* an tíogar daonna,
is mhapálamar gnéithe aiceanta
na hÉireann mar chód géiniteach
a scaoileadh i gceol diamhair tíre,
is sheoladh long ó Valparaiso
de ghlanmheabhair i gcabhair
chun luachanna ailgéabair
a chothromú ar phár na hoíche.

ÁÉÍÓÚ
dár gcothromú.

Tráthnóntaí samhraidh ar an trá
théinn ag snámh i Muir Chairbre
ar Inse an Duine sna Bahámaí
lámh le tropaicí Chloich na Coillte,
is chuala canúintí á smearadh
as na meadair ime chéanna
is leanas bóthar leáite an ime úd
ó Chorcaigh go Jamaica,
is an lá ar dhóbair don domhan
pléascadh i gcogadh núicléach
sheol an Bráthair an rang abhaile
á rá linn guí le dúthracht
go gcasfadh loingeas na Rúise
go dtiocfadh ciall chuig Kruschev,
is chonac cuntanós an Bhráthar
á chomhleá ina dhuine buartha.

ÁÉÍÓÚ
dár gcomhleá.

Thug sé Cros Cheilteach isteach
lámhdhéanta sa meaitseanna,
veairniseáilte is greanta
ag príosúnach i mBéal Feirste,
deartháir duine sa scoil
fé ghlas ar son na saoirse,
is chroch os cionn an chófra í
i bhfeighil Léarscáil na hÉireann;
chuimhníos ar lána sráide
ar na meaitseanna leathdhóite
ag téachtadh i sruth fola
tar éis sáthadh sa pharóiste,
is shil an Chros Cheilteach fuil
tríd an veairnis ar ár ngeograf.

ÁÉÍÓÚ
dár dtéachtadh.

Lá amháin a chonac é
ag imeacht ar a rothar,
dronn ar nós an droichid air
bhuail fonn mé beannú dó
ach ghreamaigh na focail
ar an teanga bheag im scornach;
leanas é go dtí an leabharlann
mar ar sheas sé leis an ráille,
ba sheanduine leathchaoch é
ag fústráil le slabhra,
bhí fonn orm teacht i gcabhair air
go dtí go bhfaca an gotha
a bhíodh air i mbun ranga,
a theanga dingthe sna fiacla
dúbailte ag pleancadh:
"Tá milseán agam duit,"
is sileadh i ngach siolla
leis an íoróin dochreidte
nuair a d'eascair as a phóca
slat chomh fada síos lena bhróga.
Bhí fonn orm a fhiafraí de
"Cad as tú?" "Cér díobh thú?"

"Mise Hurley rang scoláireachta '62"
ach chuaigh díom an tuin a aimsiú
chun na focail a chur in iúl
go ndéanfadh buíochas díobh
ar scála ÁÉÍÓÚ i dtiúin.

ÁÉÍÓÚ
i dtiúin.

AEIOU

I was no longer in the whistle class
and I made a music scale of the long vowels
in Dermo's explosive class.

I don't know if it was the explosion
that cracked with a rod on a habit
or the welt that swelled on a palm
that was the worse ailment,
but the switchforce of the rush of air
went through us with alphabetical speed.

AEIOU
terrorising us.

Ah! the desires that exploded in our heart
for the curves of the Gulf of Mexico
whether a storm or bent towards them,
they redeemed us from the isosceles
suffocation of the triangles
and we danced with the loops of Cuba.

AEIOU
redeeming us.

One day we spent
writing in by hand
the towns of Munster
on an empty map on the blackboard,
the Brother ordered Fielder
to mark Tralee and to be out.

He stood dumbfounded.
He got a sound thrashing
when he put the town west
a little south of the curve of the Bay,
and the Brother saying
between blows with a shout:

"Not there but there"
moving it east the least bit.
I saw Tralee Bay a shape
like a breast and a nipple to suck
and the Brother settled
a chalk town on the nipple
brutally.

AEIOU
brutal.

We had to wait
bolt upright in the quad
without moving even a hand or foot
when he blew
the whistle at break time,
and if there was still someone
racing and didn't hear it
he'd be called by his surname
with the penal order:
"To the office. Run."
I practised hiding
in my own body from the sharp whistle,
and boils exploded on my back
and a painful one in my crotch
and more painful still was the boil
that stayed for years in my head,
made up of official vowels.

AEIOU
official.

One day when I had to draw
the Great Lakes of America
on the blackboard
I began with Superior out

in the shape of a dog's head
as we used to make with shadows
on a wall at night in bed,
and down then to Michigan
a long strip of tongue,
and forward again to Huron
until he ordered me to stop;
"Now show where Duluth is."
And when I did it instinctively
I believed that a miracle can happen.

AEIOU
instinctive.

I brought a box of *Cadbury's Roses*
home on the back of my bicycle
as a prize for the idioms
learned in the books,
*Maidhc Bleachtair*e and *Maidhc Abú*
and *Geronimo* the human tiger,
and we mapped the physical features
of Ireland like a genetic code
that had been cracked in mystical folk music,
and a ship from Valparaiso would sail
by rote in assistance
to equate algebraic values
on the parchment of night.

AEIOU
equating us.

Summer evenings on the beach
I'd go swimming in the Caribbean
on Andros Island in the Bahamas
beside the tropic of Clonakilty,
and I heard dialects being smeared
from the same butter churns
and I followed the melted road of that butter
from Cork to Jamaica,
and the day the world almost
exploded in a nuclear war
the Brother sent the class home
telling us to pray earnestly

that the Russian fleet would turn
that sense would come to Kruschev,
and I saw the Brother's countenance
fusing into a worried man.

AEIOU
fusing us.

He brought a Celtic Cross in
handmade from matches
varnished and cut
by a prisoner in Belfast,
a brother of someone in the school
locked up for the cause of freedom,
and hung it above the cupboard
in charge of the Map of Ireland;
I remembered on a street lane
the half-burned matches
congealing in a stream of blood
after a stabbing in the parish,
and the Celtic Cross shed blood
through the varnish on our geography.

AEIOU
congealing us.

One day I saw him
riding his bike,
a hump on him like a bridge
I had a mind to greet him
but the words stuck
on the little tongue in my throat;
I followed him to the library
where he stood by the rail,
he was an old half-blind man
fussing with a chain,
I had a mind to come and help him
until I saw the appearance
of him in charge of a class,
his tongue wedged in his teeth
doubled, spouting:
"I've a sweet for you,"
and a drip in every syllable

with unbelieveable irony
when there sprung from his pocket
a rod as far down as his shoes.
I had a mind to ask him
"Where are you from?" "Who owns you?"
"I'm Hurley of the scholarship class of '62"
but I couldn't find the tone
to express the words
that would make thanks of them
in tune with the AEIOU scale.

AEIOU
in tune.

Translated, from the Irish, by the Managing Editor.

Liam Ó Muirthile was born in 1950 in Cork, where he still lives. He was for many years the Irish Language Columnist of The Irish Times. *His fourth collection of poems is* An Seileitleán agus Vérsaí Seilí Eilí *(Cois Life Teoranta, 2004).*

AN ULSTER TANDEM

John Montague

Sandwich men.

My first meeting with John Hewitt was not a success. Passing through Belfast on my way home to Tyrone, I paid the Museum a visit, and asked for the poet. A stocky, bespectacled, rather gruff man emerged from behind a glass door. (I may have been prompted to call because we both had had poems read out in a poetry competition organised by Austin Clarke on Radio Éireann, prize three guineas each.) But he clearly did not know me from Adam. Also, I was timid and tongue-tied, and he made no effort to put me at ease. We wandered silently through the gallery, where I grasped at a familiar straw by stopping before Sir John Lavery's portrait of Cardinal MacRory. "He's my second cousin," I ventured proudly. "His mother's name is Montague."

"It's a bad painting," declared the unyielding Hewitt. We were both right, but his rebuke was brusque, if not brutal.

I knew his work already, from copies of *Lagan*, bulky as a train timetable, unearthed in the dusty corner of a Derry bookshop. W.R. Rodgers was then the acclaimed Ulster poet, but I found Hewitt more to my taste, even the bigoted bits, like "the Romish pit" in his poem, "The Glittering Sod." To offset that there was his shy visit to a Catholic church in "The Lonely Heart":

> The years since then have proved I should have stayed
> and mercy might have touched me till I prayed.

It reminded me of my Protestant neighbours in Garvaghey, dour but friendly, coming awkwardly in to contribute a coin at the Funeral Offerings. (It was a dreadful "Romish" practice of the period, because the priest would read aloud not only the names of the contributors, but the amount they had subscribed to honour the dead. In this alien atmosphere the Protestants offered a token, a modest half crown or so, which placed them among the parish poor. So the last names I heard as an altar boy would have been "Robert Clarke, half a crown; Albert McClean, half a crown; George Rainey, half a crown.")

But Hewitt's essay on "some problems of the Ulster writer," called the "The Bitter Gourd," ruffled my West-of-the-Bann sensibility, along with its misuse of the term "Ulster," to describe only part of our fractured province. Yet clearly Hewitt was a thinking man, a little slow perhaps, but genuine. I was disappointed when his argument with himself, as Yeats would call it, was excluded from *No Rebel Word* (1948), his first main collection of poetry. The title seemed to suggest that he was a conservative in politics and language, alien to the Republic brought about by the Easter Rebellion and even to the 1798 Rebellion in his own beloved Antrim and Belfast. But that title does not do justice to the careful complexity of his lonely thought.

We were brought back into touch when Mary O'Malley had the generous idea of installing John as Poetry Editor of *Threshold*, the literary magazine of Belfast's Lyric Theatre. When he included some of my poems like "The Water Carrier" and saluted my first slim volume, *Forms of Exile* (1958), the austere figure I had met in the Museum in Stranmillis had definitely mellowed. (The editors did, however, amend my story about boarding school, "That Dark Accomplice," replacing "farted" with the more genteel "belched".) Slowly a working friendship was established because, meanwhile, in my small Paris studio, I was busy assembling the first serious study of Hewitt, which he gratefully described in museum terms as "building up a hairy monster from a trickle of bones". I had broken through that crusty exterior to uncover a profound loneliness. Writing from Coventry on my *Poetry Ireland* study of his work, "Regionalism into Reconciliation," he said, "I doubt if there's another mortal who has taken so much trouble to grasp its tendency."

Passed over for promotion in the Belfast Museum where I had first met him, because, he said with a grim chuckle, of his association "with Catholics and Communists," Hewitt had exiled himself to the Coventry Municipal Art Gallery. It was, in a way, a homecoming for the more English part of his psyche, and the rehabilitation of the city after the wartime bombings appealed to his socialist side, with the new, very modern cathedral soaring from the ruins. He describes "its famous steeples and its web of girders,/ as image of the state hope argued for ..." in his passionate, lonely poem, "An Irishman in Coventry". (Note he does not write "Ulsterman" and he even identifies with his old Catholic neighbours: "the whiskey-tinctured breath, the pious buttons,/ called up a people endlessly betrayed/ by our own weakness ...")

I called on Roberta (or Ruby) and himself there several times. Stratford and Shakespeare were a touristic blur, but one afternoon he brought me round to see E.M. Forster, nearly ninety, frail as a moth. John, it seemed, had been reading to him regularly, including my poem, "The Trout," which the old man remembered as "very sensuous". Imagine how I felt, as a still relatively young Irish poet, listening to a master of English prose quoting some of my own lines, particularly, "As the curve of my hands/ Swung under his body/ He surged, with visible pleasure." And I thought I was describing how to catch a fish!

Forster was staying in, and probably paying for, Big Bob Buckingham's house. Big Bob was a kind-hearted, burly former policeman, one of those sturdy, red-faced, official-looking English figures, like our postman when I was a child, Mr Blemings, whose shiny boots I had admired. I realised, of course, that this was the mythical love object who haunted Forster's later years, a male muse figure, and an image of Saxon virility in contrast to Forster's own delicacy. How some of my homosexual poet friends in Dublin would have envied me meeting this legend, but it did not seem to me that there was anything physical between them, only Forster's burning admiration for Big Bob's "fine manly form". Because Mrs Bob was also there, bustling about, serving tea, like any decent, middle-class English wife. And Forster spoke of her with great warmth. It seemed Big Bob had been quite sick, probably with a heart attack, and when he was taken to hospital, she made sure that their frail friend was kept informed of the fate of their mutual beloved. Morgan Forster's voice trembled with feeling as he recalled the ordeal.

John Hewitt and I did not discuss what we had seen in any detail: he seemed to have a kind of Protestant prudery, so that we never, for example, mentioned the childlessness which was a problem in both our marriages. Yet I carried away from that memorable afternoon a strong sense of John's unobtrusive care for his fellow man, dutiful, yes, but tender and comprehending. Looking back from my bus seat the next day, I saw John, large-hatted as Ezra Pound, waving good-bye with his stick. He was beginning to accept with pride the senior poet's role, and I was glad to have played my part, persuading McGibbon & Key, my own publishers, to also publish his *Collected Poems*. Although the selection still seemed to me a safe one, eschewing argument, and with too many final postcards from Greece, searching for solace. Still, John was glad, writing to me in October, 1968, "Publication of C.P. has meant a lot to me, coming at this time, a hope I had hugged against all apparent reason."

Our first "Planter and Gael" tour encompassed a week in late November, 1970. We had already come together for a broadcast in the curving stone studios of the BBC Northern Ireland, Belfast. John had travelled from Coventry, and I from Paris via Dublin. John was curt almost to the point of silence, still profoundly pessimistic about any possible effect poetry might have on our frozen North. "I have no audience," he kept repeating glumly, still in his Coventry cast of mind. "Maybe we'll have one after this tour," I offered, but he only shook his white head ruefully.

Nevertheless I think John and I, who were both living abroad, saw the tour not only as a return to our home territory, but as a half-serious, half-lighthearted attempt at community relations during an increasingly fraught time. And it worked very well, except that few if any Planters emerged from their fastnesses to hear us. On our first night in the Adair Arms Hotel in Ballymena, a tall, handsome blonde lady swept up to us, declaring, "I am Jane Chichester-Clarke," in a crisp, unmistakably English voice. "We don't hear much poetry round here," she continued with a dry smile. There was no sign of her MP husband, however, or his brother who would become Prime Minster of the North of Ireland. And Big Ian Paisley had not bothered to come either, no doubt scorning our different form of oratory.

Though the Gaels took Hewitt to their heart, we gradually gave up all hope of meeting Prods or Planters. Except in a formal context, like the New

University of Ulster in Coleraine and the Portora Royal School in Enniskillen (*alma mater* of Wilde and Beckett), where we were received with professional politeness. Only in the County Museum of Armagh did things become a little tense. Armagh was, after all, the scene of my own harsh schooling, and John and I walked those history-freighted streets and walls from our base in the Charlemont Arms Hotel, exchanging our different memories. He would have come down to Armagh on museum business, to see John Luke, a curiously elegant painter, or the Presbyterian pastor-poet, W.R. Rodgers. Hewitt's people had come from Kilmore in the Armagh countryside, but he did not seem to have any especially intimate feeling for that little stone city, wound round its two cathedrals.

During the Museum performance, in my commentary on my poem "Clear the Way," I spoke about visiting my favourite place of worship in Armagh, the Chapel of the Royal Irish Fusiliers in the old Protestant cathedral. And finding it empty, perhaps because so may of the families whose names were inscribed on the Roll of Honour would not feel at home there. In other words, the Roll was crowded with as many Tagues as Prods, O's and Macs galore, but their descendants doubtless felt they could not venture easily into that fine, sombre place. The heads of the two major churches were in the audience, and the Protestant Archbishop found my remark tactless. And indeed I had intended it to provoke some thought about our brutal dichotomies, in which Ulstermen from both sides of the house were united only in death, in a foreign field.

In Omagh's Royal Arms Hotel, Kitty Horisk grasped my arm: "Don't let us down the night, or I'll kill ye." And afterwards, speaking of Hewitt, "That man's no Planter. It's a rare breed of Protestant that speaks about 'getting along.'" (She was referring to John's allegorical poem, "The Colony," in which he speaks of an effort to "make common cause with the natives, in their hearts ...") Whereas a sister-in-law of mine buzzed around, complaining that some of my books, a legacy from my mother's house, were blocking her garage door. Introduced to the placid, pipe-smoking Hewitt after our reading, she said, "I suppose you're selfish, like all poets." (A conclusion hardly scientific, since I was the only example she'd met before then.)

John particularly enjoyed our night in Omagh, which he barely knew despite it being a garrison town, dominated by a stern courthouse towards which the whole town seemed to sweep. We walked through the streets at night, with old friends of myself and Ben Kiely, who gave us an insider's tour of the town. They spoke about corpulent Davy Young, the Protestant barber with an addiction to practical jokes, and the strange story of Half-hanged Norton, who survived the rope on Gallows Hill, where Kiely had grown up. There was talk, too, of pearl fishing on the Strule, with glass-bottomed boats.

That first tour, so ably arranged by Michael Longley, had been such a success, that we were asked to undertake another, the following spring. But even in that short time, the mood in the North had changed, hardened by bitter experience on both sides. Some of this had been charted by John in his pamphlet, *An Ulster Reckoning*, but it is always heartbreaking to meet such sorrow on the ground; the dejection was palpable. During the previous tour, people had truly believed the civil rights agenda would redeem the North. But now, in the Boulevard Hotel in Newry, a group of young Catholic schoolteachers explained that they intended to leave the country as soon as they could, probably heading for Canada, and we found the same growing hopelessness among young people throughout the North.

But we had a good time as well, attending the local Markets, listening to fiery Market Day preachers predicting hellfire, drinking with a former flyweight boxer in a dismal hostelry in Lurgan. After our performance in Dungannon, once again before an audience of Gaels, an old girlfriend from Glencull brought us back to her house for a party, and John was so much at ease that he danced, stiffly but resolutely, sporting a flashy weskit. But, as in Omagh, I was impressed – indeed *de*pressed – by how little Hewitt seemed to know about the North of Ireland west of the River Bann, what a geographer had called "the heartland of Ulster".

But I could have not wished for a better travelling companion. Although notoriously crusty, he also showed flashes of wry humour, like sunlight on winter ice. He professed to be greatly amused by my need for an injection of Dutch courage before our rather formal readings. For me, a stammerer, those glancing calls at the pub before a performance were an essential ritual, and in a later poem by John (set in that pub in Lurgan) he speaks of the tall poet, his speech haunted by a stammer, which shows he understood my plight. Though at the time he teased me, christening me "the droughty Gael". (It was the same droll compassion I had glimpsed in his treatment of E.M. Forster in Coventry.)

I showed him my hidden Ulster, touchstones like Knockmany Hill, which I climbed as a boy. And outside Dungannon, the coronation place of the O'Neills at Tullyhogue. I had the manuscript of *The Rough Field* with me, and he read it with pleasure and recognition, declaring at our final reading at the Arts Council in the heart of Belfast, that "it does for the North what MacDiarmid's *A Drunk Man* [*Looks at the Thistle*] did for Scotland". A heartening and timely salute, after long years of toil. At my instigation, he himself had privately published the sequence of overtly political poems, *An Ulster Reckoning*, which had drawn some friendly fire. It was a brave enough act, since he, like myself, was contemplating returning to our riven island after years of deliberate exile.

Although it is my native place
and dear to me for many associations,
how can I return to that city
from my exile among strangers?

In a letter to me, he described the nature of his plight: "My trouble is that I stand between opposites, an interloper to the Gaels with only four hundred years of Irish earth on my bones, and a disaffected person to the Stormont bullies." But I think our double tour helped assuage his fears, and that he began to sense that slight but growing audience which would sustain his later years back in Belfast, in Stockman's Lane.

Two final images haunt me from our Poets' Circuit. For me, the supreme talisman of my home territory or native place is the unmarked passage grave of Seskilgreen, locally called McRory's Fort, after the family who have worked those fields forever. ("Clan Ruadhri or Rory" is an old name from the ancient Irish for the Tagues of Tyrone. Like my Cardinal relation whose portrait Hewitt had dryly dismissed on our first meeting.) I was extremely moved to show John this numinous place from my own tradition. It was late spring, and we ambled through the high grass, past saucer-eyed cattle; then heaved ourselves over a series of sturdy farm gates, and finally came upon it, little changed in its five-thousand year sleep. The big central stones, delicately whorled, were warm with sunlight, and a bird had built its nest in a crevice. We stood gazing together in a deep, shared silence, and I remembered some lines of Hewitt, surmising and summarising our heritage.

> ... what you seek may be no more than
> a broken circle of stones on a rough hillside, somewhere.

The other powerful memory, for me, was the short period we spent in Derry. It was, after all, where I had first come to Ireland after the long voyage from Brooklyn. So I read the whole of "A New Siege," knowing full well that it would certainly annoy part of the audience, but unable to resist the provocation:

> twin races petrified
>   the volcanic ash
> of religious hatred

That morning, I had brought John to see Fountain Street, a working-class Protestant area of "Londonderry". So Protestant, the kerbs were painted red, white and blue: he professed never to have seen the like, although later such blazoning of belief would show on murals and fluttering banners all over Ulster, Irish tricolour and Union Jack, and even the Palestinian and Israeli flags!

Amongst the audience in what I would still call "Derry," was the playwright, Brian Friel, who registered every reaction around him with seismic accuracy. "They didn't like that bit," he said afterwards as we were having a drink together, shaking what I privately called "the Great Friel Head". He had clearly enjoyed himself. Brian in conversation begins slowly, almost haltingly, but when he warms up it is hard to stop him. But then I am in awe of playwrights, who, though often soft-spoken themselves, can make others speak in divers tongues.

Brian seems to me the most ambitious Irish playwright since Eugene O'Neill, always prepared to challenge an audience, and before we left, he ventured a sobering note of caution or criticism. "Why did you have to tour wearing labels like that, the Planter and the Gael?" he demanded with a snort. "Why didn't you just go round as yourselves, John Hewitt and John Montague? Not wearing placards like sandwich men!"

John Montague's most recent collection of poems is Drunken Sailor *(The Gallery Press, 2004). He is currently completing the second volume of his autobiography,* The Pear Is Ripe.

BORGES BACK IN TOWN

Glenn Patterson

Rule by the Company.

In one of his most celebrated stories Jorge Luis Borges tells how a simple lottery in the ancient city of Babylon is transformed by the introduction of unfavourable as well as favourable draws. For every thirty winners, there is one losing number, which carries with it a fine. Defaulters are sent to prison: the bigger the unpaid fine, the longer the sentence. Soon the lottery organisers have ceased to bother with the fines, publishing only their prison-term equivalents. As more and more unfavourable draws are introduced, the lottery starts to mimic, and eventually overtakes, the functions of judiciary and legislature. A sudden rise in fortune, an ignominious fall, a public execution, an unexpected erotic encounter, all are the luck of the draw. A company – The Company – is formed to manage the myriad draws necessary to control every aspect of public and private life. One of its first actions is to make the lottery free, universal, and secret: henceforth whether you choose to enter or not, you are in. After the passage of centuries the workings of the Company have become so clandestine that the very existence of a Company is a matter of conjecture and life in Babylon is considered by many "nothing else than an infinite game of chance".

This brilliant closing sentence reanimates the cliché while giving it a paranoid twist. Has the author just exposed the arbitrary nature of all our carefully constructed systems, or hinted at a hidden hand behind the most random and outrageous occurrences?

Either way, as I sit here in Belfast in the late summer of 2005, Borges's story has never felt more relevant.

I begin this three days after a Sunday newspaper reported that the Provisional IRA have perfected the forgery of the new Northern banknotes, introduced earlier this year to prevent the circulation of the £12 million in unused Northern banknotes (out of a haul of £26.5 million) the same Provisional IRA stole last December. Except of course the Provisional IRA is no longer active and, besides, it did not steal any banknotes. Honest.

I begin this a few hours after the funeral of fifteen year-old Thomas Devlin, stabbed to death as he walked home from buying sweets at a filling station on Belfast's Antrim Road: a seemingly motiveless attack, for which, it has gradually emerged, the UVF may have been responsible; has emerged and then receded again, as the suspects taken in for questioning are released without charge. This in turn recalls the aftermath of the murder, in January, of Robert McCartney, and the largely fruitless campaign by the victim's family for witnesses to come forward. The killers had notoriously removed film from the CCTV camera in Magennis's bar – had removed every speck of forensic evidence – before allowing the customers inside to leave. Those who did present themselves to the police simply refused to speak.

Although investigations are continuing into the murder of Thomas Devlin, and although two men have now been charged in the McCartney case, it is hard sometimes to shake the feeling that we are living in an age without agency. No one does anything; things just happen.

This is not just law-and-order issue, it is also an epistemological one: what can we say with confidence that we know about the society we live in? And the doubts it raises may be undermining something more fundamental than a political process. What's more, its effects don't stop at the Northern Irish border.

The Small World Theory, or Six Degrees of Separation, draws inspiration from a 1929 story, "Chains," by the Hungarian satirist Frigyes Karinthy, who is himself not separated by much – historically, geographically, temperamentally or even alphabetically – from Franz Kafka and therefore, Kafka being a presence in all Borges's work, from the writer of "Lottery in Babylon".

"There were certain stone lions, there was a sacred latrine called Qaphqa, there were fissures in a dusty aqueduct which, according to general opinion, *led to the Company*; malignant or benevolent persons deposited information in these places."

Events of the past few months have highlighted the possibility that there are far fewer than six degrees separating every one of us living in Ireland from paramilitary money and influence.

There is something *Qaphqa*-esque – I choose the spelling carefully – about the name Passage West. It was in this Cork suburb in February that a man was discovered feeding handfuls of sterling into a bonfire in his back garden. That same day another man was arrested as he stepped off a train in Dublin's Heuston station with a *Daz* washing-powder box filled with cash. Back in Cork, gardai raided the Farran home of Ted Cunningham, managing director of the Chesterton Finance loan company, and discovered £2.3 million in a compost bin. They warned anyone else who had come into large amounts of cash recently to report it to the authorities. Hours later a man walked into a Garda station with a bag containing more than £150,000.

More arrests and seizures followed, from Offaly to Dundalk, like a thread unravelling the length of the island and – if I can marry two metaphors and put one in a suit for the occasion – as far up the body politic as Phil Flynn, close associate, on the one hand, of Taoiseach Bertie Ahern, and advisor, on the other, to Sinn Fein, of which he is a former president. Flynn resigned as non-executive director of the Bank of Scotland in Ireland after it emerged that he was also non-executive director of Chesterton Finance. He flatly rejected accusations of involvement – by him or by Chesterton – in money-laundering and later, more pointed accusations made under parliamentary privilege by the Unionist Lord Laird about Flynn's relationship with two alleged IRA leaders, Brian Keenan and Thomas "Slab" Murphy.

All the same, for a short time on the cusp of spring the papers were full of revelations about IRA criminal activity and the crossover, in personnel and funds, with Sinn Fein: the Republican Movement, as it often referred to itself, was indeed indivisible. There were the millions – possibly billions – invested in properties here and across the water; there were the sympathetic accountants, solicitors, people with inside information on areas earmarked for rezoning. There was the attempt to buy a bank in Bulgaria.

From Leinster House to the White House there was the sense, if not the actual sound of welcome mats being lifted, doors slamming shut.

Even those who thought they knew a thing or two, it seemed, didn't know the half of it.

Somewhere in the middle of this five men were jailed in Dublin for IRA membership, part of a gang caught in a van with fake Garda uniforms, truncheons, CS gas, and election posters for South Dublin Sinn Fein TD Aengus Ó Snodaigh. And somewhere in the middle of this – with ever more disturbing details about Robert McCartney's murder continuing to emerge – the Sinn Fein vote went up in the Meath by-election.

One month later, and two days into another election campaign, for Westminster this time, Gerry Adams, speaking, as he said, with the authority of his office as president of Sinn Fein, made an appeal to the leadership of the IRA: "Can you take courageous initiatives which will achieve your aims by purely political and democratic activity?" Few in the media, or the British and Irish governments, deemed it appropriate to point out that only a few weeks before they were in agreement that Adams's authority proceeded from his Sinn Fein presidency and his seat on the IRA's Army Council. The gap had appeared again between the two; doors that had been shut were once more open. Stories of republican financial dealings did not disappear entirely, but they slipped off the front pages, out of some newspapers altogether.

On 28 July, the IRA responded to Gerry Adams's call with an order to dump arms. Three days later the business section of the *Sunday Independent* reported that, in the run-up to the IRA statement, businesses linked to Sinn Fein's director of finance, Des Mackin, had "suddenly lodged up-to-date accounts". Many of the businesses were cash businesses, many had deficits running into the millions, many had addresses in the Parnell Centre in Dublin and many were "ultimately owned in the British Virgin Islands and controlled by well-known Belfast businessman Peter Curistan". Peter Curistan is the founder of the Sheridan Group, which, besides being the developer of the Parnell Centre, is the largest private investor in Belfast's Odyssey Arena. (Odyssey must have seemed an apt name for an arena that was sold as a beacon for a city emerging from decades of conflict and was launched on the world with a speech by Bill Clinton.) The *Sunday Independent* quoted the auditors' reports on various of the companies: "no system of control on which we could rely," reads one; "we are unable to establish whether proper books and records were kept," reads another.

In 2004 Peter Curistan was awarded the Northern Irish Institute of Directors' Lunn Award for Excellence. I am not, any more than the *Sunday Independent* was, suggesting any wrongdoing. I am, though, genuinely amazed to learn that there are large amounts of poorly-accounted-for cash circulating so close to the surface of our economy and so close to one of our largest political parties. But, again, what do I know?

Travel up the Sydenham Road half a mile from the Odyssey, cross the Dee Street bridge and take a left into Mersey Street and you will soon find yourself at a new housing development named after one of Belfast's best-known, but, till recently, least acknowledged (I believe the term in tourism circles is "under-exploited") writers, C.S. Lewis. Sited in what was formerly one of the most densely populated – and almost exclusively Protestant – parts of the city, Lewis Square is both a major piece of redevelopment and a major piece of re-branding.

I confess I have already had a lot of sport with the idea of Lewis Square: "deceptively spacious built-in robes," etc. I confess too that I sit on a committee tasked with better exploiting the Lewis "product" ahead of the release, this December, of *The Lion, The Witch and the Wardrobe*, which is to be marked with a gala screening in the MGM multiplex at – where else? – the Odyssey.

There is to be a new C.S. Lewis trail, centred on East Belfast, which will in all likelihood take tourists past one of the several branches of Philip Johnston and Company, principal selling agents for Lewis Square. Earlier this year the company's founder and managing director was charged with money-laundering as part of an investigation into the activities of former UDA brigadier Jim Gray (a.k.a. Doris Day), himself arrested a few days earlier in a car containing thousands of pounds in cash. Council offices in County Down were also raided and planning applications examined. A Unionist election candidate was briefly questioned.

The "Lottery" conceit must be qualified by the recognition that there is more than one Company operating in Borgesian Belfast. There is more than one Company operating in loyalist parts of the city; indeed it is the protracted and bloody feuding between Companies that makes their activities so public. So public and occasionally so farcical. Another story in the press as I write this: four members of the UDA convicted of trying to tax an undercover policeman posing as an ice-cream seller in Carrickfergus. (Make that minus sixteen degrees of separation. You don't have to go out of your way to ensure that your – or your children's – money finds its way to the Company: they'll bring the means, jingling-jangling, to the end of your street.)

Then again, maybe all that is unusual about this incident is that the culprits

– evidently lacking the self-protective instincts of the people who murdered Robert McCartney – were caught on camera. In his 2004 book *Colours: Ireland from Bomb to Boom*, the *Observer* columnist Henry McDonald likens West Belfast to a one-party state-within-a-state where anything from bootlegged vodka to mini-shopping centres may be run by "the Movement," providing it with an income from this part of the city alone of £20m a year. (A recent *Sunday Times* report adds disposable razors, toothpaste and washing powder – *Daz?* – to the counterfeit commodities; bogus mortgage applications to the financial services provided.) "Sicily Without the Sun" is McDonald's term for it and he attributes the near invisibility of all this activity to the republican movement's totalitarian grip on the community.

He also draws attention to the activities of the IRA in the border areas, where it has profited hugely – and individual IRA leaders have profited hugely – from the smuggling of diesel fuel. (Cue those Flatt and Scruggs' banjos: "Come and listen to a story 'bout a lad named Slab…") For diesel to be smuggled, diesel must first be "washed," an innocuous term for a process that produces a waste so toxic that, McDonald claims, the Provisionals came within a whisker of poisoning the entire water supply of County Louth in the spring of last year. Add to this their alleged involvement in the illegal dumping of household waste, a growth industry since the introduction of bin charges in the South, and a picture emerges of an organisation dedicated to the removal of the border, profiting from its existence, while jeopardising the environment of the island whose integrity is its ostensible *raison d'être*. It is a picture as blackly comic as that McDonald paints of a Sinn Fein health minister (Bairbre de Brun) encouraging healthier lifestyles, while the IRA stole millions of pounds worth of cigarettes for re-sale in working class areas of Belfast.

Sinn Fein would deny any connection between it and these matters, as it continues to deny any link between them and the IRA; it would no doubt point to its manifesto: "We are committed to the principle of sustainable development. We believe that all economic activity and policy decisions should be environmentally proofed to ensure no needless damage is inflicted to an island environment already under severe pressure from unnecessary pollution and inefficient waste management strategies."

Borges would say, "There is nothing more contaminated with fiction than the history of the company."

If the forensic clean-up after the murder of Robert McCartney stands as one metaphor for the paramilitaries' attempt to control reality – what we can say with confidence we know – the IRA statement, as a genre, surely stands as another.

The first says something happened here, but no one did it. The second says we did do it, but *it* was not what you thought it was at the time.

IRA statements, or at least the negotiations that create the conditions for them, are like an erase function – *revise* function might be better. They turn events into non-events.

In the wake of the 28 July statement, the question has to be asked: what will become now of the investigations into the Northern Bank robbery? Will the killing of Robert McCartney be retrospectively "legitimised," as happened with the killing of Garda Jerry McCabe, whose killers' release became part of the Sinn Fein negotiations? And what will happen to the investigation into the possible UVF involvement in the murder of Thomas Devlin if, as rumoured, that organisation "responds positively" to IRA decommissioning? Already, this bloody summer now ending, there have been suggestions that the police have been standing by, or have been instructed to stand by, while the UVF pursues its latest feud with the smaller LVF, in the hope that, having wiped out its rival, the UVF, like the IRA, fades into the background; or at least, the black-economy-ground.

Certainly the UVF has nothing to learn from republicans about the contamination of history. At the end of My Lady's Road in East Belfast is one of the new gardens of remembrance that are becoming such a feature of the post-Troubles city. Standing side by side in this one are two granite memorials, the first to the men of the area who died in the Great War, the second to men, some with no connection to the area at all, who died in our own not-so-great war. This second memorial includes the names of Wesley Somerville and Harris Boyle, who lost their lives taking those of three members of the Miami Showband.

"The indirect lie," notes Borges, "is also encouraged."

In a conflict in which there were no winners – it's official – all parties get to write their own histories, paint them on walls, carve them in stone. Forget contamination, we are on the verge of a full-blown epidemic.

Or is that, to use the words with which Bertie Ahern greeted the 28 July statement, on the verge of something "momentous, historic and unprecedented"?

The organisation that six months ago was being described by government ministers as the most sophisticated criminal enterprise in the world has apparently ceased operations overnight. Things continue to happen. Every now and then it is proved that someone has done them. In Dublin the City Council calls for an end to the intimidation of the family of Joseph Rafferty, shot dead in April as he left his north inner-city flat. Sinn Fein say they support the family, but appear to be alone in thinking that Joseph Rafferty's killer is not a member of the IRA. Meanwhile the party prepares for the next Irish General Election. The signs are the vote will continue to rise. I am looking for a last line. I think Borges again, not the "Lottery" this time, but "The Immortal". How does it go? "We accept reality easily, perhaps because we suspect nothing is real." I lift down my copy of *Labyrinths* to check. Not "suspect', "intuit". And then I notice the next line: "What do you know of the *Odyssey*?"

As I sit here in my house, bought from an estate agent who has subsequently been charged with money-laundering, I ask myself what do any of us know of anything?

Postscript: About an hour after typing that final question mark I walk out on to the main road near my house and there, above the estate agent's window, where the mauve and red of *Philip Johnston and Company* should be, is a new colour scheme, a new name and a logo that on closer inspection represents a terrace of rooftops, but on first glance looks like nothing so much as a jagged line through past associations. Two days later the local free paper lands on the doorstep with confirmation: "Estate agent caught up in laundering scandal sells firm." (And, yes, part of me is disappointed it doesn't say "company".) The new owners admit they paid "a substantial sum in anyone's language," before concluding, "we believe the re-brand will give the public confidence." And do you know what? They are probably right.

Glenn Patterson was born and raised in Belfast, where he still lives. He is the author of six novels, most recently That Which Was *(Hamish Hamilton 2004).*

TWO POEMS

John Knowles

PRODIGAL

In the park, the cherry trees keep
their approximate anniversaries,
a precise white shadow of blossom
beneath their branches.

The spring must be profligate, prodigal even.
It was my father's father, before the war,
who would come home drunk,
his pockets empty, bringing flowers.

HOMAGE TO MAGRITTE

at the Ulster Folk and Transport Museum

Behind the counter, boxes for sorting letters,
pens, stationery, a variety of nibs,
but no letters. This is not a post office.

A coat is modelled
in stiff white plaster and lint behind the door
of the fisherman's cottage.

In the Transport Museum, a dark-suited mannequin
sits in a railway carriage
with perfect lack of expression.

The time is not the time on the station clock.
The map of the countries
is not the map of countries on the schoolroom wall.

John Knowles works as a librarian at The Queen's University of Belfast. His poems have appeared in a number of Irish journals.

TED HUGHES AND TRUTH

Daniel Weissbort

In search of the ur-text.

I
The Early Translations

Ted Hughes and I founded the journal *Modern Poetry in Translation* in 1965. We co-edited it for ten issues (until 1971) and he continued to take a close interest in it. For its part, *MPT* brought a number of poets to his attention: notably the Israeli Yehuda Amichai, the Hungarian Janos Pilinszky and the Yugoslav Vasko Popa. Poetry by the first two he translated and the last he did much to promote.

The magazine itself was Hughes's idea, one he had conceived while he was still living in America with Sylvia Plath. He mentioned it to me, at a New Year's Party, 1962-63, after his return to England and shortly after Plath's death. It took about two years to get the magazine launched, but I began to investigate the international scene, so to speak, and was fortunate enough almost immediately to come across Amichai and Popa, along with a number of poets from Eastern and Central Europe. Some of these – for instance, the Czech poet Miroslav Holub – Hughes had personally encountered at the Spoleto Poetry Festival. The barriers between Eastern and Western Europe, at least culturally, were becoming increasingly permeable in the decade following Stalin's death in 1953.

Ted Hughes was particularly interested in the post-War East European poets of the generation immediately preceding his own, who had lived through the war as young adults and had survived in politically and culturally oppressive circumstances. As he observed in his Introduction to Anne Pennington's translation of the *Selected Poems of Vasko Popa*, the Yugoslav poet who became a personal friend, these circumstances had "brought their poetry down to such precisions, discriminations and humilities that it is a new thing".

Though he might not himself have put it so bluntly, since he was a tactful and modest man, there is, I believe, a connection to be made between the strivings and accomplishments of the writers of this first post-War East European generation and Ted Hughes's self-distancing from the highly wrought idiom inherited from such as the American John Crowe Ransom – between their poetry and his own experiments with a more direct language that eschewed the Hopkins-like linguistic density of his earlier work. As he wrote in a letter to me:

I suppose [that] what I see as their common quality is their simple and

> direct presence – even within quite elaborate fantasies. Each phrase has a matter of fact tone.

Hence also, perhaps, the allurement for him of the kind of English produced by, say, Yehuda Amichai when translating his own Hebrew poems into English, or the literal renderings from the Hungarian of Janos Pilinszky by another Hungarian poet, a friend of both Hughes and Pilinszky, Janos Csokits. Hughes was struck by the forcefulness of these non-native English versions.

He expressed his confidence in the translatability of poetry, when introducing the first Poetry International in 1967. This conviction has been characterized as sixties idealism, but I think it has more to do with a curiosity about the foreign as such:

> However rootedly-national in detail it may be, poetry is less and less the prisoner of its own language. It is beginning to represent as an ambassador, something far greater than itself. Or perhaps it is only now being heard for what, among other things, it is — a Universal language of understanding, coherent behind the many languages in which we can all hope to meet.

That the magazine and Ted Hughes's early translations do not represent a passing phase is shown, of course, by his continuing work in this area: Seneca's *Oedipus*, Racine's *Phèdre*, Frank Wedekind's *Spring Awakening*, Lorca's *Blood Wedding*, Ovid's *Metamorphoses*, Aeschylus's *Oresteia*, Euripides's *Alcestis*. Towards the end of his life, he was also working on a version of *Sir Gawáin and the Green Knight* and had plans for a staged version of *Gilgamesh*. Ted Hughes's last known poem is, in fact, a translation, a version of Pushkin's "The Prophet" (see below). By any reckoning, this amounts to a substantial body of work, especially bearing in mind how considerable was Hughes's output as poet, playwright, children's writer, anthologist and essayist.

The use Ted Hughes made of translation evolved from his early interest in and literalistic renderings of poets of the first post-War generation (Amichai, Pilinszky) to his late, apparently much "freer" adaptations of Ovid and of Greek Classical drama. (While his Introduction to *Tales from Ovid* does not comment on the translation process, and while there is no translator's introduction either to his *Alcestis* or *Oresteia* versions, a comparison of the translations and their sources – the source texts themselves and earlier translations – makes it possible to characterise his strategies.)

Baldly stated, Hughes was looking for the Truth, that which underlies language and which survives translation, even if Robert Frost claimed that it was precisely the poetry that was lost in translation. *What is the Truth?* (1983) is one of Hughes's books for children. Subtitled "A Farmyard Fable," it contains some of the author's most striking animal poems. The plot is roughly as follows.

God reluctantly accedes to his Son's request for them to descend to earth and learn what humans can teach them, but warns him that he will be disappointed. On earth, God summons a number of country people from their sleep and asks them, "What is Truth?" In sleep, it seems, they are closer to the Truth than when awake; in a series of poems – evidently they are closer to poetry too – each human spirit tells of this or that creature, trying to convey its essence, the truth of itself.

But what seems also to be happening is an interrogation of poetry, of Hughes himself or the kind of poet he has been and clearly is still capable of being. So, is the Truth discoverable? The book ends with God the Father having left, and the Son finding himself alone on earth, at the start of a new day, in the countryside that has just been depicted. The Truth, it seems, is not to be conveyed through description, however mimetically powerful.

Of course, Hughes is here keeping his particular talent in trim, the talent that brought him to public notice with his first book, *The Hawk in the Rain* (1957). But *What is the Truth?* had been preceded by *Crow* (1972), *Gaudete* (1977) and *Moortown* (1979), where, in various ways, he seemed to be distancing himself from this earlier manner; so, when it comes to his "adult" work, Ted Hughes is writing, as it were, less "poetically". Still, it looks as if, after all, he is not jettisoning his earlier strengths. Contrary to what some commentators have claimed, Hughes advanced, throughout his career, on a broad front. Translation of such poets as Amichai and Pilinszky evidently helped him to pare English down, while at the same time it uncovering new possibilities in it.

This is, after all, what translation has always helped its practitioners to achieve. Who among us, as George Steiner has remarked (*The Penguin Book of Modern Verse Translation,* 1966) can read, for instance, the Bible, Shakespeare, Pascal, *The Brothers Karamazov*, the poems of Li Po, and *A Tale of the Genji* in the original? "Without translation," Steiner adds, "we would live in arrogant parishes bordered by silence." Charles Tomlinson, who edited *The Oxford Book of Verse in English Translation* (1980), has written that "English poetry happens to be so rich because of what it managed to incorporate into itself 'in the guise of translations.'" All this has repeatedly been pointed out, and yet translation, especially of poetry, is often still seen as problematical, pointless, impossible even.

Ted Hughes's collaboration, first with Assia Gutmann and later with Amichai himself, on the translation of the latter's poetry, originates in our early discovery of this poet and publication of translations by various hands in the first issue of *MPT*, in 1965, two years before the first Poetry International reading in London. We were both greatly moved by Amichai's poems in the translations available to us, and at once set about obtaining more versions in

English, since the poetry seemed to us eminently translatable. To this end, Hughes showed his versions to his friend Assia Gutman, who had been raised in Israel and who knew Hebrew. He began to produce more English translations of Amichai's poetry, which were later to appear in a volume published by Cape Goliard (1968) and in a Penguin collection (1971).

Hughes's introduction to Amichai's poetry, in 1963, obviously came at a critical point in his own life. The Israeli poet, in any case, continued to occupy a special place for him. As he wrote, contrasting Amichai's poetry with that of some of his Eastern European contemporaries:

> Somehow Amichai's verse attracted and held one's affection as well. It became involved with one's intimate daily experience in a curious way.

Perhaps it was the combination of metaphoric richness and perennial wisdom in Amichai's poetry that proved so heartening, his ability to write at a personal, almost confessional level, while drawing sceptically but also affectionately and humorously on an ancient and yet accessible tradition. That Hughes's involvement with Amichai's poetry was no mere infatuation is evidenced, of course, by his further collaborations with this poet on two collections: *Amen* (1977) and *Time* (1979). Amichai sent Hughes his own English versions of the Hebrew originals and (as he characteristically put it) the two of them then reconstituted or reconstructed them in English, "as though performing some kind of plastic surgery on the English roughs". Actually, they were not so rough, Amichai's English being very good. In any case, these being the poet's own versions of his poems, their authenticity was not in doubt.

Hughes had more than a little to say about that. Indeed, he was quite clear about his approach to the translation. From his point of view – and from Amichai's too, of course – there was more to it than plastic surgery. As he wrote in his Introduction to *Amen*:

> The translations were made by the poet himself. All I did was correct the more intrusive oddities and errors of grammar and usage, and in some places shift about the phrasing and line endings. What I wanted to preserve above all was the tone and cadence of Amichai's own voice speaking in English, which seems to me marvellously true to the poetry, in these renderings ... So, as translations these are extremely literal. But they are also more, they are Yehuda Amichai's own English poems.

And as he wrote in an early editorial (*MPT 3*, 1967):

> A man who has something really serious to say in a language of which

> he knows only a few words, manages to say it far more convincingly and effectively than any interpreter, and in translated poetry it is the first hand contact – however fumbled and broken – with that man and his seriousness that we want.

The claim that these translations were also "Amichai's own English poems" was no idle boast. I have looked at several of the poet's drafts and Ted Hughes is true to his word. Nevertheless, the procedure remains audacious. From a translation point of view, I think what we are witnessing in these collaborative versions is an act of attentive listening on Hughes's part, resulting in what might be called creative non-intervention. Amichai, I believe, was a sort of guide, a Virgil, for Hughes in this ancient world, but at the same time an incomparable companion. To translate is sometimes to walk in the footsteps; in the case of Amichai and Hughes, however, it was more like walking side by side.

Obviously, Hughes was trying to arrive at a definition of *literalism*, the kind of text he himself needed so as to experience the otherness of a poet writing in another language, the kind of text that, as he saw it, was already half way there, requiring minimal intervention on the translator's part. (Clearly, selflessness of this order is a far cry from what most poetry translators aspire to.) What ideally he wanted was, in any case, obtainable only where the foreign poet, or an inspired and dedicated stand-in, like Janos Csokits, could act as interpreter in English. Hughes, it seems, was after a kind of ur-text. He was moving in the direction of plainness, directness; he experimented variously, for instance, with what has been called the "super-ugly language" of *Crow*, the limited lexicon of his translation of Seneca's *Oedipus*, commissioned by Peter Brook, and even more radically, the invented language, or pre-language, *Orghast*, that he developed also during the time of his association with Brook (see A.C.H. Smith, *Orghast at Persepolis*, 1972).

As regards *Orghast*, Peter Brook quotes Ted Hughes himself (*The Epic Poise: A Celebration of Ted Hughes*, 1999):

> I listen to the patterns that arise in the deep level of the brain, when impulses become sounds and syllables – and before they shape themselves into recognizable words.

One is reminded of what Hughes wrote about the Yugoslav Vasko Popa's poetry, regarding which "no poetry could carry less luggage or be freer of predispositions and preconceptions" (Introduction to *Vasko Popa: Collected Poems*, translated by Anne Pennington, 1978):

> There is a primitive pre-creation atmosphere about his work, as if he were present where all the dynamisms and formulae were ready and charged, but nothing created or only a few fragments.

For all his admiration of Ted Hughes's work, Janos Pilinszky, in the Hungarian, was a very different poet. Of course, Hughes was perfectly aware of this, but what he homed in on was the passion of a Christian sensibility in confrontation with the Holocaust. He describes this in his Introduction to Pilinszky's poetry (*Janos Pilinszky: Selected Poems*, translated by Ted Hughes and Janos Csokits, 1977):

> The silence of artistic integrity "after Auschwitz" [a reference, of course, to Theodore Adorno's famous comment that after Auschwitz there could be no lyric poetry] is a real thing. The mass of human evidence of the camps, and of similar situations since, has screwed up the price of "truth" and "reality" and "understanding" beyond what common words seem able to pay ... [Pilinszky's] poems are nothing if not part of an appeal to God ...[a] God of absences and negative attributes, quite comfortless.

This draws, no doubt, also on Janos Csokits's perceptions. Csokits read the poems in Hungarian to Hughes (he has written, in Hungarian, an account of their collabortion). Hughes also met with Pilinszky himself several times (Pilinszky read at the Second Poetry International, in 1969, directed by Ted Hughes and Patrick Garland). Hughes had no Hungarian and Pilinszky little English, but they were able to converse in French. Pilinszky, it seems, had intended to translate *Crow* into Hungarian, but he died, suddenly, just before the International Festival in Cambridge (1981) which he was due to attend.

Ted Hughes was particularly impressed by Pilinszky's own comment on his linguistic resources. The following passage comes from a 1969 interview with the poet, quoted by Hughes in his Introduction:

> Should someone ask, what after all is my poetic language, in truth I should have to answer: it is some sort of lack of language, a sort of linguistic poverty. I have learned our mother-tongue from my mother's elder sister, who met with an accident, was ill, and got barely beyond the stage of childlike stammering ...

This "linguistic poverty," a kind of elemental language, was of perennial interest to Hughes, hence partly his attraction to the so-called minimalistic poetry of the first post-war generation of Eastern European poets. Although his life experience was very different to theirs, he identified to some extent with their work, even reaching back to World War I – his father was a survivor of the Gallipoli campaign – and the poems of Wilfred Owen, as well as to World War II and those of Keith Douglas, a selection of whose poetry he edited in 1964.

It would presumably have been less arduous for Hughes to imitate his first successes. Instead he continually attempted to reach beyond or through all this brilliance and dexterity towards something more primal, to the dismay of many admirers of his early work. About *Gaudete*, for instance, he wrote to me:

> I once wrote a film scenario about a priest who turns all the women of his parish into his coven ... I just re-wrote it, much altered, in a sort of verse, *very crude lead-pipe verse* ... He gets killed at the end but then resurrects and writes a lot of poems which I quite like. They started being vacanas – as in that *Speaking of Siva* book – but then took off on their own.

Speaking of Siva (Penguin, 1973), incidentally, is a book that greatly impressed us at the time. Translated by the poet-scholar A.K. Ramanujan, it is a collection of free-verse *vacanas* or sayings, religious lyrics of the mediaeval saints, characterised by their spontaneity, all speaking of or to Siva, translated from the south Indian language Kannada. In his translator's note, significantly enough, Ramanujan challenges the more conventional (or, as we might now say, "domesticating") approach to translation:

> In the act of translating, "[it's] the *Spirit* killeth and the *Letter* [that] giveth Life." Any direct attack on the "spirit of the work" is foredoomed to fuzziness. Only the literal text, the word made flesh, can take us to the word behind the words. I have tried therefore to attend closely to the language of the originals, their design, detail by detail; not to match the Kannada with the English, but to *map* the medieval Kannada onto the soundlook of modern English ...

In an essay written for *MPT* (1983), Hughes summed up the translation boom of the previous decade or so, while at the same time re-formulating our bias towards literal translation. He refers to a work that for him represented a kind of model of translation, *Specimens of Bushmen Folklore*, collected in the 1870's by the German-trained ethnographer and philologist William Bleek:

> Ideally we would have liked to see at least some poems translated ... as meticulously as Bleek's translation of Bushman lore – though we understood the limited appeal of anything so raw and strange.

As in the early *MPT* editorials, he inveighs against translations that aim to produce a "parallel equivalent" of some original's unique verbal texture. He comments that, in fact, "most often we found what we were after in translations made by poets whose first language was not English or by scholars who did not regard themselves as poets." (Which, I suppose, is where Bleek comes in. Hughes had read archaeology and anthropology in his third year at Cambridge, after his flight from "Englit".)

Hughes's progress towards a concentration of his native idiom, a dissolving of the formal constraints of his earlier work, in a way replicated that of the poets of Eastern Europe already alluded to. Pilinszky, of course, also belonged to the generation that had directly experienced the war. However, for him, "the death camp was his imaginings come true"; it was as if the war simply confirmed his pre-existing vision of human suffering. The Polish poet and playwright, Tadeusz Rozewicz, in an attempt to explain the bareness of his own language had famously remarked (see Michael Hamburger, *The Truth of Poetry*, 1969):

> I cannot understand that poetry should survive when the men who created that poetry are dead. One of the premises and incentives for my poetry is a disgust with poetry. What I revolted against was that it had survived the end of the world, as though nothing had happened.

What Pilinszky called his "lack of language," however, was ascribed by him, as we have seen, to his learning the language, in the first first, from a brain-damaged aunt. That is, he ascribed it to his personal biography rather than to the calamitous historical circumstances. It may be partly for this reason that Hughes, who was a little younger and who himself lived out the war at a remove in England, not at the catastrophic centre, was drawn to him.

In an article that he wrote (somewhat reluctantly) at my request (*Translating Poetry: The Double Labyrinth*, edited by Daniel Weissbort, 1989), Csokits declared that Hughes did not want smooth renderings in what he called "magazine English". So Csokits stuck to the meaning, while trying also to convey Pilinszky's poetic idiom, "without", as he significantly put it, "exaggerated respect for the host language". Inevitably the English text sounded odd, but this was exactly what Hughes wanted. Here is Csokits's account:

> It is almost as if he could X-ray the literals and see the original poem in ghostly detail like a radiologist viewing the bones, muscles, veins and nerves of a live human body. The difference is that X-ray pictures do not show the human face, whereas Hughes can see and visualise the whole astral body of the poem. I saw the result of this operation in the corrections made to my literals and saw it happen several times. Pilinszky witnessed it, too, and was duly impressed. It is eerie when it happens, one can almost hear the humming of a high tension line, but the effect is not that of a technical device; it has more to do with extra-sensory perception.

And here is Ted Hughes's comment (in a letter to me):

> I wrote a longish introduction mainly to explain why my translation

> was as literal as it could possible be made … why I eschewed any "imitation" of rhythms of which I couldn't possibly have the faintest idea, whose real components I couldn't even guess, and why Pilinszky's poetic temper seems to me absolutely the last one to be served in any way by "liberties," or the approximations of re-invention. If you can't like the literal crib of a Pilinszky poem it seems to me he's one poet you'd better leave unliked …

Later, in another letter (*circa* 1975), he returned to the theme. He had just finished work on the Pilinszky selection and was moderately pleased with the results. He was, however, absolutely convinced that his rigorous collaboration with Csokits was the way to go. Just as Pilinszky, a poet of suffering, was the poet for him at that time in his life, so Csokits was the ideal collaborator.

Clearly, Hughes felt he had got as far as he could get. He had done what he set out to do. What he needed initially was an *ad verbum* version. He was delighted when, as with Amichai, he found he had to make only minimal changes in the texts with which he was supplied by the poet. He did not believe in change for its own sake, still less did he wish to interpose himself, his own poetics or poetic personality (his own poetic "medicine-bag", he calls it) between an original – at least, insofar as it was present in the form of an almost *ad verbum* version – and the reader:

> Very many lines of his [Csokits's] rough draft have been impossible to improve, as far as I could judge, and besides that odd inevitability and "style" which a poet's translation into a language other than his own often seems to have…

One recalls what he had said in that early *MPT* editorial, especially about translations by native speakers of the source language: "The very oddity and struggling dumbness of a word for word version is what makes our own imagination jump." So

> besides that odd inevitability and style which a poet's translation into a language other than his own often seems to have, he [Csokits] retained naturally an unspoiled sense of the flavour and the tone of the originals — that very intriguing quality which is the translator's will-o'-the-wisp, the foreignness and strangeness. That most important thing was something I developed a feeling for, wherever Janos Csokits captured it, but I could not begin to re-invent it where he did not, or where I had to re-align his wording. Instead, I was too often conscious of reducing Pilinszky to the worn tracks and familiar locutions of workaday English. The best way to escape this claustrophobic feeling of locking up foreign uniqueness in home-

> grown commonplace, is to re-invent — so that the over-drive exhilaration of new imagination freshens the task. But this way I decided not to take.

And why, in this particular case, did Hughes resist the temptation to re-invent? He himself saw it as

> a natural decision ... in translating a poet whose chief characteristics are economy and accuracy. As it happens, the very thing that attracted me to Pilinszky's poems in the first place was their air of simple helpless accuracy. Nothing conveys that so well as the most literal crib, and I suppose if we had the audacity that is what we should be printing here. As it is, we settled for literalness as a first principle.

Finally, I should emphasize that it is a question here of a particular kind of poetry, the poetry of a particular generation really. The "theory" of translation propagated by our journal, *Modern Poetry in Translation*, in the first years of its existence, seemed to us to serve the purpose we had in mind, which was to provide a platform for poets such as Pilinszky and Amichai.

That being said, underpinning Ted Hughes's approach to translation was a particular view of the art:

> In this Festival, poets from nine different countries will take part [actually eight, as the Soviet authorities did not permit Bella Akmadulina to attend]. The idea for such a gathering was suggested by the great and growing public for poetry which is making itself felt in London just as surely as in Moscow and New York. However rootedly-national in detail it may be, poetry is less and less the prisoner of its own language. It is beginning to represent as an ambassador, something far greater than itself. Or perhaps it is only now being heard for what, among other things, it is — a Universal language of understanding, coherent behind the many languages in which we can all hope to meet.
>
> We now give more serious weight to the words of a country's poets than to the words of its politicians – though we know the latter may interfere drastically with our lives. Religions, ideologies, mercantile competition divide us. The essential solidarity of the very diverse poets of the world, besides being a mysterious fact, is one we can be thankful for, since its terms are exclusively those of love, understanding and patience. It is one of the few spontaneous guarantees of possible unity that mankind can show, and the revival of

> an appetite for poetry is like a revival of an appetite for all man's saner possibibilities, and a revulsion from the materialist cataclyms of recent years and the worse ones which the difference of nations threatens for the years ahead.
>
> The idea of global unity is not new, but the absolute necessity of it has only just arrived, like a sudden radical alteration of the sun, and we shall have to adapt or disappear. If the various nations are ever to make a working synthesis of their ferocious contradictions, the plan of it and the temper of it will be created in spirit before it can be formulated or accepted in political fact. And it is in poetry that we can refresh our hope that such a unity is occupying people's imaginations everywhere, since poetry is the voice of spirit and imagination and all that is potential, as well as of the healing benevolence that used to be the privilege of the gods.

These remarks at the opening of Poetry International in 1967 have an idealistic ring to them. Intended as a kind of fanfare for the poetry games, Hughes's comments seem also to posit a "universal language," a language *between* languages, to which both original and translated texts have access. Beneath the "rootedly national' lies the "universally human". If this now sounds grandiloquent, one should perhaps cast one's mind back to that earlier period, with its insularism, suspicion of or distaste for anything foreign, a time when Philip Larkin, for instance, could wittily remark that it would be fine to visit China provided one could be home in time for tea. My point, though, is that beneath Ted Hughes's uncompromisingly severe approach to translation lay a belief in poetry's ability to transcend linguistic frontiers, provided that the translator did not interpose himself overmuch. We were not entirely alone in thinking that the key to this was for the translator to stick to the literal text, to the words themselves and, as far as possible, even to the syntax of the original – even if it was not easy to distinguish this procedure from that of a dry academicism.

The question perhaps arises as to what Ted Hughes was actually doing, as against what he imagined he was doing, in his translations, say, of Pilinszky or even of Amichai. Clearly, a decision was taken to focus on the text itself, as a verbal artefact, to admit a minimum of lexical changes, even to reproduce the foreign syntax where possible, insofar as it preserved certain features lost once that syntax was standardized. It followed that no attempt should be made to imitate the formal structure of the source text, since this entailed reckless sacrifice of literal sense.

Translating Pilinszky or Amichai was also Ted Hughes's way of reading these poets, of coming closer to them. This was a two-way affair, as it had to be. Since he was, to say the least, an extraordinarily attentive reader, so his readings or translations of these poets are illuminating, both in themselves and as pointers to developments in his own work. Beyond this, though, it seems to me that an apprenticeship of sorts was being served which led to the later "free" adaptations (*Phedre*, *Metamorphoses*, *Oresteia*, *Alcestis*). There is a literalistic component in these later works of Hughes, which amounts, in our time, to a "new way" of translating – and recalls the "new way" of Cowley and Co in the seventeenth century.

II
The Last Translation: Pushkin

Ted Hughes's last known poem is a translation: a version of Pushkin's "The Prophet". Valentina Polukhina and I provided him with the literal version, some historical notes, and notes on the prosody. He had been invited to contribute to *After Pushkin* (1999), edited Elaine Feinstein, to mark the bicentenary of Pushkin's birth, and had chosen "The Prophet". His translation was first published in *The Daily Telegraph* on 9 January, 1999.

"The Prophet," evidently, is a poem Hughes had for some time wished to translate. The political implications of this poem, based on Isaiah 6:1-13, are clear enough, but it was surely the exaltation of the visionary's role that drew Hughes – that, and the specifically shamanic nature of Pushkin's treatment of his subject.

Hughes's interest Pushkin dates back at least to the early sixties when he wrote a review of a selection of Pushkin's letters (republished as "Opposing Selves," in *Winter Pollen*): "Pushkin gives a peculiar impression of being something utterly different from his fellow Russians – not just a genius, but different in kind, like some sort of changeling from outer space." He sees Pushkin as being two people, the sophisticated, Frenchified aristo and the solitary sufferer, a kind of spiritual outlaw, a primitive: "he liked to think of his private monopoly of primitive African passion".

The same year, 1964, Vladimir Nabokov's translation of and commentary on Pushkin's novel-in-verse, *Eugene Onegin*, was published. Hughes had the four-volume Bollingen Foundation edition. Though he was not alone in regarding Pushkin as the classic case of an untranslatable poet, with so much depending on the verbal texture, he also sensed apparently something primal in Pushkin's highly sophisticated poem, or in the language, insofar as he could tell from the English versions he had read. Perhaps he also had in mind the elemental nature of "The Prophet," with its Biblical associations and its evident rehearsal of the shamano-Christian journey or ordeal through death and resurrection to knowledge, as evidenced by a preternatural sensitisation: "the shudderings of heaven,/ the huge wingbeats of angels,/ the submarine migration of sea-reptiles/ and the burgeoning of the earth's vine" (see below). The poem recalls shamanic practices, even to the insertion of something rock-like in the to-be-resurrected body: "He split my chest with a blade, / Wrenched my heart from its hiding, / And into the open wound/ Dropped a flaming coal." Hughes's interest in Shamanism is well-known and much of his own work bears witness to it (most typically, *Crow*), from his early libretto based on the *Tibetan Book of the Dead* to this translation, in effect his last poem.

It is worth noting again that Hughes always asked for as close literal versions as possible, this not always being understood, as translators, even those providing so-called "trots," tend to feel that word-for-word literalism may be misleading, given the differences in syntax between languages and the inevitable subjectivity even in literal translation. Hughes, on the other hand, presumably believed – many readers would not agree – that the *ad verbum* texts better represented the author in question. Knowing this, Polukhina and I presented him with a "kit," comprising a transcription of the original Russian text, an interlinear *podstrochnik*, or word-for-word, making it possible to match individual Russian words with the English ones and giving some sense of the differences in syntax between the two texts or languages, and a "literate" version, based on the *podstrochnik*, but normalizing or Englishing the syntax. This was the method used, for instance, by the late Max Hayward, when he collaborated with the American poet Stanley Kunitz in the translation of the selected poems of Anna Akhmatova; it was also, by and large, that used by Csokits and Hughes in the translation of Pilinszky.

That Hughes nevertheless transformed the text is evident from the last six lines of "The Prophet," the literal and literate versions of which read, respectively:

> Like a-corpse in the-desert/wilderness I lay
> And of-god the-voice to me called out:
> "Arise, prophet, and see [archaic], and hear
> Fill with-will mine [carry out my will]
> And passing/wandering-by seas and lands,
>
> With- the-word burn the-hearts of people.
> I lay like a corpse in the desert,
> And the voice of God called out to me:
> "Arise, prophet, and see, and hear,
> Carry out my will,
> And passing by sea and land,
> Burn the hearts of people with the word."

Hughes translates this as:

> I lay on stones like a corpse.
> There God's voice came to me:
> "Stand, Prophet, you are my will.

Be my witness. Go
Through all seas and lands. With the Word
Burn the hearts of the people."

The full text of the translation is given below. For the present purposes, I shall examine these last six lines of the poem. The literal version above makes use of hyphens to represent the Russian inflexions (note, also, that Russian does not have definite or indefinite articles).

I lay on stones like a corpse.

What strikes one here is Hughes's translation of "desert" or "wilderness" into *stones*, a graphic simplification. He sacrifices, that is, the association between Old Testament prophet and desert or wilderness for the sake of a more immediate representation of the scene. *Stones* can be felt, except that a corpse cannot feel; so, the deadness to feeling of the corpse-like self is emphasized. *Stones* seems to relate more to wilderness than to desert. The line is terse, hard in every sense, conveying the reader directly to the next line even if Hughes's text ends with a full-stop, unlike the original.

There God's voice came to me.

In English, *There* links the two more dramatically than does "And". Hughes thus modernizes while retaining something of the rhetorical force of the Biblical structure. He articulates the drama, by pausing (minimally) at this point, emphasising God's final pronouncement. Interestingly, he separates God's voice from the lying "on stones" or "in a wilderness".

With *came to me*, Hughes suggests the passivity of the subject. The focus remains on the prophet, rather than on God. So, despite the break, there is more psychological continuity between these two lines in the Hughes version than in the original. *Came to me* suggests revelation, and yet is also rather casual.

Stand, Prophet, you are my will.
Be my Witness. Go
Through all seas and lands. With the Word
Burn the hearts of the people.

Hughes stays closer to the literal than to the literate. He retains the exact wording but breaks a line, highlighting *Word*.

The lineation and punctuation here are dramatic, suggesting an acting or speaking text. The original four lines are metrically regular, with no break, whereas Hughes breaks three times, and uses two enjambments.

Go, like *Word*, is stressed. God's utterance is divided into four sentences.

These are more distinctly articulated in the Hughes version than in the original. Going *through all seas and lands* receives almost as much emphasis as *with the Word*.

There is an abruptness, even jerkiness in Hughes's ending, as against the seamlessness of Pushkin's text, with its Biblical resonances. Of course, the Biblical note is there in Hughes too, but there is also a makeshift, provisional quality.

You are my will is pure invention, although the literal's "Fill with my will" is perhaps awkward enough to have precipitated so drastic a solution; in any case, "Fill" chimes too strongly with "will". (Hughes's formulation – the abruptness, too – might recall his characterizations of God or of Crow, in *Crow*, although the present context does not admit such carnivalesque grotesquery.) *Be my witness*, a separate sentence, may have been prompted by the "see and hear" of the literate version. (Also, of course, there could be a problem in using "see", because of the proximity of "seas".) So, while making this more explicit, more contemporary, and also retaining the Biblical allusiveness, Hughes reverses the order of these two items. In so doing he is able to end two lines with stressed monosyllabic words, *will* and *Go*. *With the Word* forms the climax of the poem, the very last line, rhythmically, functioning as a kind of coda.

In general the lineation here makes the reader linger over these lines. God sets the Prophet in motion. For the outcome, however, we must pass beyond the poem.

From 1965 to 2003, Daniel Weissbort edited Modern Poetry in Translation, which he and Ted Hughes founded. His most recent book is Letters to Ted *(Anvil, 2003), and he has edited several anthologies of Eastern European and Russian poetry. His* Selected Translations of Ted Hughes *is forthcoming from Faber. He is currently completing a book about Ted Hughes and translation.*

See page 55 of this issue for Daniel Weissbort's translations of Inna Lisnianskaya.

"The Prophet" appears on the following page.

THE PROPHET

Translated, from the Russian, by Ted Hughes

Crazed by my soul's thirst
Though a dark land I staggered.
And a six-winged seraph
Halted me at a crossroads.
With fingers of dream
He touched my eye-pupils.
My eyes, prophetic, recoiled
Like a startled eaglet's.
He touched my ears
And a thunderous clangour filled them,
The shudderings of heaven,
The huge wingbeat of angels,
The submarine migration of sea-reptiles
And the burgeoning of the earth's vine.
He forced my mouth wide,
Plucked out my own cunning
Garrulous evil tongue,
And with bloody fingers
Between my frozen lips
Inserted the fork of a wise serpent.
He split my chest with a blade,
Wrenched my heart from its hiding,
And into the open wound
Dropped a flaming coal.
I lay on stones like a corpse.
There God's voice came to me.
"Stand, Prophet, you are my will.
Be my witness. Go
Through all seas and lands. With the Word
Burn the hearts of the people."

The following historical note accompanied the literal translation given to Hughes: "Pushkin wrote this poem in 1826, at the time of the Decembrist Rising. The language is archaic, Biblical (Isaiah 6, etc), even though Pushkin is famous for introducing colloquial Russian into the language of poetry. Legend has it that this poem was in his pocket during a secret interview with the Tsar, soon after the Rising. Pushkin sympathized with the Decembrists, aristocratic reformers, many being his friends."

PORTFOLIO

Mélina Gacoin

Kilometre 28

Km 28, Rosslare

In September and October 2004, the photographer Mélina Gacoin and the documentary filmmaker Arnaud Devroute toured Ireland on motorbikes. From Rosslare to the North of Ireland, they followed the seaboard and finished 44 days later, having travelled some 4,000 kilometres. This trip along mainly country routes was punctuated by a stop every 28 kilometres, in order to take a single photograph. The number 28 was chosen because this was Gacoin's age at the time. "My aim," she has written, " was to create a book of visual and geographic exploration where a singular Ireland might be discerned. A personal gaze which sought out colours, forms and details. Places chosen by chance which unfolded with sequential iteration so as to evoke the landscapes of Ireland in its entirety, without the distinctions of tourism."

Mélina Gacoin was born in 1976, studied photography at the University of Paris VII, and now lives in Lille, France. Her work has been exhibited in Paris, Lille and Reims. Her first book of photographs, Guyane: Détails Pays (French Guyana: Native Detail, *Editions Photographiques*), *appeared in 2003.*

Km 196, Youghal

Km 336, Timoleague Road

Km 532, Healy Pass

Km 756, Valencia Island

Km 840, Killorglin Road

Km 868, Annascaul Road

Km 1064, Ballybunnion Road

Km 1764, Bangor Village

Km 1792, Pollatomish Road

Km 1820, Belderg

Km 2104, Ballina

Km 2408, Fahan Village

Km 2492, Carndonagh

Km 2884, Rathfriland Road

Km 2940, Carlingford

PORTFOLIO

is generously supported by Nicholson & Bass Ltd. Belfast.

HEANEY'S BLACKBIRD

Chris Agee

Wide-angled in the light of time.

(SAMHAIN INTERNATIONAL POETRY FESTIVAL, OCTOBER 2004)

In my second collection, *First Light,* the title-poem is a small *hommage* to an old pastime of mine, beachcombing. The poem arose out of an hour-or-so's walk along a long crescent of sand in southern Rhode Island early one summer morning in 1994. By the time I had returned to my starting point at the southern end of the crescent, the poem was inwardly complete, bar the tweakings and finessings that always come with committing the imagined construction to paper. The beach itself, Crescent Beach – as it has been known for perhaps three centuries – is the western rim of a small pear-shaped island, Block Island, named after a Dutch trader, eight miles by five, lying between the better-known Martha's Vineyard and the eastern tip of Long Island.

It is a place where I partly grew up in a biographical sense, but more metaphorically, also in an emotional sense, having spent a decade of summers there from childhood to young adulthood. Its once-pastoral topography of rolling meadows, stone walls, wind-licked grasses, marine scrub, dunes and beaches wide open to the Atlantic – so reminiscent of certain landscapes in the West of Ireland, I would later discover – I still have imprinted on the mind like the proverbial back-of-the-hand. If there is one place that is my emotional *patria* – one place, as Auden puts it in his "In Praise of Limestone," I am "constantly homesick for" – then this island microcosm is it. It is, as another poem in *First Light* has it, with a nod to the ineffable, "that place/ I first felt its deep offing" – this "offing" representing, I would say, the offering of life pure and simple, without metaphysical gloss, here and ahead, whatever it may bring. Those landscapes of childhood and youth somehow enter one's deepest being as one enters, through them, more fully into the adventure of life. One's first narrative is the polestar to which all later divagations must align and configure. About a third of the poems in my first collection, *In the New Hampshire Woods*, explore my feeling for this island landscape backdropped by a coming-of-age, including several that take their particulars from the long arc of Crescent Beach.

I like the aformentioned title-poem for its simplicity and straightforwardness. Not something I always seek or, indeed, can always achieve. There is nothing in it that does not deal directly, empirically, with both the outward and inward experience of that hour of beachcombing. No detour of image, no metaphor or buried allusion, not even the final inward turn, takes us away from the actuality of the walk. This cleaving to "the bastion of sensation" is one of my poetic ideals; and whilst it certainly aligns with my temperament, especially as it was moulded by an early and deep exposure to North American wilderness, it also reflects, unquestionably, as with so many other poets, a debt to the poetry of Seamus Heaney, characterized, as it is, by an almost preternatural beauty of language, cleanness of line, and depth and breadth of sensibility.

Nonetheless, I think most readers or listeners of this small poem of mine will have little trouble discerning an extension of meaning beyond the cleaved-to particulars of beachcombing. From the opening "one begins not knowing" to the final "looking back," "First Light" could be read as extended image for the way the psycho-dynamics of poem-making come to mix the unexpected, the rhythmic and the random in a single forward creative motion; or even as a little parable for the life journey itself, for consciousness-in-action, and the way we can never quite apprehend the past steps that have brought us to our present moment. In other words, like several others in the collection, "First Light" is also self-reflexive, about the torque of its own creation: it mirrors and transcribes, step by step, almost self-scientifically, the movements of one poet's imaginative circuitry. Part of the alchemy of the successful poem lies in this ability to create a space, an imaginative *agora*, so to speak, where such extensions of meaning are given leave and thus expected, and so encouraged and cultivated. Poetry, you might say, is the art of meaningful extension *par excellence*.

Looking back at the genesis of the poem a decade ago, I am struck now by how much personal experience in and around Crescent Beach predated its sudden composition. I probably did not think of this personal background at all during the walk itself, the conscious mind plunged into a trance of composition, like that dawn's half-moon sunk into the blue of morning. Those childhood days, for instance, playing around the mussel-encrusted breakwaters, or by the high stilted seats of lifeguards. A teenaged tryst with a girlfriend, sitting awkwardly on a blanket before the sea's ravishing moonlight. My father, still hale and handsome, striding along the beach, a few weeks before I left for Ireland. A walk with my grandmother, during my first island stay in 1966, hoping with child's hope for a message-in-a-bottle – which, fairy tale-like, came my way a moment later, in the form of a bottled postcard from the US Navy, requesting a return-by-mail with geographical information on its washed-up whereabouts.

No trace of any this is there in the poem, but I find myself thinking now that my long history of time on this beach would certainly have primed that hour's alertness to "what the mind will beachcomb from the radiant flux/of things in the intertidal zone". In the event, nothing much happened, apart from the marvel of being alive in the visible universe. And not so long ago, it came to me that perhaps my first real aspiration to write a poem took form on this beach, when I noticed my shadow following me along the slick gloss of the tide's aftermath. Which, come to think of it, is a sound image I ought to use some time. But I lacked even the most rudimentary poetic muscle then – and for many more years to come.

That poetic musculature, it goes without saying, thrives on both technique and sensibility. Somewhere Paul Muldoon remarks that every good poem is "an adventure in language," to which might be added it must also be an adventure in experience, on some level, often of an extraordinarily subtle and inward nature, like the finest tones of a photograph. If the ability to touch posterity constitutes the natural selection of literature, then the two adventures entwined make for the survival of the fittest. The ability to excel in both adventures, folded into a voice whose suppleness approaches consciousness itself, is of course the special genius of Seamus Heaney's poem-making. Truth to tell, I number him among the very greatest in the English language, the sort of poet that comes along only few times in any one country, in any one century. There is a Shakespearean coherence and roundedness to the whole meteoric arc of his career. What might he still produce as he moves through further years that Shakespeare, gone at 52, never saw? I remember the moment when this particular subliminal penny dropped, and that atmospheric dawned; not so much as some critical parallel, but rather as the stuff of metaphor. Heaney had just faxed me a poem, in connection with some editing I was doing, and as I ripped the sheets from the machine, I found myself murmuring without pre-reflection: *like getting a fax from Shakespeare…*

But to return to beachcombing, which is also an apt image for one's delight in certain poems. The puzzle of beachcombing is this: why does the eye delight in one thing, and not another? Why this pebble, this shell, this bit of seaweed, this bird, and not another? It is quite similar, indeed, with poetic composition: amongst the myriad available, why this image, and not another? Why does the mind beachcomb this force or form or pattern or creature in nature, for instance, and not another? Can we divine in such innate selectivity some correspondence between the psychic and cosmic orders (or disorders), or is that just idle anthropomorphism? (Two sea-poems in *First Light* explore this train of thought). Likewise with reader-response: why does one poem impact more powerfully than another of obviously equal quality? What exactly has clicked? And what does this *click* tell you?

I will now cut to the chase. This small *discursus* on beachcombing and the Nobel Laureate has an upshot. For as a reader as well as a poet, I am a something of devotee to the beachcombing method. Compared to the poetic *genius loci* of Gortahork, my editorial comrade, Cathal Ó Searcaigh – who reads very deep and very wide, as is well-known among his literary peers – I read mainly deep, being hooked by a certain limited number of writers whom I then follow over time with avidity and thoroughness. For the rest, I rely on the luck of the beachcomb. A poem, an essay, a book washes up on the day's psychic strand. If it touches my beachcomber's eye, it goes straight to the psychic strong room, as one drops a beachcombed shell or pebble into one's coat pocket, for future display on the shelf of the mind.

Actually, because I am such a literary magpie, especially with poetry, I find it hard to choose from among this shelf of literary valuables and to nominate, for instance, particular poems as favourites, though, of course, as with friends, I like to spend time with some more than others. Choosing between great poems is rather like choosing between beautiful faces: an invidious task, compounded by the fact that taste is a mystery. Indeed, why have the legions of bad poems become a kind of folk knowledge, but not the contrary observation, just as true?

Speaking as an editor as well as a poet, I am inclined to admire any poem that is originally realized and individuated in the terms of its *own* imaginative ecology, however aslant to the reigning ecosystem of styles. The strong poem is always a true species, never the imitation decoy. Language used with high artistic consciousness, out of whatever current and using whatever psychic materials, is my reader's holy grail. As A.R. Ammons writes in his marvellous *Garbage* – a long philosophical poem set in a Florida dump:

> I say to my writing students – prize your flaws,
> defects, behold your accidents, engage your
>
> negative criticisms – these are the materials
> on your ongoing – from these places you imagine,
>
> find, or make the ways back to all of us, the figure,
> keeping the aberrant periphery worked
>
> clear so the central current may shift or slow
> or rouse adjusting to the necessary dynamic ...

One's own practice demands, of course, this dowser's interest in the achieved poem of others. What makes it tick? And what makes it click for you? I now want to use a recent poem by Seamus Heaney to lift the veil a little from this backstage understudy of other work, a core activity.

"The Blackbird of Glanmore" was sent to me a few months ago and I keep returning to it. It possesses a subtle alchemy of effects that is one of Heaney's hallmarks. Heaney is an especially good example of the difficulty of nominating favourite poems. His work is so steady and magisterial, so without real dip in quality, that the exercise would soon become academic. There is a strong sense, too, that each poem is one uniquely fitted piece of the jigsaw from a radiantly inward geography that he appears able to mine inexhaustibly. The surpassing coherence and extent of this psychic excavation, especially as it relates to interlocking patterns of imagery and tonality across his whole oeuvre, is another of the things that sets him apart quite dramatically.

On a first reading of "The Blackbird of Glanmore", I was immediately struck by its conjoining of two things: a restrained, quotidian, quiet mood, and its undertows of extraordinary power. At the same time, I remarked to myself how easy it would be to glide through this poem, admiring yet another sterling emanation from the Heaney mint, but failing to twig on to the muted genius of his interlacing of experience and language. Deep and real feeling as here is never *grand guignol*, it has often this quotidian, matter-of-fact setting. So in his short line here there is a deliberate flattening of poetic effect away from the lushness and exuberance of language on display, say, in his major sets of sonnets or sequences of untitled poems. Helen Vender has remarked on Heaney's unrivalled ability to create continuously varied linguistic structures fitted to the finest graduations of consciousness, and the power of this poem's psychic snapshot lies in its fidelity to the exactitude of a rare mood.

With further readings, I began to marvel at the compendium of discrete verbal beauties that could culminate in such poetic power nonetheless heightened through its deliberate curbing. This is poetry as wisdom. How does he work the alchemy? Let us take a closer look. I will say a something about the poem in general, followed by a few words about each stanza.

THE BLACKBIRD OF GLANMORE

On the grass when I arrive,
Filling the stillness with life,
But ready to scare off
At the very first wrong move.
In the ivy when I leave.

It's you, blackbird, I love.

I park, pause, take heed.
Breathe. Just breathe and sit,
And lines I once translated
Come back: "I want away
To the house of death, to my father,

Under the low clay roof."

And I think of one gone to him,
A little stillness dancer –
Haunter-son, lost brother –
Cavorting through the yard,
So glad to see me home,

My homesick first term over.

And think of a neighbour's words
Long after the accident:
"Yon bird on the shed roof,
Up on the ridge for weeks –
I said nothing at the time

But I never liked yon bird."

The automatic lock
Clunks shut, the blackbird's panic
Is shortlived, for a second
I've a bird's eye view of myself,
A shadow on raked gravel

In front of my house of life.

Hedge-hop, I am absolute
For you, your ready talkback,
Your each stand-offish comeback,
Your picky, nervy goldbeak –
On the grass when I arrive,

In the ivy when I leave.

(first published by The King's Library Press as a limited edition keepsake for the Yeats Summer School, August 2004)

Overview

This is a Wicklow poem. Some of Heaney's most celebrated work, like "Exposure" at the end of *North* and "Glanmore Sonnets" in *Fieldwork,* has had as its locale his cottage in Glanmore, in the Wicklow Hills. It was here he first moved with his family after Loyalist threats contributed to his decision to depart the North. So Glanmore is not only a place where important work has been done and continues to be done, a second home and working retreat, but also a *locus classicus* in his poetry for meditations on the poetic art and his own grapplings with his public role as a poet. Wicklow has served him as the physical landscape *par excellence* for the conjoining of the lyrical and the ethical in the practice of his art.

"The Blackbird of Glanmore" is also one a series of car poems scattered across his oeuvre, where driving, or roadside halts, become the occasion for a meditative taking-stock in the midst of the life journey. Recent poems of this mould are "Postscript" at the end of *The Spirit Level*, "Ballynahinch Lake" in *Electric Light*, and "Nonce Words" published in the second issue of *Irish Pages*. In the first of these, the car is not stopped, since in light of the surrounding beauties that are blowing through him, it is "useless to think you'll park and capture it/More thoroughly." But in each of the others there is a roadside halt where an extraordinarily subtle, yet universally recognizable, mood and apperception are netted, recorded, and so made transparent from out of the more opaquely lived quotidian.

Stanza One

One notices at once all the little taut interlacings: the riffs of assonance (*arrive, life, ivy; ready, very, ivy*); the internal rhymes (*filling*, *stillness*); the half- or slant rhymes at the end position (*arrive, move, leave*), the colloquial rightness of *scare off* ; the plain and mainly Anglo-Saxon vocabulary; the simplicity of the set-off line and its song-like self-identification. Not one of these effects is beyond any competent poet, but the totality of interplay is pure Heaney. And although the poem as a whole has no set rhyme-scheme, each of the other stanzas-plus-outrider possesses the same interlacing interplay of image and ear, making the feat, in the very absence of said fixed scheme, still more impressive.

Stanza Two

More simplicity in the very casualness, the precise usualness, of the monosyllabic verbs (*park, pause, take heed, breathe, sit*). The beautifully demotic *take heed* is very characteristic. Then from verbs to the nominative double-take of *lines*, and an acceleration into intertextuality with both another poet and himself. Literature itself, of course, is a profound and pervasive presence in his work. Not for Heaney the strange populist idea one gleans off some critics and poets that allusions to literature should be kept out of literature. The quote itself, with that touch of Ulster in *away* and echo of Gaelic in *clay* (from *cré*), is quite surprising, really quite striking, when one keeps in mind the autobiographical context. Who would have thought Heaney could share the fleeting desire to give it all up? His life and career appear to be so charmed, as he himself admits in one poem: "lucky lucky lucky," he says of himself . But there it is, a feeling for grief's black road, one of history's secret forces.

Stanza Three

And then the plunge, the still-deeper swerve, into the naturalness of the memory of the death of his four-year old brother, commemorated in an early poem in his first collection, "Mid-term Break," written forty years before, and ending: "A four foot box, a foot for every year." Minded that the twin of grief is silence, the curt economy of feeling here, brightened nonetheless by the memory stirring in the mind, cannot but deeply impress, all of it lashed together with more superb touches: the odd but perfect "little stillness dancer" echoing the description of the blackbird in the second line; the trinity of *er* words (*dancer*, *haunter*, *brother*) not only creating a compound image of Christopher's life and afterlife-in-memory, but echoing *father* above; the diminuendo assonance of *o* through *home*, *homesick* and *over,* suggesting, ever so slightly, the desolation of the loss itself; and *haunter-son* suggesting how the little boy must have ghosted his namesake, Heaney's own son, the nephew he would never see.

Stanza Four

That *think* shorn of its personal pronoun, like the verbs in the second stanza, partakes of the telegraphese of actual thought and so keeps us close to the poet's stilled moment of memory and breath-awareness seated before the steering wheel. Likewise, the baleful words of the Ulster neighbour swim into his stream of consciousness, as such a distinct recollection would. What does the Ulsterman's blackbird suggest, in contradistinction to the one on the grass at Glanmore? I would say the dreadful existential fear of the world and its works that the aftermath of great traumas can induce. So Heaney sees this thing, too. This breadth of insight, beyond the deep reserves of emotion asparkle with technique and intellect, strikes me again as Shakespearean. The shed's blackbird seems a tonal entrance, as well, into the older Ireland into which Heaney the countryman was born, though only in its purely negative aspect; a blacker and bleaker Ireland of charms and omens and cures, crabbedly poetic (for the image is extremely powerful), more fear-blighted and death-haunted, more ancestrally marked by traumas, naturally and anciently alive to the malignancy and suffering of existence.

Stanza Five

But this is not Heaney's Ireland, or Heaney's blackbird, or at least no longer so. Heaney is a Modern who has left the *Agraria* of Bellaghy, the up-to-date car lock clunks shut, and the memory of the neighbour's fear-struck blackbird dissipates in tandem with the panic of the living blackbird on the grass before him. So this is also one of the many poems in his oeuvre, beginning with the first in his first collection, "Digging," that marks his psychic and professional progress from the pre-modern "den-life" of the Co Derry smallholding he describes in his Nobel Speech. That we are meant to identify the bird with the poet's sensibility, even his *credo* for living, clear enough from the alchemy performed by these lines, is nonetheless underscored by the imaginative levitation in the phrase "a bird's eye view of myself". The identification of the bird with the poet, the feather with the pen, is of course a classical-beginning trope, and one Heaney has often used. There is thus the suggestion in the succeeding image, the strange and beautiful wide-angle of his smallness in the light of time, of the shadowy and transient life that leaves behind its poems. An image not so different, really, from that shadow of self on Crescent Beach thirty-something years ago.

But if his own life is suggested by its shadow, why, then, is he only in front of the "house of life"? The phrase harkens back, to my mind unmistakably, in a further instance of the self-intertextuality already seen in the second stanza, towards another Wicklow poem, one to which I have returned many times, and which I would venture to call one of my Heaney favourites, a first-among-equals. Notice how much work is done by the title and the dedication, giving an off-stage temporal and geographic setting for this traditional African tale, grounding, in other words, the mythological in the personal, or vice versa:

A DOG WAS CRYING TONIGHT IN WICKLOW ALSO

in memory of Donatus Nwoga

When human beings found out about death
They sent the dog to Chukwu with a message:
They wanted to be let back to the house of life.
They didn't want to end up lost forever
Like burnt wood disappearing into smoke
Or ashes that get blown away to nothing.
Instead, they saw their souls in a flock at twilight
Cawing and headed back for the same old roosts
And the same bright airs and wing-stretchings each morning.
Death would be like a night spent in the wood:
At first light they'd be back in the house of life.
(The dog was meant to tell all this to Chukwu).

But death and human beings took second place
When he trotted off the path and started barking
At another dog in broad daylight just barking
Back at him from the far bank of a river.

And that is how the toad reached Chukwu first,
The toad who'd overheard in the beginning
What the dog was meant to tell. "Human beings," he said
(And here the toad was trusted absolutely),
"Human beings want death to last forever."

Then Chukwu saw the people's souls in birds
Coming towards him like black spots off the sunset
To a place where there would be neither roosts nor trees
Nor any way back to the house of life.
And his mind reddened and darkened all at once
And nothing that the dog would tell him later
Could change that vision. Great chiefs and great loves
In obliterated light, the toad in mud,
The dog crying out all night behind the corpse house.

(from The Spirit Level, *1996)*

With "The Blackbird of Glanmore", one could feel, of course, that "my house of life" carries the same literal denotation as the similar phrase in the African tale, extending the shadow-image into its generalized gloss. But Heaney never uses any resource of language without discernible intent (another of his greatnesses) and I think there is a migration of meaning introduced here, through the spatial "in front of," that is carried through and amplified in the concluding stanza.

Stanza Six

Notice again the beautiful economy and mimicry of all the effects in this small space: the perfect visual and aural fit of *hedge-hop*; the unusual, colloquial yet somehow classical Heaney *absolute for you*, with its sly assonance; the repetition and chimes of consonance in *talkback*, *comeback*, *goldbeak*; the further adjectival assonance (*ready*, *picky*, *nervy*, *ivy*) as in the first stanza; the repetition, with a new investiture of meaning, of two lines from the opening stanza. With true poetic alchemy, the stanza manages to mimic the actual physical jerkiness and nerviness of the blackbird in a way that, nonetheless, becomes metaphorical for something that Heaney admires, in contradistinction to the Ulsterman's blackbird of fixity and death. Heaney's blackbird is full of adjectival readiness, talkback, distance, comeback, acquisitiveness, and beauty. So what is he pointing at by *meaningful extension*? With this Glanmore blackbird he has seen and loved so often, in this place where so much work has been done, a cottage of art and not of farming, one is put in mind not only of certain qualities of his own work, but of the very recorded origin of poetry in Irish and in Ireland, the small poem commonly entitled "The Lagan Blackbird," with its goldbeak and chirrup, an anonymous monkish gloss from the ninth century, written not far from his home ground.

Coda

"My house of life," I think, is the house of poetry. This is the route to which he has dedicated his life, the route that took him away from his people, his home place, his dead. In this poem Heaney the man, ready for the work, stands before this more enduring house of poetry; the shadow of the life which produces the work will dissolve, like his lost brother's, "like burnt wood disappearing into smoke". By pausing, in the course of the life journey, by taking heed and breathing deeply, he enters this house from time to time, but only under imaginative conditions, or *geasa,* concerning his own essential attitude to life. What the blackbird of Glanmore represents seems, above all, what he has left to the blackbird on the shed. The key phrase in this poem, I feel, must be *scare off.* Look at those opening four lines: surely, also, a description of the making of a poem. Poetry is the sense of talkback, comeback, fight-back against a dog barking in Wicklow. In this sense, and perhaps this sense alone, poetry is fully congruent with life itself. The Blackbird of Glanmore is a talisman for entrance from the quotidian into the house of poetry. Thus it is that the bird, unscared-off for the duration of the imaginative visit, is "on the grass when I arrive,/ In the ivy when I leave."

This essay was delivered as the plenary address on 31 October, 2005 at the Samhain International Poetry Festival, Gortahork, Co Donegal. The annual speaker is asked to discuss several favourite poems.

Chris Agee is the Editor of this journal. His second collection of poems, First Light *(The Dedalus Press), appeared in 2003, and his anthology,* Scar on the Stone: Contemporary Poetry from Bosnia *(Bloodaxe Books), in 1998.*

From BIRD SWEENEY

Seán Lysaght

THE ROOST IN THE TOWER

Since God had cursed him with wings,
Sweeney believed he owed nothing
for his artifice of feathers.

He was a brolly collapsed
around the stem of his vigil,
his body riddled with quills.

He dreamed of other extensions
as pike-loads and oars
and clattery ladders.

When the day thinned in the ivy,
he reached the great span of himself
for an armful of air

and the tower delivered him.
He twisted his cockpit
as he worked the rush of his feathers.

Magpies were out in the fields,
inspecting the cages of sheep
they had picked clean.

The bodies of sea-birds were tossed,
in a tangle of seaweed,
beyond the sea's fiction.

Sweeney kept going.
He stayed clear
in the metre of his flying.

NORTH TAWTON

Sweeney flew on
to a yew-tree
in North Tawton.

The church steeple was the shape of a witch's hat,
the village in mourning,
everyone dressed in black.

A hearse prowled across the square
with a seaman's coffin
draped in a Union Jack.

Then Sweeney surged into the blue
above them, a dove in mourning.

He jingled the keys of a robin's song
beside a gardener.

As a house sparrow,
he arrowed into their eaves.

He mimicked the stars among their starlings.

When he flew back withershins
among the swallows, they took no notice.

The blackbird answered his blackbird calls.

Even a tawny owl was taken in
by a note he commandeered from a woodpigeon.

But when he came to the crow
he couldn't find any black.
They had taken it all for the mariner's funeral.

The best he could manage was a grey mantle.

At once, the crows saw through his disguise
and mobbed him over the hill.

THE HAWK IN THE ORCHARD

A sparrowhawk flashed through the orchard
on the line of a previous sparrowhawk.
His centred eyes and instrument of feet
holding the thrush almost too far down
for the hooked bill to reach
told Sweeney how his kill would be.

The thrush was in the hawk's fate
as it flailed the evidence of shells
on a makeshift anvil. Lynchseachan
could piece together how it had happened
where his slow, obscure footsteps
led to feathers in the silvered grass.

It may have been him who first spoke
the hawk in the orchard, having seen it;
and then Sweeney, on the trail of his follower,
finally shot past everything into his own
appearance as the panic of the orchard,
such was his hunger to come level
with what he had foreknown.

SWEENEY TRANSLATES

I'm the first flight
under dawn light,
hen of heather,
mason of the egg.

Yellow on red,
siobhán of the fuchsia,
my song carries
in the blowy lane.

When they tried to fix
my wings to a crucifix
they couldn't decide
which quill was my wrist.

So I slipped the bite
of their cold pins
and sing again
within the song of myself.

A WAGTAIL GLOSS

Sweeney danced
        on the peak of a roof,

little alpinist in his crampons
        after a fly,

so high and light!
        Then he settled again,

ahead of his own long wobbling tail —
        only to vanish in a flit,

not caring how the scribe's pen
        had to labour after him

in his economy and freedom.

Author's Note: "This sequence – twenty poems in all – approaches the traditional Sweeney story with some of the precisions of natural history: Sweeney in a series of transformations as different bird species."

Seán Lysaght lives in Westport, Co Mayo. His fourth collection of poems is Erris *(The Gallery Press, 2002).*

POEM

David Wheatley

ST JOHN AND THE EAGLE

Lindisfarne Gospels

In the beginning was something
or other – what was it? The saint's
parchment is blank, but from
the badger's snout will come the hair

for the brush, from the calf's
martyred back the vellum,
from Ireland the adze-headed scribes,
their insular majuscules, the DNA

coils of frets, trumpets and key steps
weaving a carpet of pages for you
over the sands at low tide:
from gall and indigo the green

and blue of your tunic, from heliotrope
the pinks and purples, and wrought
to its uttermost lapis lazuli
from Badakshan of the peaks

from which the eagle will swoop,
scattering doves as he goes.
Evangelist's bird, tired
of the easy kill, the flocculent hare

and deckchair legs of the deer
folding under a ton's worth of rapt
persuasion in its claw: from a thousand
yards up the eagle has spied

and will snatch from your hands
your book, leaving you only
a feather with which to scatter
and sow the Word in his

fugitive image, *imago aquilae*:
no sooner will you have finished
this page than talons will
puncture and carry it off.

A native of Co Wicklow, David Wheatley is the Editor of Metre *and teaches at the University of Hull in the North of England. His second collection of poems is* Misery Hill *(The Gallery Press, 2001).*

LETTERS TO ELIOT AND AUDEN

Louis MacNeice

From the scrap-album of the literary life.

Editor's Note: The following 10 letters, all from the 1930s, are included in The Selected Letters of Louis MacNeice, *edited by Jonathan Allison, which will be published by Faber in 2007. They are held by the Bodleian Library, Oxford and are published courtesy of Jon Stallworthy on behalf of the Louis MacNeice Estate and David Higham Associates. Jonathan Allison teaches at the University of Kentucky and was Director of the Yeats Summer School in Sligo from 2002 to 2005.*

To T.S. Eliot
April 19 [1932]

Highfield Cottage
28 Selly Park Road
Birmingham

Dear Mr. Eliot

I met Father D'Arcy last week and he tells me that you have some poems which you received without any letter or explanation and which he thinks are mine. I think this is probable, as I sent you a large number of poems in January with a letter enclosed. The letter must have been lost owing to my use of a double envelope; I must therefore apologise.

As for the poems themselves I think that only a few of them stand on their own merits, but that as a collection and arranged in a certain order they would supplement each other and make an aggregate of some value. Whereas if I chose a dozen individuals, they would remain, perhaps, merely individuals. It seems to me (as far as I can see myself) that I am not sufficiently in a school for my poems to be readily significant; therefore they have to build up their own explanation. This is my apology for what may seem a haphazard mass of indifferent or casual verses.

My hope was that Faber and Faber's might publish the collection in book form.

Yours sincerely,

Louis MacNeice.

P.S. (In case the poems, which Father D'Arcy mentioned, are not mine) the first poem in my collection is called TO VUV and the last 'Neurospastomnenos.'

To T.S. Eliot
June 16th [1932]

Highfield Cottage
28 Selly Park Road
Birmingham.

Dear Mr. Eliot

Very many thanks for your letter; I must apologise for my delay in answering it.

I should very much appreciate the publication of any of my poems in the 'Criterion'. I may be in London towards the end of this month and should be very much pleased if I could discuss this with you.

I should add that I have recently received a suggestion as to the publication of some of these poems as a volume; but this, if decided on, would not, I think, be for some time.

Some of the poems which you have, have already been published in 'This Quarter,' 'Oxford Poetry' etc. Of the remainder I should myself propose 'The Green Bird,' 'Everyman his own Pygmalion', 'Hustled by Wind' or 'Colonel X speaks from his Coffin'.

Yours sincerely,

Louis MacNeice.

To T.S. Eliot
Jan. 15th [1936]

Highfield Cottage
128 Selly Park Road
Birmingham

Dear Mr. Eliot,

Thank you for your letter. I will try the Longinus if you like.

Do you mind my consulting you on the following question? For various reasons I should rather like to go to the U.S.A. this summer in my long vacation and I wondered if there was any chance of doing this profitably, or at least less expensively, by means of giving lectures. Either academic lectures, literary lectures, or just lectures. Is there an organization to which one applies for these purposes? If you could give me any information on this subject or refer me to a source of information, I should be extremely grateful.

Yours sincerely,

Louis MacNeice.

To T.S. Eliot
May 28th [1936]

Highfield Cottage
128 Selly Park Road
Birmingham

Dear Mr. Eliot,

My translation of the 'Agamemnon' is not quite ready. I gave it to my Greek professor, E.R.Dodds, to vet and he is suggesting certain changes. I hope to have it ready in three or four weeks' time.

A friend of mine is anxious to meet you. His aunt wants to do a production of 'Murder in the Cathedral' in the cathedral of Lahore! I shall probably be in London next week. I wonder if he and I might possibly come round to see you at Russell Square?

I am just applying for a rather absurd job at Bedford College for Women, London—not because I want to teach women but because I should like to live in London. I gave your name to them among others for purposes of reference. I hope you don't mind?

I have a play of my own which I am writing for the Group Theatre. I wonder if you would like to see it also sometime.

Yours sincerely

Louis MacNeice.

To T.S. Eliot
28 March 1937

4a Keats Grove, NW3

Dear Eliot,

Thank you for your letter. The report about the Hebrides project is quite true. It did not occur to me till I saw Wystan the other day that there was any question of my having committed a breach of etiquette because the proposal was made to me like this. Curtis Brown wrote and said that there was a publisher (who turned out to be Longmans) who wanted someone to do a book about the Hebrides and that, if I liked, they could get this job for me. So it seemed to me that the choice was not between my doing a Hebrides book for Longmans and doing it for you (or for anyone else) but between Longmans having their book done by me and having it done by someone else. So, as I badly need money and it seemed an easy, if frivolous piece of work, I agreed to do it for them. I am sorry, however, that I did not mention it to you at the time but it really did not occur to me that under the circumstances you would object to my doing this.

Wystan and I have gone carefully into the criticisms of the Iceland book made by your reader. I shall be bringing back the Mss tomorrow and perhaps I could see either you or Mr de la Mare about it? I shall ring up before I come. Wystan has gone back to Birmingham for sometime but I think he has now done his worst with the text so we hope that it will really now be able to go safely to press!

Yours sincerely

Louis MacNeice.

To T.S. Eliot
October 4th [1937]

Bishop's House,
Malone Road, Belfast
(as from 4a Keats Grove, N.W.3.)

Dear Eliot,

Thank you very much for your letter. I am glad to hear that the Poems may soon need reprinting but I am not at all sure that it is a good idea to include my new poems in the book. I now have nearly twenty, including three long ones, which would almost make a new book by themselves. From talking to people I am pretty sure that while many of the people who bought the original volume of 'Poems' would buy an entirely new book, very few of them would buy a new edition of the original book even if it were announced as containing some new poems.

I do not feel like trying a detective story at the moment, but someone has made a suggestion to me which I think rather good. Namely, that I should write a shortish book about my experience of the teaching of the Classics (at two English schools & three universities.) Not however in the form of a treatise but impressionistically—e.g. presentation of the classroom or lecture room, specimens of Greek & Latin literature as they appear in translationese, some good translations for contrast, the point of the whole thing being to show the very different & distorted ideas people in schools (& universities) get of the 'Classics'. One might have also a few words against pseudo-Hellenism etc. Some of the book could be in verse.

I am over here for the weekend; coming back on Wednesday.

Yours sincerely

Louis MacNeice.

*To W.H. Auden**
21st October, 1937

Dear Wystan,

I have to write you a letter in a great hurry and so it would be out of the question to try to assess your importance. I take it that you are important and, before that, that poetry itself is important. Poets are not legislators (what is an "unacknowledged legislator" anyway?), but they put facts and feelings in italics, which makes people think about them and such thinking may in the end have an outcome in action.

Poets have different methods of italicisation. What are yours? What is it in your poetry which shakes people up?

It is, I take it, a freshness—sometimes of form, sometimes of content, usually of both. You are very fertile in pregnant and unusual phrases and have an aptitude for stark and compelling texture. With regard to content, the subject-matter of your poems is always interesting and it is a blessing to our generation, though one in the eye for Bloomsbury, that you discharged into poetry the subject-matters of psycho-analysis, politics and economics. Mr. Eliot brought back ideas into poetry but he uses the ideas, say, of anthropology more academically and less humanly than you use Marx or Groddeck. This is because you are always taking sides.

It may be bad taste to take sides but it is more a vital habit than the detachment of the pure aesthete. The taunt of being a schoolboy (which, when in the mood, I should certainly apply myself) is itself a compliment because it implies that you expect the world and yourself to develop. This expectation inevitably seems vulgar to that bevy of second-rate sensitive minds who write in our culture weeklies.

"Other philosophies have described the world; our business is to change it." Add that if we are not interested in changing it, there is really very little to describe. There is just an assortment of heterogeneous objects to make Pure Form out of.

You go to extremes, of course, but that is all to the good. There is still a place in the sun for the novels of Virginia Woolf, for still-life painting and for the nature lover. But these would probably not survive if you and your like, who have no use for them, did not plump entirely for something different.

Like most poets you are limited. Your poems are strongly physical but not fastidiously physical. This is what I should expect from someone who does not like flowers in his room.

Your return to a versification in more regular stanzas and rhymes is, I think, a very good thing. The simple poem, however, does not always wear too well. At first sight we are very pleased to get the swing of it so easily and understand it so quickly, but after first acquaintance it sometimes grows stale. A. E. Housman, whom I join you in admiring, was a virtuoso who could get away with cliché images and hymn-tune metres, but, as you would, I think, admit, his methods are not suitable to anyone who has a creed which is either profound or elaborate.

I am therefore a little doubtful about your present use of the ballad form. It is very good fun but it does not seem to me to be your *natural* form as I doubt if you can put over what you want to say in it. Of course if you can put over half of what you want to say to a thousand people, that may well be better than putting over two thirds of it to a hundred people. But I hope that you will not start writing down to the crowd for, if you write down far enough, you will have to be careful to give them nothing that they don't know already and then your own end will be defeated. Compromise is necessary here, as always, in poetry.

I think you have shown great sense in not writing "proletarian" stuff (though some reviewers, who presumably did not read your poems, have accused you of it). You realise that one must write about what one knows. One may not hold the bourgeois creed, but if one knows only bourgeois one must write about them. They all after all contain the germ of their opposite. It is an excellent thing (lie quiet Ezra, Cambridge, Gordon Square, with your pure images, pure celebration, pure pattern, your scrap-albums of ornament torn eclectically from history) that you should have written poems about preparatory schools. Some of the Pure Poets maintained that one could make poems out of anything, but on the ground, not that subject was important, but that it didn't matter. You also would admit that anything can go into poetry, but the poet must first be interested in the thing in itself.

As for poetic drama, you are now swinging away from the Queer Play. This, like the formal change in your lyrics, is also a good thing and also has its danger. But the danger is not so great for you as it would be for some. Whatever the shape of your work, it will always have ideas in it. Still, when authors like Denis Johnston, who can write excellent straight plays, feel impelled to go over to crooked plays and "poetic writing," there must be some good reason for it and it may appear perverse in you to forget your birthright and pass them in the opposite direction to a realism which may not be much more natural to you than poetry is to them.

These are the criticisms which occur to me at the moment. I have no time to expand on your virtues, but I must say that what I especially admire in you is your unflagging curiosity about people and events. Poetry is related to the sermon and you have your penchant for preaching, but it is more closely related to conversation and you, my dear, if any, are a born gossip.

Yours ever,

Louis MacNeice.

*"Letter to W.H. Auden" *New Verse* 26-27 (November 1937), pp.11-12.

To T.S. Eliot
Nov 29(?) '38

16A Primrose Hill Road
N.W.3.

Dear Eliot,

Here are some notes on 'Autumn Journal' for the Spring Catalogue in haste,
Yourssincerely [sic]

Louis MacNeice.

Autumn Journal.

A long poem of from 2,000 to 3,000 lines written from August to December 1938. Not strictly a journal but giving the tenor of my intellectual & emotional experiences during that period.

It is about nearly everything which from firsthand experience I consider significant.

It is written in sections averaging about 80 lines in length. This division gives it a dramatic quality, as different parts of myself (e.g. the anarchist, the defeatist, the sensual man, the philosopher, the would-be good citizen) can be given their say in turn.

It contains rapportage [sic], metaphysics, ethics, lyrical emotion, autobiography, nightmare.

There is a constant interrelation of abstract & concrete. Generalisations are balanced by pictures.

Places presented include Hampshire, Spain, Birmingham, Ireland, & – especially – London.

It is written throughout in an elastic kind of quatrain. This form (a) gives the whole poem a formal unity but (b) saves it from monotony by allowing it a great range of appropriate variations.

The writing is direct; anyone could understand it.

I think this is my best work to date; it is both a panorama and a confession of faith.

L.M.

To T.S. Eliot
Sept.14th (1939)

The Abbey Theatre.Dublin.

Dear Eliot

My plans are rather in the air at the moment. I will try & finish the Roman Smile – although I am no longer an academic by profession.

Would you by the way consent to my doing a short book of about twenty short poems for the Cuala Press here? A limited edition of about 300 copies for subscribers. Yeats had most of his poems done by them first & subsequently – in bulkier collections – by Macmillan's. It would be good Irish (&, I think, American) publicity & I should like to do it for the sake of someone connected with the press who has done a lot for me. If you preferred, there need be no copies sent out for review. They could publish it Christmasish & by late spring. I could add enough new poems for a book from Faber's.

I have also a scheme for my first serious creative prose book – to be called something like Plaudits & Aspersions or Blessings & Curses. Autobiographical but not in the usual way. A series of quick shots – with some more drawn-out-ones – of the signficant events of my life, not so much things I have done as things I have met; the padding left out & a pattern appearing through variations on several recurring themes; some of it – the more personal parts – in disguise, possibly fantasy. Roughly, in chronological order, it would cover: – The North of Ireland, child's nightmares, Ulster mentality, Ulster religion, sadist mother's help, zany gardener, Orangemen: the last War, preparatory school in Dorset, a Dorset Powys, a 1919 Oxford aesthete : public school (Marlborough), games etc., sex fantasies, a dream about the Crucifixion, public school Picasso fans : Oxford, Auden & Spender, etc., dons, drink : Jewry & marriage – treated obliquely : Birmingham, pigeon-fanciers, the Birmingham surrealists, provincial universities – maybe classical digressions : divorce treated obliquely : London from 1936, various odd travels, the Left : Barcelona New Year 1939 (a whole chapter): New York : finally Ireland again ending with news while in Galway of Germany invading Poland. This was the sort of book I mentioned to Robert Hale & they were prepared to contract for it – to be delivered within twelve months. This is of course confidential but a young man on the firm told me I could get £150 advance for it. I had much rather of course that Faber's did it & should in that case be prepared to drop £50 but I should like £100 advance as I now have no money at all. Being an Irish citisen I am exempt from conscription, so shall no doubt have time to write it long before a year's time.

I hope you will approve the Cuala Press scheme,

Yours ever,

Louis MacNeice.

P.S. Please reply to me c/o the Abbey.

To T.S. Eliot
October 6th [1939]

Bishop's House
Malone Road
Belfast.

Dear Eliot,

I was glad to hear from you about the Cuala Press (they won't send any review copies outside Ireland) and also that you are willing to do the prose book. Yes, I intend to be all prose. It would be convenient if, as you say, I could have the contract at once. 80,000 words will be all right. I am pleased at the prospect of writing prose for a change (it will be rather different from my pot-boiler prose), especially as in verse at the moment I can write nothing except short – almost Greek Anthologyism – lyrics.

I have been asked to apply for the Chair of English Literature at Trinity College, Dublin. Of course I don't know anything about Eng. Lit. by examination standards but I am going to put in for it. I wonder if you could send me some sort of testimonial. If, as is likely, I don't get it, I still hope to try to crash America for a three months' lecturing visit starting in January. The consulates however are very difficult these days.

I am still labouring at this terrible book on Yeats but I hope soon to be able to finish 'The Roman Smile' (when I can get hold of the right books) and the translation of Hippolytus. One – rather grey – advantage over here is that there is nothing to do but read and write. Especially now that the Irish weather has returned to type.

Yours sincerely

Louis MacNeice.

Louis MacNeice was born in Belfast in 1907 and grew up in Carrickfergus, Co Antrim, where his father was a Church of Ireland clergyman (later Bishop of Down, Connor and Dromore). He was educated at Marlborough and Oxford, and in the 1930s was associated with the Auden group of left-wing English poets. The most celebrated of his nine volumes of poetry, Autumn Journal, *was published by Faber in 1939. Between 1941 and 1961, he worked in London as a producer for the BBC, for which he also wrote many radio plays and features. He died in 1963, and his* Collected Poems *(Faber) appeared posthumously in 1966.*

AFTERTHOUGHTS ON THE MUG'S GAME

Michael Hamburger

Necessary subversions.

To me, my life and work are a jigsaw puzzle with more pieces than I can ever put together. I tried once, thirty years ago now, for a book about my early years I called not an autobiography but "intermittent memoirs" – intermittent because even then I was too conscious of the holes in my memory that could not be filled with the documentary evidence I did my best to collect. One reason why I never wrote the projected sequel about later years is that my own case became less and less interesting to me, except as a gauge of phenomena and developments outside myself that did continue to concern me. But the essence of such experience had gone into my chosen medium of verse, by that process of condensation which Ezra Pound distinguished from the processes of functional prose by deriving the German word *dichten* – to make poetry – from the adjective *dicht* – dense or tight. This etymology is spurious, but *ben trovato*. Pound's enemies could have pointed out that *dichten* derived from nothing less prosaic than *dictare*, probably going on to connect this derivation with Pound's leaning towards dictators. Even thirty years ago I also knew that any autobiography I could have written would have been a work of fiction – a selection from the events and concerns of my life and work, a collaboration of memory with imagination, with which it is inextricably bound up; not a chronicle, like the one I had attempted, but a transmutation of the material. And after one abortive novel written in my youth I recognised once and for all that a full-length work of prose fiction was not for me – not even as a translator!

By 1972 I had also begun my retreat from the literary scene in Britain and the USA, with the consequence that my book of memoirs received no more attention than my books of poems in Britain, and none at all in the USA, where the book was not published, and that my British publisher at the time was discouraging about the sequel or complement I might have produced. Then, in my late middle age, after the Thatcherite cultural revolution, I did experience something like alienation, feeling that all I had done or might still do had no place or function in the new order. Over the centuries British institutions had been formed by a tug between conservative pieties – dismissed as hypocritical or snobbish by those who did not share them – and radical ferment, leading to compromises and equipoises like the capacious Anglican Church with its many mansions, a monarchy hedged in not by a constitution but by parliamentary proceedings and our post-war welfare state, in which class differences were levelled upwards, generously and benevolently. The new money free-for-all put an end to both traditions. Old Conservatives who had assented to the welfare state, together with Liberals and Socialists, were eliminated one by one as "wets". "Democratic" was confused with "demotic," the culture levelled down, "dumbed down". The new "Conservatism" was as little about the conservation of anything but the growth of profits as New Labour was to be about productive skills and labour or the radical tradition it found it expedient to incorporate into its name. "Modernization" now meant not progress in any direction – the culture itself having become "post-modern" – but the maximization of profits. In this would-be egalitarian society a new underclass was created, that of the losers in the rat race, now excluded from the solidarity that had sustained the former working classes, who since the nineteenth century had become upwardly mobile by education, self-education fostered by their social "superiors".

Anything I could now write in plain prose – or plain verse, for that matter – had become too plain to be noticed or understood, when double-talk, duplicity, "spin," "sound bites" and "rip-off" had taken over in the public realm; and for most of those at the receiving end – always and everywhere – it's less uncomfortable to make what use they can of a devalued coinage than to reject and resist it. In that climate it was best for me to concentrate on the "non-events" of my latest long poem, cultivating that silence from which the music of poetry has always sprung, with only rare intrusions of other noises.

Here I can't help thinking of my paternal grandfather, who had written under the family name or the pseudonym Burghammer. My mother told me that before he died, at about the time of my birth, he had not only been silenced as a writer by the pressures of earning a living, but reduced to total silence by the professional dishonour inflicted on him by two of his five children, a dishonour that broke his heart. If, more than once, my heart came close to being broken, it was also mended again and again, by love and defiance. Had my grandfather been a poet, rather than a critic and mediator, even his terminal silence could have elicited words of a kind – words addressed to no one or anyone.

So I doubt that my case would have been essentially different if I had not been displaced at the age of nine from one country, one language, to another. I can imagine no personal or literary development in the world as it is that could run in a straight line or a closed circle. When I still practised literary criticism, which I have given up, I looked for the truth about writers in their contradictions, that quarrel with oneself which Yeats said generates poetry, as distinct from rhetoric – though Yeats may now seem a rhetorical poet. My one book-length critical work, *The Truth of Poetry*, was a study in tensions and extremes that clashed and met either within the work of a single writer or in the possibilities of all poetry within the temporal and linguistic bounds of my enquiry. In order to write that book, over a period of at least ten years, I had to break with my academic specialisation as a teacher of German, in which I had always felt uncomfortable – as in any specialisation whatever, other than in the craft of poetry, the mug's game to which I had chosen to devote my life.

A Mug's Game was the title of my book of memoirs, the first version of it, though I changed the title for a second version published in 1991, not wishing by then to make too much of its derivation from a remark by T.S. Eliot about the vocation, and substituting a title drawn from a poem of mine, *String of Beginnings*. Though the Eliot epigraph, too, had to be replaced, all my later experience had confirmed its truth – not only for Eliot but for poets less eminent than he was when he made a remark so uncharacteristically personal and confessional, however general its formulations: "As things are, and as fundamentally they must always be, poetry is not a career but a mug's game. No honest poet can ever feel quite sure of the permanent value of what he has written: he may have wasted his time and messed up his life for nothing."

Well, not only did the posthumous edition of Eliot's letters have to be suspended after one volume, because it had come up against a consensus adverse to him, but "permanent value" has become too big a mouthful for any poet to perpetrate in public, even if in his or her heart it remains the only possible incentive and justification for what cannot be a career. At the height of his fame T.S. Eliot had been invited to address the Conservative Party, on the strength of his professed allegiance to the established Church and the monarchy. It was to be a government that called itself Conservative which made the royal family subject to income tax, therefore competitive in the market economy and symbolically redundant. T.S. Eliot will have turned in his grave.

The aspiration to the (immortal) fame which to Milton was "that last infirmity of noble mind" became mere delusion and vanity when fame had turned into instant, promiscuous and often fortuitous celebrity; and even before that state of affairs it had been quite possible for a poet to keep up the mug's game in total obscurity or rejection. At the age of 18 or 19, in a Soho pub, I asked my friend John Heath-Stubbs whether he had ever had a poem anthologised, thinking in my naivety that this made all the difference between being called and being chosen. A few decades later I had to clear out a hundred contributor's copies of anthologies, in which I was represented with poems or translations, keeping only those I thought of some significance. Decades after that, far from having graduated to immortality by anthologisation, I had amassed a new lumber of such volumes, including many in foreign languages or scripts in which I can't even make out my name – from Arabic to Chinese; but in my country was now omitted as a poet from all anthologies treated as representative. Cultural correctness now disposed of me with the phrase "better known as a translator" or simply ignored the poems I have written. The same cultural correctness now tends to be racist, nationalistic, sexist (or genderist, to use the current term), classist and ageist, perpetually rubbing in the differences while proclaiming a would-be egalitarianism. (Real equality begins where it's taken for granted, not asserted or enforced.) Whatever competent or distinguished critics had written about my work in the past, these omissions could always be justified on other grounds, the dubious "permanent value" a poet can never be sure about in his or her own case; and criticism itself has been largely diverted from texts to the personalities of their author.

The most drastic change since T.S. Eliot's lifetime is the degree to which electronic media have replaced the written word – and the spoken word, for that matter, where it has become a gabble in competition with the abbreviati of those media, because time is money. The effect of this on generations that receive most of their knowledge not from immediate experience, nor from original texts, but from the television screen or from computers is so blatant that it needs no elaboration here. Its effect on poetry – its reception, if not its production – is not only a psychic one, in that more and more young people have grown incapable of sustained attention to anything whatever, other than images and sounds projected for instant consumption or instant distraction – distraction from what?, one begins, to ask oneself – but a practical one that extends to the non-career. The Internet is not subject to those copyright laws that gave authors some measure of control over the use of their work and a minimal share in the form of royalties or fees. If a poem is used on a website the author need not be so much as informed, let alone paid for publication now treated as an advertisement; and even the most vain of authors cannot live by advertisement alone. Needless to add, the question of "permanent value" does not arise at all in media that are random, insatiably and indigestibly cumulative, conveying information about this, that and anything without end.

I have written elsewhere – in an essay included in my book *Testimonies* of 1988 – about the survival of poetry in any historical circumstances or conditions of which I am aware. Poems were written or recited even in extermination camps – or preserved in one person's memory, like the later poems of Mandelstam. As long ago as the first industrial revolution in Britain the end of poetry was predicted, as by Thomas Carlyle. The prediction was proved wrong, both because the squalor brought in by that revolution created a need to escape from it – the Romantic Movement – and because an expanding readership, even for poetry, could be served by the mass production of written texts. The reversal of that development may now look like the end of a whole culture, the literate one, in which literacy was bound up with an awareness of the past – a selected past, therefore "elitist" in the terminology of those who confuse class resentments with considerations of quality. This reversal is still resisted here and there, by dwindling minorities, but other threats of environmental, economic and political disasters detract again and again from the urgency of the resistance, now that it is not the continuity of one culture, one civilisation, but of life on our planet that is in question. Any prediction about the future of poetry would rest on the complacent assumption that the larger destruction can still be averted.

So much had to be said before I could bring myself to write anything more about my own case, displacement from Germany to Britain in childhood or the multilingualism that seems as natural to me as the opposite seems to others. Throughout a millennium and more, educated Europeans had to be proficient in a dead language, Latin, if not Greek and Hebrew also – a Latin that was not dead where it functioned as the *lingua franca* in the Babel of modern languages and dialects in Europe and beyond – much as English can still do in India. Milton wrote poems in Italian, and in the next century William Cowper translated Milton's Italian and Latin poems into English, the language in which both of them had been born to speak and write.

What's more, migration, dispersal and resettlement have become the rule, rather than the exception, in many parts of the world, as throughout recorded history, not least that of Britain and America. When a Welsh nationalist critic described me as a "rootless cosmopolitan," I had to tell him that in fact I had become a stick-in-the mud as a poet, drawing most of my imagery from a single region of England that has become my home. It is plants, not human beings, that are physically rooted; and long ago Remy de Gourmont distinguished the uprooted – *déracinés* – from the transplanted. This applies even to non-human nature, plants and animals. Most of the trees most widespread in Britain were introduced from foreign parts at one time or another. One of the most prolific weeds or wildflowers in Britain and continental Europe now is the Himalayan balsam. An American grey squirrel has displaced the European red squirrel in all but the wildest parts of Britain. One of our commonest birds now is the collared dove which until a few decades ago was confined to Eastern Europe. Until exterminated by genocide, the South American coypu, a large vegetarian rodent, spread all over the East Anglian marshlands on which I live. In my East Anglian garden, exposed to fierce winds from the North Sea, trees from America, even Mexico and Nicaragua, as from China and Japan, do as well as trees regarded as indigenous since the records began. Much the same is true of culture and the arts, from agriculture and horticulture, their products and implements, to architecture, sculpture, painting, musical composition and the verse forms dear to traditionalists.

As for me, my bibliography attests that I have translated and written about more German language authors than I can enumerate here. Though at school I began to specialise in Modern languages, I could not take up the Exhibition (scholarship) I had won to Christ Church, Oxford, without passing an entrance examination in what is not a modern language, Latin, still obligatory at that time, 1941, for students of any subject; and in retrospect I wish that my early specialisation had not been forced on me, at the expense of the Ancient Greek I should otherwise have learnt. The first and main modern language I did learn was French, and there was a time when my French was better than what remained of my childhood German and the book German that complemented it. My first book of translations, completed at the age of 18 and published when I was 19, was from the German poet Hölderlin, on whose difficult texts I was to go on working off and on for half a century; but my second book of translations was from the French of Baudelaire, done in 1944 when I was an infantry soldier in the Shetlands, and still in print with an American publisher, City Lights. With very few exceptions, foreign influences on my earliest poems were more French than German. What impelled me to make German my main subject when I returned to Oxford after military service was my renewed contact with the spoken language as an interpreter for German prisoners-of-war in Austria and as headmaster of an Army boarding school staffed with Austrian civilians, as well as British teachers. As a soldier in Italy I had also taken up Italian, at first reading Dante in a bilingual text that could easily be carried in a kitbag, the Temple Classics edition. Though it was already too late for me to pick up another language in the way I had plunged into English as a boy, I was to translate one Italian poet, Franco Fortini, with his help and the odd howler, a few Italian poems by others needed for my critical book and – more recently – two poems by Leopardi I had long lived with. More recently still it was some lines of Dante used as an epigraph for the latest book I have translated, W.G. Sebald's *After Nature*, which also called for a version of a Latin epigraph from Vergil. *The Truth of Poetry* had also elicited versions of poems in Spanish and Portuguese, languages I can't begin to speak. When the Romanian poet Marin Sorescu asked me to translate poems of his I was able to do so because Romanian is a partly Romance language and because the virtuoso German poet Oskar Pastior allowed me to cannibalise his excellent German versions of these poems. When I tried to translate from languages I can neither speak nor guess at, by way of literal cribs or trots, I found myself groping in the dark for Hungarian and liberated by ignorance for the one poem I was asked to translate from the Chinese, so much so that I could place this version in my *Collected Poems* and it has been translated in turn into German as a poem of my own – a *chinoiserie*. Because my curiosity about the state of post-war Europe drove me into Displaced Persons' Camps out of bounds to British soldiers in Austria, camps filled with refugees from the Baltic, Ukraine and Tito's Yugoslavia, I was brought up against the limits of my capacity to absorb more languages, including Russian. It had been hard enough at first to adjust to the Carinthian dialect, when my brain sponge was reaching saturation point for languages.

Here I must mention that when I was presented with a gold medal by the Society of Linguists, only its receipt by post saved me from having to refuse it or suffering painful embarrassment at its presentation, since I don't think of myself as a linguist at all, only as a person with a boundless interest in what can be communicated and not communicated verbally, in literary texts or other media. From earliest childhood onwards this interest extended to animals and mute plants. In later years I wrote a poem called "Conversation with a Blackbird," only one of several in which I tried to transcribe or translate animal sounds. So the many translations I have done, to me, were not linguistic exercises but responses to the most diverse phenomena – explorations less of affinities than strangeness. The more difficult and strange a text, the more challenging it was likely to prove, like the texts of Hölderlin and Celan. From Celan's poems I could take nothing I am aware of for my own; from Hölderlin nothing more palpable than a way of breathing. Accessibility, in that process, had more to do with empathy than with knowledge of any kind, linguistic, historical or textual.

The crux of my displacement at the age of nine, from Berlin to Edinburgh, is that it occurred at an age when adjustment is either immediate or impossible. I compared the sudden change to a child's being thrown into water so that it can learn to swim – for survival. My Berlin childhood had been so oppressed by restrictions, even before the Third Reich, that when I was quite able to swim I dropped like a stone into the water of the Havel, at Kladow outside Berlin, and had to be rescued from an unconscious wish to drown by the second of the governesses who had oppressed us – not a benevolent disciplinarian like our first, but a sadistic one with a resentment that had contributed to my state of mind. In Edinburgh, without governesses at last, I recovered my will to survive. This meant acceptance into a community of schoolboys, made possible only by almost immediate linguistic assimilation – and by my plunge from the highest springboard of a swimming pool, to the admiration of fellow pupils not as familiar as I was with water, thanks to my grandfather's house at Kladow and perhaps to earlier seaside holidays on the Baltic coast. I was then invited to join a street gang from the school, George Watson's, that picked fights with boys wearing the uniforms of other Edinburgh schools – when in Berlin my three siblings and I had never been allowed to go anywhere but to school without adult supervision, or play with children not approved by the supervisors.

So the fall from upper middle-class prosperity and status – my father had been a professor of paediatrics as well as a family doctor, and in Germany professorships were prestigious – proved my liberation from an increasing introversion that had become morbid. But my father had to sit all day long over textbooks in a language still foreign to him during the year's crash course in all branches of medicine he had to absolve so as to be allowed to practice in Britain – where paediatricians did not work as family doctors and no professorship awaited him – on money borrowed to pay the rent of the furnished Edinburgh house, since he had made over what savings he had to his widowed mother, who stayed behind in Berlin until transported to her death, probably in Poland. All we ever knew, from a Red Cross message, was that she had "gone on a journey". Within a year of that, in 1940, my father succumbed to an incurable illness. Meanwhile, in a Britain still civil, I had been able to outgrow the necessary macho phase, though a few fights were still needed at later schools.

But the phases are recorded in my memoirs; also, that assimilation had governed my forebears ever since the eighteenth-century Enlightenment, the emancipation of the Jews from their ghettos and the *Code Napoléon*, whose solution to the "Jewish Problem" was the opposite of Hitler's in that the Jews were to disappear not by genocide but by their absorption into the majority. This earlier trend was to be reversed, on the basis of a eugenics drawn from cattle breeding, adopted out of a resentment with mass appeal. Just because the ideology was absurd, it had to be implemented with an unprecedented thoroughness and bureaucratic efficiency, so that the method would justify the madness. Had the Third Reich lasted longer, its "final solution" would have extended to those of partly "non-Aryan" provenance, as intended, then those of Slavic or other non-Germanic descent. If it had, the German population itself would have been reduced not only to the "purity" but the size of an aboriginal tribe – a logical conclusion hardly compatible with world domination, quite apart from the losses incurred by war and the increasing risk of internal revolt.

What had not struck me when I wrote the memoirs was the French sympathies of both my grandfathers – one born in Prussian Silesia, the other in Mainz, in whose ghetto his ancestors had lived. My paternal grandfather, Leopold, attempted to introduce French Naturalism into Germany, a decade or more before there was a Naturalist movement in Germany, and long before the Dreyfus affair. Because all this grandfather's papers were lost when his widow was taken out of her Berlin flat, all I have of his literary remains is a few letters to him by Alphose Daudet and Zola. (It was the editor of a book of Zola's letters who passed on what little he could discover about my grandfather's publications.) It can't have been an accident that my maternal grandfather's first name was Bertrand, and his father's Louis – both not German, but French forms; or that this grandfather, too, was a reader of Zola and other French writers.

The social assimilation, though, was such that I never saw the inside of a synagogue until my friend Erich von Kahler took me into one in New Jersey, in the sixties or seventies, not for worship but for a lay speech he was delivering there. When my paternal grandmother, born in Poland, spoke of going to the "Temple," I imagined a Greek one. No one else in the family ever mentioned such a place. The very first prayer I learnt by heart was a childish jingle taught me by our Roman Catholic governess; and Hebrew was not among the languages of which I was given so much as a smattering. One of my great-uncles, who survived the Third Reich in Berlin, had become a Lutheran and married an "Aryan" of the landowning class – killed there in a mugging after the war throughout which she had stuck by her "non-Aryan" husband. Another great-uncle fled Berlin only at the last moment, surviving the war with his wife under an assumed name, with no ration cards, as itinerant farm labourers. That survival made a mockery of the biological race laws: assimilation had gone so far as to invalidate them in practice; and on a visit to my family after the war this great-uncle was outraged by an anti-German remark, leaping up from the dinner table to protest that he was still a German – after being condemned to death as such, robbed of his house and possessions, deprived even of the pointer hound of whose loss he told, with tears not shed for his murdered human friends. My mother became a Quaker; and one of the last books read by my agnostic father was a selection from the works of Kierkegaard, when he was working on a psychological book he did not live to finish. (I was to write a little piece on Kierkegaard, included in my collection *Testimonies*).

So it came about, too, that I was sent to distinctly Anglican schools after Edinburgh and spent most of my formative years in very British institutions – a Hampstead prep school, a public school, Westminster – attached to the Abbey – Christ Church, Oxford – attached to the Cathedral – and the British Army – up to the age of 24. As the poet I was already trying to become, I got some encouragement and assurance from being at a school, Westminster, which had produced poets for centuries, from Ben Jonson – a working-class pupil when the school was a truly public one – George Herbert, Henry King, among other excellent minor poets of the "metaphysical" kind, to Dryden and Cowper, in the earlier centuries. It was a clever and precocious fellow pupil, Richard Wollheim, who read some of my first, still somewhat Tennysonian, apprentice pieces and advised me to toughen up my verse by reading Dryden. My first published essay, written in 1942 or 1943, while I was waiting in London for my military call-up, was on "John Donne and Metaphysical Poetry"; and my last academic job, in Britain, was a temporary part-time professorship that demanded only one weekly lecture and seminar on twentieth-century English and American poets.

My inflated early poems, which made up in rhetoric for what they lacked in sensuous roughage, also remind me how much, at this period, I took to heart the religious worship in which I participated in all those institutions, although I never became a member of any Church or sect, and the theological teaching at Westminster, called "Divinity," was decidedly liberal, if not positively ecumenical. Many later quarrels with myself were to arise between the life-long effects of this taking to heart and a need just as strong for independence of mind. The security to be found in any co-operative membership had become suspect to me at an early age. If that was to leave me an outsider everywhere, in spite of loyalties that could not be formalised or formulated, so it had to be.

Because George Watson's had prided itself on "pure," standard English, this was the vernacular into which I was initiated, and nothing was ever to shake that foundation, not even when my English had to become basic in the barrack-rooms I shared with other infantry privates, the lowest of the low in the class order only beginning to be loosened at that time. If my father's crash course had taken him to Glasgow, and my first British school had not been a private one, my linguistic initiation would have been very different indeed and my case complicated by regional, as well as class, divisions. Later, I was to teach some ten semesters at universities and colleges in the USA as a visiting professor, also travelling widely there for readings and lectures from New Hampshire to Texas, from Montana to South Carolina. Even in Britain this vernacular of mine has become an anachronism; but other vernaculars could serve me only for satirical and polemical purposes, the "low mimetic" also demanded for solidarity in barrack-rooms – small price to be paid for the considerateness and kindness I received in these, so that at times I could even work at poems while sitting or lying on a palliasse, no table or chair provided for the lowest of the low. However assimilated, I never anglicised my surname, and didn't need to for these barrack-rooms; nor later, when my surname had become the name of a junk food, or because I was serving in a war against the country that gave my family that name.

My first translations may have been my way of bridging the displacement from that county, separation from the relatives and friends left behind, from the open spaces around Kladow to which I owed my first moments of freedom and exhilaration, the diverse animals I had collected and looked after there, and what had been my family's culture – though it was music not language, that was my earliest love in the arts, and one practised by my father and mother. Had I been a few years older when the displacement occurred, I might well have had to return to my first language as a writer of poems. My friend Franz Wurm, born in Prague into a German-speaking family also fluent in Czech, was shipped to England in a children's transport at the age of 13 and educated at an English boarding school, then Oxford. Because, unlike me, he had lost his immediate family, when told by an English friend that he would never make a good English poet, he reverted not to German but to French for his early verse – his German lost to him by association with the more grievous loss. "It was only then that I turned to German, which for quite a while came from my reading rather than from the language spoken at home," he writes in a letter. He was then moved to re-emigrate to a German-speaking part of Switzerland, a neutral country by association, and become a German-language poet as linguistically inventive and idiosyncratic as his friend Paul Celan – who was even more multilingual by circumstance, but clung to German for poetry when he talked and corresponded with his wife and son in French, out of his very obsession with his *mother* tongue and the wound inflicted on his family and friends under the German occupation. Erich Fried, one of the most widely read German-language poets of his time, came to England at the age of 16, remained resident there but never became wholly bilingual other than as a translator of texts ranging from Shakespeare to Dylan Thomas and Sylvia Plath. Many other cases could be cited, each distinct for reasons too intricate to be unravelled here.

When towards the age of 30, I was induced to write unambitious critical pieces in German, they proved acceptable, though my syntax, like my attitudes, tended to be more English than German and my grammar could be shaky; but the attempt to function bilingually, at least in prose, precipitated an identity crisis for a year or two, leaving me stranded in a no-man's land. For a time I was able to produce German versions of English poems of mine that had found no other translator or to collaborate with my earliest German translators if necessary. To resolve the crisis, though, I had to put an end to the pretence of bilingualism. The three tiny poems I wrote in German – for friends with little English – only brought home to me that my childish-cum-bookish German lacked the resources needed for poetry – resources of lived experience and association more than linguistic proficiency. For better or for worse, it is the English language in which I feel at home – its wealth of short words, its range of many-layered meanings, its laxities and lazinesses even, its shedding long ago of cases, declensions and inflections, its freedom from grammatical compulsions, leaving most English speakers scarcely aware that there is or was such a thing as grammatical rules, if they were never drilled in a foreign language as law-abiding as Latin or German. (Christian Morgenstern made fun of the bureaucratic and pedantic proclivities of his language in his well-known "Werwolf" poem. The Dadaist Kurt Schwitters subverted them in his best-known poem, "Anna Blume.")

I, too, was told early on by a friend that no one not born in an English-speaking country would ever write a good English poem. I defied that warning as one of many risks incurred and defied throughout my life, not only by my choice of the mug's game. At a reading in Washington D.C. my fellow British poet George MacBeth introduced me as "the best German poet writing in English," and I can never know whether that was a back-handed compliment of a kind I have got used to or a critical judgement. I also gather from a recent four-volume German anthology of British and American poetry that I am the most widely translated poet – into German – of its living contributors. This, again, could be due to non-literary judgements; accidents of politico-cultural correctness or a generous act of restitution towards my person; and it could mean that the translatable gist of my poems does appeal more to German-language readers than to the English-speaking. Interesting as the sociology and psychology of reputations may be in themselves, after 60 years of the mug's game I can't speculate how they apply to my case. Whatever the reasons and motivations, I have received more prizes and more serious attention for my work in the German-speaking countries than in Britain; but this points to general differences in the status of the arts and the status of their practitioners. Poetry especially is an overcrowded occupation, because, as Yeats wrote, there are always too many of us, and it's simply too easy to produce something that looks like a poem but fails to sound or work like one. No wonder, then, that in Britain most of one's fellow practitioners – called "colleagues" in Germany – turn out to be competitors, often mean ones at that. With his tongue in his cheek or not, the magnanimous English poet Geoffrey Hill once spoke of "the rabble of one's so-called peers". The book in which he did so, I was told, received no review in our country other than one I wrote. From Germany I receive letters in which the formal address *geehrter* (honoured) is heightened to *verehrter* (admired or revered). The British response to that is likely to be embarrassment or amusement, but there is more to it than an archaic formality. Because I cannot bring myself to enter for any of our countless poetry competitions, the prizes I have been awarded were unsolicited, therefore honours as well as subsidies. At a session of the Royal Society of Literature founded by a Hanoverian king to subsidise writers like Coleridge, who discovered very soon and painfully that the funds were no longer available, so that later elected Fellows of the Society have had to pay a subscription fee for the honour – Lord Butler, its President at the time, presented a prize to John Wain for a book on Samuel Johnson, going on to say he was sorry to have gathered that John Wain now intended not to write another book of that kind but to return to his hobby of writing poems. Most German poets I have known would have felt this to be a disparagement of their chosen vocation. In England, for England, it was an instance of good sense – not a literary judgement or a personal one, but a confirmation, by a statesman, that the mug's game is not a career, since no living can be made by it.

In Britain this state of affairs makes for a humility that may or may not be a genuine one. There is a kind of pride, also known as integrity, that one must allow others to see as arrogance, just as there is a seeming humility, often combined with bonhomie and charm, that lends itself to opportunist climbing. No one could have been more proud in his dealings with the world than the poet of love and religious orthodoxy, Dante – humble enough, too, towards his pagan predecessor Vergil to make him his poetic guide – up to the point of separation.

This brings me to the mediating of mainly, but not exclusively German texts as a translator and critic – for which I was "better known," at least until given larger coverage in a British newspaper as a grower of mainly obsolete apple varieties. A few of the translations have been reprinted, enlarged and revised over a period that seems long for such work. Of my critical books only *The Truth of Poetry* remains in print in Britain, not in the USA, has appeared in German three times, Italian, Spanish in Mexico, and is about to appear in Portuguese in Brazil. In retrospect I wonder how I could possibly have turned out so many books – by choice, not commission – much of the time while doing odd jobs or teaching for a living, travelling not for relaxation but more work, with energy to spare for physical labour in gardens when we had gardens to tend, as we did most of the time. For the last 26 years it has been three and a half acres of land, on which I planted more trees than I have published books; and I think it is the physical labour of their conservation that has kept me going to the age of 80. Most translation and criticism are as ephemeral in effect as my cyclically repetitive gardening chores – and as one can't stop hoping a few of one's poems are not, with the potentiality at least of outlasting the grower like a tree.

Beyond that I have little to say about my translations and criticism, subject as both are to market forces, the reputation stock exchange, its brokers and the fluctuations of all these. Since auto-psychoanalysis is another mug's game that does not attract me, I shall not pretend to understand why or how I was drawn to one text rather than another. It is German-language critics who have tried to put the jigsaw-puzzle pieces together in books and essays on my work – though a student of James Dickey in South Carolina came as close as anyone, for my early poems only, in the USA, telling me things I did not know about them. Every translation I have done and every critical piece I have written also belongs to the jigsaw puzzle, each a requirement of its own in the first place. If I can risk a generalisation now, only about my translations from the German, it is that they were of texts I considered different in one way or another from anything written in English, therefore not unnecessary as additions to a literature already inexhaustible in its variety and range. It could be the few mediaeval lyrics I attempted by Walther von der Vogelweide, a baroque sonnet by Andreas Gryphius in lines so irregular that it does not look like a sonnet, or later poets to whom I devoted whole books; and it could be short prose by Novalis, Kleist, Büchner, Georg Heym or my contemporaries Eich, Grass, Heissenbüttel, Bichsel and Adolf Muschg unlike any others I knew. Of my Goethe translations, plays and poems, the one that gave me most trouble and pleasure was the least-known, the late dramatic fragment *Pandora* in which each speech is in a metre appropriate to the mythical speaker, an invention that transcends the stage it was written for and in which the heroine never appears, though she is present throughout in the speakers' minds. Hofmannsthal's play *The Tower* is another play that strains the possibilities of the stage; but I translated it as a text to be read, and it made a powerful radio play, like plays written for radio by Günter Eich and Peter Weiss I also translated, when what was our Third Programme still had a use for the "elitist" minority medium, an acoustic one in which poets have excelled. Again it is in Germany that this medium still flourishes, in the teeth of television, which once seemed to threaten it with obsolescence – for how much longer is uncertain, when resistance to the junk and advertising culture may be crumbling even in that so Platonic (Egghead) Republic.

Despite the hints I have dropped here, I don't know and don't care whether or not some foreign residue characterizes my work as a whole. As I write this I have received an article on my work – in German – quoting me as having distinguished between two phases in my writing, one of mimicry, imitation of models, the next of "word-scepticism," a certain distance between the matter communicated and the words chosen. All learning, of course, is imitation of one skill or another, and very few poets indeed seem to have come into their own without an apprenticeship of imitation. Foreigners, it's true, are supposed to be recognisable by the meticulousness of their way of speaking. But poets, too, pick their works if they aren't out for automatic writing or an indiscriminate spontaneity; and, if they try to write prose that is accurate, they will be picking their words also, often with the many "buts," "ifs" and "perhapses" for which Eliot was notorious in his essays. Eliot was not as blatant an expatriate as Conrad, Joyce or Beckett, yet in his time the great divide between American and British English, American and British attitudes had already opened.

Reading two posthumous volumes of texts by Paul Celan now – his correspondence with his devoted friend and searching critic Peter Szondi, and a collection of miscellaneous prose drafts and notebook jottings – I am struck by two things, other than by the fact that such books can still appear in Germany, meticulously edited and annotated. One is the confirmation in both books of the damage done to an incomparable poet by malicious and fabricated accusations of plagiarism. (These had already been fully documented in a separate study.) At times Celan could dismiss this campaign as the psychopathic phenomenon it was; but subliminally it precipitated his own paranoia, when a demented widow's charges were taken up by accredited critics and academics, rubbing poison into the wound inflicted on him by earlier persecution and the murder of his parents in concentration camps. The campaign began with the appearance of his first collection of poems in Germany and continued even when he had been driven into breakdown and suicide.

The second is reflections on his own poetry, and so on the paradox that poetry shares a medium, language, with many other forms of communication, but not with their functions, which it may find it necessary to subvert; in his own case, an insistence on the essential darkness that was not obscurantist, for all the scientific and esoteric allusions in his poems, and not hermetic, since he never ceased to hope that his necessarily cryptic messages could be received. His poems were a groping in words for what he could not know before the poem found it, becoming not his but anyone's. Once the poem was finished, its author might not be able to elucidate it at all without betraying the darkness. Hence Celan's refusal to provide clues in the form of notes. Any one poem's itinerary could be neither retraced nor repeated, preoccupied as a poet must be with the next poem's groping in the dark, up to the final silence.

Mutatis mutandis, this accords with my experience, with what Keats meant by the "negative capability" of poets and with the doubt built into the vocation itself so startlingly voiced by T.S. Eliot, a poet seemingly much more deliberate, more self-assured than Celan in his public stance and pronouncements. It has a bearing, too, on why, ever since Plato, the place of poetry in any *res publica* – not least one as philosophical and ideal as Plato's – has been suspect; and why many intelligent persons have no use for its processes.

But it is in classical Chinese poetry, produced over a period of some two millennia, that poetry's imperviousness to social and political change is much more conspicuous than in any Graeco-Roman or Judaeo-Christian tradition. Wars, massacres, upheavals of dynasties, even the differences between successive religious creeds were intimated here and there by these poets – most of whom were civil servants when they could not or would not retire from public affairs – but not so specifically as to constitute a record of systems or events, just as the individuality of these poets was subordinate to their continuity – and the continuity of human life as such among the ten thousand things.

And the laconic revelation in Celan's previously unpublished jottings is his remark that he had learnt more from the work of W.B. Yeats than from the surrealists always included among his antecedents. This, too, rang a bell for me, recalling a time when a critic wrote that I was "ghosting for the ghost of Yeats" – not without justification, at that formative stage of my work; but it would hardly have occurred to anyone to connect Celan's work with Yeats's since the affinity was not one of manner, diction or form, but of what Yeats called "heart mysteries".

The Russian poet Svetayeva once remarked that all poets are Jews, probably meaning not their stubborn clinging to a minority faith and identity – the alternative to assimilation that has led to the present cruel impasse in Palestine – but that they remain classless, never wholly accommodated or uniform. What counts in the end is not how we are labelled and classified, least of all by ourselves, but how we have coped with the identities partly imposed by circumstances, partly assumed by positive and negative responses to the circumstances. Whether we accept the Fall as a dogma or as an incontrovertible myth, that separation from non-human nature gave each of us a measure of freedom and choice in the matter of who we are and aspire to be; but the judgement of how far the things we have done and made accord with the aspiration is not ours, and by writers must be left to critics as fallible as they are. This is where an egregious mug's game may link up with the human condition.

TERMINAL HOUR

1

"Stay put" she said. "This is it.
Starting-point, destination
Both Nowhere on your tickets.
Sit in the lounge – or quit
If a car for your recall
Was parked by you or summoned.
Your luggage? It's too light
For our scale's registration.
How, why, by whom this flight
Was booked, computerised
We have no means to tell."

"Nor I. So thanks. Amen
To every complication.
Just let me share again
Air hostess litanies
Of safety, of salvation,
Jet organ introit,
A choir's unearthly swell,
The step marked *vox humana*
Become angelical;
And clouds reversed in ice-light
Perversely let me praise."

2

Landed indeed, I blink at the white and gold
Of so much baroque, such plump angels tumbling,
Walk what I'm told is the Prater, where nearly sixty years back
On leave from alpine service, more wondering
I strayed from the Hotel Sacher, conquerors' rest-house then,
Street map redundant now, guidebook discarded –
Indirection will see me through, between no-more and not-yet –
Among the few faces recognised, the many half-placeably strange
And those at work here once, removed, if not for ever.

Then off cross-country through plains past hills to high summits,
Through towns with names just remembered and names never noted,
Flashes of rail-side wildflowers, their guessed-at shapes

Blacked out too soon by tunnels –
Though the train also sang, hosannas,
Polyphony wordless from bass to descant,
Diaposon for blocked ears, fulfilled in its fading.

3

But herded again, penned in
For departure; a little hitch
In transit, the first plane detained,
A zigzagging sprint through the maze of gates,
The right leg, aching, intent
On late retirement, the left,
Its grim propeller, bereft
And, oh, the one bag heavier –
But the craft already boarded,
Four hours to kill till the next,
A driver waiting in vain and leaving
On the other side of the sea
For the thirty-mile final stretch.

Nowhere once more. Blankness,
Dusk, advertisement-lit
While on the unseen, foreknown
Inaccessible city outside
Not wholly homogenised yet
The real sun shines.

Michael Hamburger, a poet and translator, lives in East Anglia. He is the author of 22 volumes of poetry, published between 1945 and 2004, most recently From a Diary of Non-Events *(Anvil, 2002) and* Wild and Wounded *(Anvil, 2004).*

FIVE POEMS

Gerard Smyth

VILLA FLORICA

In the villa that evening
the birds in the ivy were full of *bonbomie,*
up in the minstrel gallery
warbling their benedictions,
whistling their hearts out.

In the dead heat the thunder shifted
from far beyond to close behind.
Enclosed by trees of great height
we were listening, attentive
to the poet from Lesbos

and the poet who intoned his Balkan elegy
for a homeland that had altered shape.
In the mansion they gave us
a place at a table:
the wine was served from cool carafes,

after that the soup and then the salad
of cucumber and tomatoes.
The dictator's name could not be mentioned
without a chill to break the enchantment,
a theatrical stir in the sylvan camouflage.

ANNA'S SANCTUARY

We find it through a hidden entrance:
the arboreal courtyard, Anna's sanctuary
of little rooms that still exhale
the atmosphere of Russia in the age
of forbidden truth.

In this, her church of premonitions,
the ink on her petitions
fades; a shrine is made
of the icon in the icon-corner,
the empty samovar.

And there in Napplebaum's
haunted image Cassandra lives.
Poet with the inward look of the savant
the look she gives is stoic, chiselled,
black-rimmed beneath a Cleopatra fringe.

TK'S TERRITORY

Beyond Swift's Hospital
and the grey slab wall,
down the lane where you remember
Paul Henry cottages,
it's all breeze-block and brick,
electric gates and double windows.

But this was once a sward
of city vegetation: blackberry fields
where you picked your way
through a rivery smell
and the smell of clay
shared with gull and pigeon.

Beyond Swift's hospital,
in the hollow glade
on the hillpath like a pilgrim's walk,
it was late September,
summer's cadenza of final warmth.
There was shunting

in the distance: the evening train,
the departure whistle.
The hopstore harboured bitter grain.
In the cooperage a craft was dying
there among planks of wood,
hoops of iron.

CROSS OF MOONE

What startled us was the rattle of gridiron,
the gravel track twisting under the tyres.
We were driving east, clocking the distance.

Oozing in the heat of late afternoon
the black tar was viscous
on the motorway of our Iliad.

We were driving east but stopped off
at the Cross of Moone, symbol of the creed
Of fatherland and mother-tongue.

It was one of the first of the last days of summer.
The tops of conifers brightened and dimmed
and filled with birds with only one song.

Song of innocence, prayer without words.
It was not the beginning and not the end
but the in-between time before Amen.

WONDERLAND
(after Nick Miller)

Snow when it falls is a snowy blanket.
Numinous. Galactic. Like plumage
on the scrawny branches.

It is a good landscape for hide-and-seek
in the cold shadows
of whitethorn and maple.

Power-line and telephone cable
catch the rain and let it fall on gorged-on acres,
borderland, forsaken territory.

In this high country roads twist north
into mountains,
into the corona of dense cloud.

The trees work up a chant of incantation
and sing to the lakes:
Lough Arrow and Lough Gill.

The western gale leaves its razor-scrapes.
It is a ragged landscape
of watery illuminations, a wonderland
for the fisherman with patience.

Gerard Smyth works as a journalist with The Irish Times. *His most recent collection is* Daytime Sleeper *(The Dedalus Press, 2002).*

THE BLOOMSDAY PERIODICAL

Malcolm Ballin

What could Leopold Bloom have been reading? Plus ça change …

I want here to discuss the nature of the periodical market in Dublin on June 16 1904, the first "Bloomsday", to consider how it is represented in *Ulysses,* and to discuss Joyce's relations with literary journalism. Bloom could, if not otherwise much engaged, have had access to over fifteen titles without resorting to English imports such as *Tit-Bits*. Opinions about the press were often critical. In the "Aeolus" episode of *Ulysses,* set in the offices of *The Freeman's Journal,* J. J. O' Molloy, the distressed barrister, refers disparagingly to the Harmsworth press and to "his American cousin of the Bowery gutter sheet not to mention *Paddy Kelly's Budget, Pue's Occurrences* and our watchful friend *The Skibereen Eagle*". He goes on to declare that "sufficient unto the day is the newspaper thereof". This reflects some of Joyce's own ambivalence about literary journalism: Declan Kiberd (*Ulysses: Annotated Students Edition,* 1992) describes him as "a hater of the bookish" who "loved to twit literary types."The mockery of literary styles in "Oxen of the Sun" exemplifies this attitude as does the representation of Stephen Dedalus as a literary poseur. Leopold Bloom's rather inflated claim to "follow a literary occupation" as "author-journalist" earns him much obloquy from Beaufoy who identifies him as "a plagiarist. A soapy sneak masquerading as a literateur". In *Ulysses,* the future of journalistic production lies in the wrapping of meat parcels if not, indeed, as in the case of *Tit-Bits,* in even more prosaic uses.

Joyce often wrote about newspapers and journals satirically and in later life sometimes refused to engage with them. However, in his youth, he wrote many articles for journals, actively sought employment in this line, and was not above misusing his press card for personal expenses. His first appearance in print was his precocious essay on Ibsen in the *Fortnightly Review* in 1900 when he was eighteen. Apropos of his work in the Trieste journal, *Il Piccolo de Sera* in 1907, he remarked to his brother, Stanislaus, that "I may not be the Jesus Christ I once fondly thought myself, but I think I have a talent for journalism." He used international periodicals, such as *The Egoist, The Little Review, Criterion* and *transition* to provide advance publication and to circumvent censorship; he wrote letters to magazines and was highly sensitive to the reviews of his work. He was mortified by the *Münchner-Augsburger Nachwriten's* description of the first-ever performance of *Exiles* in 1919 as "all that noise for an Irish Stew". His contacts with journals also created and sustained relationships with some major sources of financial and critical support, including Harriet Weaver, Ezra Pound,

T. S. Eliot, Richard Aldington, Hilda Doolittle and Rebecca West.

It is convenient to divide the periodicals on sale in Dublin in 1904 into two main categories. There was a range of weekly journals, typically priced at one penny, such as *The Freeman's Journal* itself, together with *The Irish Homestead,* the *Dublin Penny Journal*, the *Shamrock,* the *All Ireland Review* and the overtly nationalist weeklies, such as *The United Irishman* and *The Leader.* Then there were the more expensive monthly or quarterly productions, many of them priced at sixpence, such as *Dana,* and *Uladh* (from the North). There were specifically catholic publications such as the *New Ireland Review* or *The Irish Monthly Magazine,* and more sporadic productions like Yeats's *Samhain* or the Trinity College magazine, *St. Stephens.* Their editors are intensely aware of each other's competing stances and struggle to access and retain particular readerships. Yug Mohit Chaudry (*Yeats, the Literary Revival and the Politics of Print,* 2001) shows how "meaning - both intended and received - is invariably linked to cultural contexts, and the significance and value of utterances depend on the context and pre-dispositions of the audience for whom they are intended." These periodicals all seek to establish particular images of Irishness for differing audiences both within and outside Ireland.

The Freeman's Journal for Thursday, June 16 1904 presents itself in broadsheet newspaper format, with a front page devoted to births, marriages and deaths, and a range of advertisements for laundries, pawnbrokers and great shipping sales. But it is more than just a newspaper; it covers a miscellany of topics relevant to national and international events. It appears to aim at pleasing a number of opposed constituencies. It has a report on "Orangeism in Action" that deprecates the storms of protest about a Catholic woman, Rose Sweeny, appointed to a Presbyterian School at Canntall near Omagh. A County Councillor, William Coote, responding to criticisms of the graffiti daubed on the Church door, blames the Presbyterian Minister for provocation. Parliamentary reports, by way of balance, deal with the debate about Constable Anderson, allegedly dismissed because of "Catholic bigotry". International coverage supports Russia's right to base troops in Manchuria and the English capture of a Lama in the Tibetan campaign. Mrs. Bandsman-Palmer's performance as Hamlet at the Gaiety Theatre is favourably reviewed. Sports reporting covers both Gaelic Athletic Association events and English county cricket scores. Excitement is reported in Homburg as preparations escalate for the forthcoming Gordon Bennet motor race, remarked on by Martin Cunningham in the Hades episode. Joyce's placement of the "Aeolus" episode in the offices of the *Freeman's Journal* suggests that he saw it iconically as representative of the press in Ireland. In 1912, while staying in Galway, Joyce wrote an article for the *Freeman's* himself, about the prevention of foot and mouth disease, also destined to be the subject of Mr. Deasey's letter to the *Evening Telegraph.* The *Freeman's Journal* illustrates how information is often produced journalistically, in bite-sized portions, influenced by the space available as well as by the perceived demands of the reader. Robert Darnton, (*The Kiss of Lamourette,* 1990) demonstrates that news reporting "is heavily influenced by stereotypes and by preoccupations of what the story should be", a point neatly encapsulated in his chapter-heading, "All the News that Fits We Print".

George Russell (AE) was a more literary editor and was entrusted with Joyce's manuscripts when he first left Ireland for Paris in 1904. Later in that year Joyce sent Russell the first hundred pages of *Stephen Hero* and, in response to an appeal from Russell, he wrote "The Sisters", the beginning of the creation of *Dubliners,* for publication in *The Irish Homestead* on August 13. Famously, he declined to sign it, according to Stanislaus because he was ashamed of publishing in "the pigs' paper", and it appeared, instead, over the pseudonym of "Stephen Daedalus". The story was one of a series under the heading "Our Weekly Story". These stories did not actually appear in the magazine every week but other offerings in the series include romantic love stories and comic accounts of country life. Joyce may well have felt uncomfortable in this company, but his desire to be read - always, according to Richard Ellmann (*James Joyce,* 2nd edition, 1993), greater than he would have admitted - overcame his distaste. "Eveline" appeared in September and "After the Race" in December. However, so many complaints were received that the editor of the day, W. H. Norman, asked for further instalments to be deferred and, in the event, they never appeared.

Founded in 1895, *The Irish Homestead* was primarily designed as an agricultural journal. Before becoming his own editor in 1905 Russell wrote articles about co-operative banking and on Tolstoy's relations with the Russian peasantry. He sought to combine capitalist individualism with socialist brotherhood. In September 1900, "Our Cycle Expert and the Gaelic Revival" mocked the ghost of George Moore's support for the Gaelic language: "Ye are only to use the Saxon when ye are feeding pigs or the like. It is not the policy of the Gaelic League that it is fit for more." Many issues of *The Irish Homestead* in this period have little or no literary material. However, the one for June 4 1904, in addition to the usual agricultural topics, includes (reinforcing the "pigs' paper" soubriquet) an article on developments in the Irish bacon industry. It also has a sympathetic review of a village hall concert in Kinnity, together with a sentimental poem of exile, starting

Take a blessing from my heart to the land of Ireland,
The fair fields of Ireland O!

At this stage of its development *The Irish Homestead* appears to take literature lightly, but later, when Russell was personally responsible as editor, it devoted considerable space to original writing and to reviews.

Shamrock, a story magazine lasting for more than fifty years (1866-1922) is wholly devoted to entertainment. It is printed cheaply on poor quality paper, and has a populist nationalist tone. The issue for June 11 2004 opens with a serial story about loveable rascals, including Mick McQuaid, a former gombeen man who, is the confederate of a smuggler named (surely coincidentally) Jack Joyce. There are romances, such as "What a Kiss Did", "Two Roses" and "A Bride's Secret". Between the stories are "filler" items designed to fill up vacant spaces in the columns, typically comic verses or solemn aphorisms. Leopold Bloom recalls, in "Ithaca" that he submitted his first piece of original verse, written at age 11, to a competition run by the *Shamrock*. There is a biographical piece about Miss O'Neill (later Lady Wroxham Beecher) an actress said to have rivalled Mrs. Siddons and to have partnered Keane in *Macbeth* in a performance attended by Maria Edgeworth. The tone of these contributions is nostalgic, playing to a stereotypical romantic Ireland. It is intriguing to speculate about the likely readership. Perhaps there is a clue in the presence at the back of this issue of a series of advertisements giving the dates of Civil Service Examinations, offering coaching services for them and also advertising clerkships in the Guinness brewery and in the offices of the Great Southern and Western Railway. Could the magazine, perhaps, have been catering to the potential clerks' *mothers*?

Another popular offering is the *Dublin Penny Journal*, according to Tom Clyde, "a lightweight production" – which is certainly true of its literary content. Its cultural ambitions have, however, a wider scope. The issue for June 11 1904 has much antiquarian material, such as an account of Athcarne castle, a report of an academic lecture on the whereabouts of Tom Moore's first editions, and an excerpt from a history of the O'Hanlon clan. There are translations from Hungarian and Romany love poems and there is a "weekly story" of a romantic kind. It also has edifying articles about scientific topics, including part of a lecture by the late Isaac Butt, deploring the rise of Darwinism, and a technical description of the workings of submarine mines. The *Dublin Penny Journal* mixes the tradition of the self-improvement magazine with that of nationalist popular journalism. It is far more demanding than *The Shamrock* and seems to be aimed at an unusual audience combining limited educational attainments with quite sophisticated interests and aspirations.

Standish O'Grady's *All Ireland Review,* was dominated by its mercurial editor, a high proportion of its material being contributed by him personally. O'Grady was intent on wide coverage. A single issue contains, for example, articles on "The Land Conference", on "Irish Literature and Literatures", a memoir of Dublin's streets, an account of the fundamental laws of Ireland, a study of surnames, and a mythological excursus on the "Classic Gods of Ireland". There are readers' letters and dissenting comment from the editor. Despite his "high nonsensical words", as Yeats recalled them, O'Grady was a formative figure in the genesis of the literary revival. *The United Irishman,* in its June 11 1904 issue, remarks caustically that Standish O'Grady's historical work is "amusing and delightful", because "replete with ignorance". W. J. McCormack

(*From Burke to Beckett,* 1994) derides his literary criticism as "a comic failure". O'Grady's puff for Eustace Gildea's novel, *Foughilotra,* serialised in the magazine in 1904 and described by him in a special note as "the greatest Irish story product me-day", does rather bear this judgement out. However, the *All Ireland Review* also gave space to distinguished critics such as T. W. Rolleston, AE, Yeats, Lady Gregory, John Eglinton (W. K. Magee), Stopford Brooke and Dowden and thereby adequately redeemed the balance.

Arthur Griffith, the editor of *The United Irishman,* was annoyed by James Joyce's unsigned review of the patriotic poems of William Rooney (for the much-derided *Daily Express* in December 1902). So much so, indeed, that he pointedly used Joyce's phrase about patriotism – "those big words that make us so unhappy" - derisively in Griffith's advertisement for Rooney's book. Joyce defiantly gives Stephen the same expression in "Nestor". Bloom comments, in "Eumaeus", recalling the breaking of *United Ireland's* presses by Parnell's supporters, that the adjective "United" is "a by no means [...] appropriate appellative". In 1904 *The United Irishman* was in competition (especially with *The Leader*) for the nationalist constituency and also saw itself threatened in a different way by *Dana*, the new monthly, edited by two of its own former contributors Frederick Ryan and John Eglinton. By 1906 Joyce thought that *The United Irishman* was the only journal of any merit in Ireland, still arguing, however, that much of its material was absurd, "educating the people of Ireland on the old pap of racial hatred." Bloom is said by John Wyse in "Cyclops" to have given Griffith the idea "to put in his paper all kinds of jerrymandering, packed juries and swindling the taxes off of the government and appointing consuls all over the world to walk about selling Irish industries".

The United Irishman for June 11 1904 shows Griffith in typically combative mode in the "All Ireland" editorial column. He deplores the discrimination implied in the be-flagging of Ireland for the King's visit but not for the *feiseanna* held in Waterford, Killea and Tuam. Lady Carina's dancers betray her ascendancy origins: they represent "the worst kind of stage Irishmen". Griffith also finds much to disagree with in the second number of *Dana:* John M. Robertson's article betrays his Protestant prejudices; AE, O'Grady (as we have seen earlier) and Frederick Ryan all produce criticisms of Irish life that are likely to be much resented. In characteristically nationalist vein, this issue of *The United Irishman* continues a series on the ballad history of Ireland, celebrates the triumph of Hungarian nationalism some thirty years before and praises the work of the Gaelic League in relation to the Irish language. The editor deplores the appointment of an ex-sergeant of the British army to the Dublin Corporation and anticipates his factional support for the conduct of soldiers in O'Connell Street.

Daniel Moran's *The Leader* had a special place in the affections of Irish Ireland. Moran argued that in the interests of national unity the people must "go back to their national traditions, get permeated with their own literature, create a drama, resurrect their customs [...]," inaugurating a discourse of exclusivity that was later to be further elaborated by Daniel Corkery. In its pursuit of an authentic Irish culture *The Leader* does not spare Irish society from the lash any more than Joyce did. In its first number it asserts that:

> This is not a country inhabited solely by injured saints, and it will be part of our business to point out the many respects in which we are a nation of unsuccessful fools.

The issue for June 11 1904 urges support for Irish manufacturers, including starch, aerated waters and coffins, to the extent of identifying unscrupulous shopkeepers from Cork who display exclusively Irish wares in their windows but sell inferior British equivalents inside the shop. The Newcastle West Orchestral Society's concert is attacked for playing to stereotypes:

> The orchestra played "Coonland" [...] and probably Newcastle West would survive if the orchestra went to Coonland and stayed there.

Sir Horace Plunkett's book on the economy is criticised for its assertion that Catholicism is hostile to progress and is "anti-economic". Later issues of *The Leader* become especially concerned with the importation of "dirty periodicals". Moran advocates the use of the criminal law and welcomes the statement of the Dublin Vigilance Committee that it "had been instrumental in reshipping back to England some tons of filthy literature that had been imported into this country." Doubtless this would have included *Tit-Bits.*

Tit-Bits for June 11 1904 is, as it happens, not particularly lubricious. It has numbers of lame jokes, often class-based put-downs, including one Bloom may have taken to heart - about a gentleman who belongs "in the misfit department". He might, however, have been cheered by an article about "Aliens who have done England a Good Turn", including Disraeli, the Rothschilds and Ernest Cassell. The sexiest items in this issue are an account of Mrs. Melba's luxurious bed and an advertisement for "Domen belts and Belt Corsets, designed to give *Comfort* and *Support* and an *Elegant Figure* to those inclined to *Corpulency*", illustrated by a drawing that bears some resemblance to descriptions of Molly.

I now want to turn to the second group of journals, those with substantially greater intellectual ambitions, catering for the devotees of high culture. In 1904 John Eglinton who edited *Dana* with Frederick Ryan, refused the first version of *Portrait of an Artist*, telling Joyce; "I can't print what I don't understand." In the "Lestrygonians" episode "John Eclecticon" tells Stephen that "you are the only contributor to *Dana* that asks for pieces of silver". The June 1904 issue is liberal in tone: the editors print a criticism of their earlier articles about Catholicism in Ireland, but reply to it thus:

> In the interests of "mental efficiency" a man may properly criticise a belief or policy which he regards as wholly false or vicious. The conditions are that he shall be courteous, that he shall never substitute abuse for argument, and that he shall fairly listen and give publicity to the opinions he criticises. That certainly is the ideal of *Dana*.

Dana regularly questioned the terms of discourse in contemporary Ireland. The magazine attacked over generalisations, hypocritical pietism ("we are not all saints but we all have to behave as if we were") and nationalist truculence ("the belligerent expression of opinion") alike. F. M. Atkinson's contributions, "A Literary Causerie" displayed enthusiasm for other literary publications, such as *Ulad* and *Samhain*. In its brief life (1904-5) - according to Joyce's friend Francis Sheehy-Skeffington - *Dana* "pricked the bubble of the Gaelic Leaguers". Joyce would have found much to empathise with in *Dana's* key ideas, though his omni-present sense of the ridiculous surfaced in relation to the literary solemnity he associated with Yeats.

Tom Clyde (*Irish Literary Magazines*, 2003) points out that Yeats's magazine, *Samhain* (1901-8), was well established by 1904 as the platform of the Irish Literary Theatre. Its expensive and stylish presentation marks its links to modernism. The strategy of printing the texts of plays such as *Cathleen ni Houlihan* or *Riders to the Sea* mark it as more distinctively literary than most other magazines discussed here. The September 1903 issue has a pencil sketch by AE of Augusta Gregory. Joyce offended Lady Gregory by his hostile 1902 review of her *Poets and Dreamers* in the *Dublin Daily Express* in March 1902. Buck Mulligan tells Stephen that "Longworth [editor of the *Dublin Daily Express*] is awfully sick about what you wrote about that old hake, Gregory". Mulligan goes on to tease Stephen about his inability to display the graceful "Yeats touch". Yeats's recognition of the need for tact does appear conspicuously in *Samhain,* for example in an article about the reform of the theatre, where he describes his wish to become "the rough and ready conscience of the newspaper or the pulpit in a matter so delicate and difficult as literature." Yug Mohit Chaudry points out that Yeats's diplomacy could tip over into manipulation as he collaborated with editors "with a view to the given political situation and the sensibilities of his intended readership." This emphasis on stylish and topical presentation of literary and especially theatrical material also appears in *Uladh,* the first Northern Irish literary magazine of the century. Bloom would have had to wait until November 1904 to see the first issue in its distinctive brown cover, featuring a Celtic warrior attended by an Athene figure. *Uladh's* declared style was "more satiric than poetic" and it aimed to keep the young men of Ulster from "the sloblands of American or English language work."

In 1904 Joyce was still engaged with his difficult relations with *St. Stephens,* the University College magazine. *St. Stephens* had refused to publish his iconoclastic essay, "The Day of the Rabblement," in 1901 on the grounds of its inclusion of a brief reference to the indexed *Fuoco* by D'Annunzio. Following the article's private publication alongside a feminist broadside by Frank Skeffington, *St. Stephens* then prophesied that its writer would have nothing but "ill success". This did not stop the magazine publishing Joyce's paper for the Dublin University Literary and Historical Society on James Clarence Mangan in May 1902, after it had been praised by the *Freeman's Journal.* In June 1904 *St. Stephens* took a liberal view on many topics. It expressed interest in new journals such as the *Irish University Advocate,* produced for medical specialists and *The Cross,* a Canadian review praised for simultaneously fighting Protestant intolerance and Catholic abstentionism. The editors of *St. Stephens* remark that "it might have been written in Dublin." The tone of the journal's literary criticism is represented by its assertion that Wordsworth's "Ode on Intimations" makes one "mildened and purified." It admires the "grotesque humour" of Richard Dalton Williams , the founder of *The Irish Tribune* in 1848, and publishes complaints from "Una" about the "woeful lack of anything like a University life" in the Ladies' Colleges.

Dublin University was the original sponsor of *The New Ireland Review.* This was originally founded in1858 as *The Atlantis* and later continued as *The Lyceum.* In all its guises the magazine, sub-titled "A Catholic Magazine of Social, Agrarian and Literary Interest", was relentlessly serious, aiming "to promote a higher Catholic literature, and to discuss questions of scientific and literary interest from the Catholic point of view."The magazine married nationalism to Catholic feeling and published the powerful political essays by Daniel Moran which were to be collected in 1905 as his influential *The Philosophy of Irish Ireland.* The June 1904 issue runs to more than two hundred and fifty pages. The opening article by George D. Clancy about the unfairness of the current tax regime and the failure to distinguish between earned and unearned income might have intrigued Bloom, who muses in "Lestrygonians" on the best way of painlessly supporting poor children out of taxes. Anticipating the tone of de Valera's St. Patrick's Day broadcast some forty years later, Elion McGregor writes of a vision of the rebirth of a people:

> grandsires, grandmothers; men and women in the prime of life; young men and maidens; happy laughing little children, all wearing alike an air of sober earnestness that denoted no ordinary purpose, no mere intent on pleasure.

Haines, the Oxford Englishman who went off to Gill's to buy Hyde's *Lovesongs of Connaught,* might possibly have also wanted to read the translations of the same writer's *The Religious Songs of Connaught*, serialised at length in *The New Ireland Review* over the whole of 1904. *The New Ireland Review* set a high tone for Catholic discourse at the turn of the century.

In this it was not alone. *The Irish Monthly Magazine,* almost as venerable, enters in July 1873, according to its first editor, the temperance campaigner Father Matthew Russell, "on the discharge of its holy functions as a memorial and remembrancer of that national consecration [...] devoted to the service of Faith and Fatherland." Originally concentrating on Catholic apologetics and discussion of Catholic social policy, it soon became more literary, publishing writers such as Katherine Tynan, Kickham and Mangan. By June 1904, however, it had moved down market, becoming significantly less heavy-weight than *The New Ireland Review.* It still carries some serious reviews and articles, such as a plea for more equal rights for women, together with some middle-brow stories - but it also prints some truly dreadful doggerel verse, the nadir of which, by a poet simply designated as "W. A," commences, without apparent irony

> I've a darling little chum
> Sweet as any sugar plum...

These Catholic magazines were the forerunners of twentieth-century religious periodicals, such as the Jesuit magazine, *Studies,* the sociological journal *Christus Rex* and the *Capuchin Annual*, a miscellany which mixed wholesome entertainment with serious commentaries.

In the introduction to her book of essays, *Ideals in Ireland* (1901), Lady Gregory identifies three categories of Irish citizen: "the baker", who "has all the virtues of the peaceful citizen"; the "butcher", whose sectarianism "separates Trinity College from Ireland"; and the "candlestick-maker" who is an idealist and a seer. The first two groups are loftily excluded from serious discourse: "they have their newspapers, where all who desire may see their views and the views they attribute to each other." Among the makers of candlesticks, however, she numbers the contributors to her current volume, including Daniel Moran, W. B. Yeats, George Russell, and Standish O'Grady. All these, except the last, worked as editors of journals that feature in this article. In these essays, as in their periodicals, they explored the key themes and issues associated with the literary revival that dominated Irish production at the turn of the century. These include many of the concepts that preoccupied Joyce and that are simultaneously celebrated and subverted in *Ulysses. Ideals in Ireland* proclaims the triumph of cultural nationalism and links it to future political developments. Russell argues that, in order to fulfil his idealistic belief that "an aristocracy of lordly and chivalrous heroes is bound in time to create a great democracy by the reflection of their character in the mass" it is necessary for Ireland to reject English imperialism. Moran contests the importation of cheap English periodicals and the "increasing and spirit wearying flow of romances" in the penny magazines. Yeats believes that the current massive increase in books and journals on Irish subjects "will bring a new national agreement, and the political tumult [will] arise again." All these writers are striving for the attention of new audiences for their work.

Joep Leerssen (*Remembrance and Imagination,* 1996) has credited Joyce with rejecting Ireland's "ingrained discourse of marginality". These magazines are, on the other hand, much preoccupied with national as against international events. In 1904 world-wide reactions against imperialist ambitions were reflected in many global conflicts, including the Russian- Japanese war, the Sumatran rebellion against the Dutch and the Tibetan uprising against the British as well as in Casement's sensational report on the Congo. Few of these world events found much space in the Irish journals of the day and some of Joyce's scepticism about the role of journalism may have been occasioned by the relative provinciality of the publications. But, to counter these criticisms, Francis Phelan, in his unpublished dissertation from University College Dublin ("Aspects of National Literature in the *United Irishman* and other Periodicals of the Anglo-Irish Literary Revival", 1996) has described "the spectacular burst of magazines and newspapers of real merit" that originated in the period between 1899 and 1906 and has shown how new readerships within Ireland were much stimulated by these productions. *The Irish Homestead's* earnest efforts to improve agriculture and national culture simultaneously, the antiquarian material in the *Dublin Penny Journal*, the trenchant social observation of *Dana,* the theatrical criticism and dramatic material in *Samhain* and *Ulad,* all sought to engage a wider constituency for a heady mix of nationalism and intellectual expansion. O'Grady, according to Lady Gregory, "holds up his torch in the dusky chamber where the gentry of Ireland have lain through their hundred years' sleep."

On the other side of the rhetorical balance lie, ironically, Moran's own sectarianism in *The Leader,* the pugnacious polemic of Griffith, the stereotypes of *Shamrock,* and the apologetics of the Catholic journals. Doubtless some of these publications were influenced by economic considerations, especially the search for advertising and the associated need for a popular market. According to Jurgen Habermas (*The Structural Transformation of the Public Sphere*, 1992) this was a period when the market for cultural goods was expanding rapidly and the transition between products previously confined to cultural élites and those taking more commodified forms was creating incompatible strains in literary society. Habermas fears the breakdown of audiences into minorities serving uncritical mass readerships. The intertextual awareness of these Irish publications, however, actually seems to me to have served the cause of dissent and dialogue. The evidence of the embattled editorial exchanges between *Dana* and *The United Irishman* or the supportive relation between *The Leader* and the *New Ireland Review* speaks of an engaged public sphere where the parties eschew tepid neutrality and set about the issues. These battles of the periodical books may have been rather less physically threatening than those between Bloom and the Citizen in "Cyclops". However, the tensions in that episode between the one-eyed worldview of blatant nationalism and the binocular vision of tolerant liberalism were also played out in the pages of contemporary periodicals.

Francis Phelan observes, at the outset of his dissertation on turn-of-the-century journals, that "the footsteps of Leopold Bloom across Dublin [...] are annually trodden by an army of scholars seeking for epiphanies, while nearby, in the National Library, lie periodicals and newspapers relatively neglected." I have tried here to place some of these periodical ephemera in the context of the week-to-week experience of literary journalism in James Joyce's time. Joyce was, himself, sufficiently sentimental about his own career in this field to work into *Ulysses* a passing reference to *The Irish Beekeeper,* of which journal, according to Richard Ellmann, he was the assistant editor for a grand total of twenty- four hours during December 1903. Stephen Dedalus, in "The Wandering Rocks,"wanders down Bedford row and, is offered the "tattered pages" of *The Irish Beekeeper* for two pence – such being the typical deflation of journalistic endeavour. I have, I fear, like O'Molloy, failed to mention *Paddy Murphy's Budget, Pue's Occurrences* or, indeed, the *Skibereen Eagle* with its legendary watchful eye on the Tsar of Russia. But I hope that the coverage of the penny press and its more prestigious sixpenny rivals in the Dublin of 1904 will have persuaded the reader to excuse these egregious omissions.

Malcolm Ballin, a literary scholar, is a Research Fellow at the University of Cardiff in Wales.

DÁNTA ÓN FHRAINC

Michael Davitt
(1950-2005)

Ar fán in iardheisceart na Fraince.

AN APPRECIATION

For more than three decades Michel Davitt was a luminous presence, a liberating force in Irish language poetry. A tuned-in, amped-up, street-wise cosmopolitan, he set the fads, the lingo, the stances. For a lot of us who took to poetry in the seventies, he was the rather raffish, maverick lyric tenor of our bohemian rhapsody. We adored the sounds he made; the jazzy urgency of his style that made Gaelic go bebop in the night with a swinging, snazzy self-confidence. It was compelling stuff: funky, defiant and free.

Davitt was a child of the sixties, a freewheelin' follower of the new vision, a believer in that costumed counter-culture that put a rosy glow in the mind and a rainbow show in the wardrobe. He brought all of that expanded mind-exuberance to bear on the writing of poetry in the Irish language.

In the early seventies he took us out in the carefree caravan of his poetry to a lovely mellow-yellow domain somewhere between Dylan and Dún Caoin.

In recent years the creative flow showed no signs of abatement. The poems kept on coming, as fresh as ever in their urgency and utterance, their stylistic assurance, their rhapsodic sonority. Lately, in poems that are pitched skillfully between plainness and a pulsating lyricism, he speaks with the persuasive powers and the passionate authority of a great poet. These are richly human poems brought back from the edge of the abyss, from a zone of fear and desperation. They are poems of bewildered tenderness, poignant attempts to make sense of the world's grief and the soul's despair.

Michael Davitt, more than anybody else, has been responsible for the remarkable renaissance of Irish language poetry in our times. His is an eloquent achievement, a merging of the old and the new in a triumphant synthesis.

He was an audacious pioneer, a latter-day Johnny Appleseed, scattering seeds out there in the still-uncharted territories of Gaelic poetry. Gúrú maith agat, Michael. "On apple-bright September mornings," we will all benefit from those flourishing seeds you sowed.

Ba i nGort A Choirce a casadh Michael Davitt orm den chead uair. Maidin Domhnaigh a bhí ann, bhí mé thíos sa tsráidbhaile le paipéirí an Dhomhnaigh a cheannacht. Fad is a bhíodh an sagart ag léamh an Aifrinn bhíonnse ag léamh na bpaipéirí. Tá ár mbealaigh féin again uilig leis an bhriathar Diaga a chomóradh is a cheiliúradh. Bhí mé ar mo bhealach chun an Ostáin le beart nuachtáin faoi m'ascaill nuair a tchím ag teacht chugam é ar an chosán; fadchosach, catach, a cheann "lán de chasadh na Gráige", b'fhéidir, nó ag cur thar maoil le Dylan.

Bhí sé i gceannas ar *Eachtra*, cúrsa amuigh faoin spear a bhí a reachtáil ag Gael Linn an Samhradh sin sa Cheardscoil I nGort A' Choirce. Bhí aithne shúl agam air, dar ndóighe, ó ghrianghrafanna sna h-irisí ach ní fhaca mé riamh ina bheatha é go dtí an mhaidin chinniúnach úd agus é ag siúil chugam go grástúil, é ard, aigeanta, ainglí. Aisteach go leor lig mé do siúil tharam gan gíog nó míóg a ligean asam. Bhí m'anáil I mbéal mo ghoib le faitíos. Bhí glas na heagla ar mo theangaidh agus mé I láthair mo laoch, mo ghile mear. Bhí faitíos orm, go ndeirfeadh sé "But it ain't me, babe; no, no, no, it ain't me, babe, it ain't me you're looking for, babe".

Cúpla bliain ina dhiaidh sin chuir muid aithne ar a chéile agus is I meadaíocht agus I mbuaine a chuaigh ár ndaimh le himeacht na mblianta. Is mór an briseadh croí domh a bhás ro-thobann, Dia go deo leat, a thaiscigh.

Ma b'iad an Riardánach, an Direánach agus Máire Mhac an tSaoi a thug filíocht na Gaeilge – an tSeanbhean Bhocht – isteach sa fichiú haois, b'iad bunadh *Inntí* agus Davitt ach go háirithe a chuir coiriú na seascaidí uirthi. Thug sé dathanna niamhracha amach as *wardrobe* a aigne agus ghléas sé go barr na méar í. Chuir sé ag caitheamh "*cannabis*" í. Chuir sé an ceol aríst ina cuislí.

Mar atá ráite ag Seán Ó Tuama b'é Michael Davitt an "*Pied Piper*," ruaig sé luchóga móra an leadráin as Hamlyn na hÉigse agus ansin mheall sé an t-aos óg dána siar go Dún Caoin – *Haight Ashburg* na Gaeilge. Thaispeáin sé dúinn an dóigh leis an dán a thabhairt ó leibhéal go leibhéal" agus chonaic muid le soineantacht súilfhoscailte an linbh "an oíche ag titim gleann ar ghleann"

Tógadh Michael Davitt le béarla ach bhí an ghaeilge ar a thoil aige. Thuig sé thar aon duine eile an dóigh a bhfuil an dá theanga ag coraíocht le chéile inar n-aigne. Thuig sé go rímhaith scitsifréine teanga ghleann seo na nGealt agus bhain sé leas chruthaitheach as an choimhlint sin chun scóip na teanga a shíneadh. Thuig sé go raibh teorainneacha úra teanga le trasna again, *frontiers* nua le aimsiú again I ngaeilge. Sé atá ina dhánta féin I ndairíre na pictúirí de Oileán Úr a shamhlaíocht.

Tá sé ar shiúil uainn chun na síoraíochta agis is mór ár gcaill. Ní deora atá de dhiobháil air lena chaoineadh, lena cheiliúradh ach dánta. Cloisim é ag rá liom I nGaeilge gan chaim …

Dá bhféadfainn breith ar mo hata
Atá Caite i mbéal geata
Ní bheifeá ag sá do shúl
Chomh sotalach síos im anam dorcha

Cathal Ó Searcaigh

AN SIOC

do Ghabriel Fitzmaurice

Cad eile 'bheadh uaim sa tsaol:
cead teachta is imeachta
gan aird ar éinne

is an oíche ag titim le faobhar
is an sioc ag tuirlingt ón spéir
is an fuacht ag crapadh na réalt?

Cad eile 'bheadh uaim sa tsaol:
bheith neadaithe isteach
fé charn blaincéadaí

is an sioc amuigh ina shuí
is an fuacht ag siúl timpeall an tí?
Cad eile 'bheadh uaim sa tsaol:

muga breá tae le héirí gréine
is canta aráin agus im air
agus subh bhreá mhilis shú craobh

is an dúthaigh chomh bán le heala
is an lá chomh cruaidh le speal
is an intinn chomh geal is chomh géar?

Mí na Nollag 2004

DÉIRC

do Mhoira

Níor leor na silíní fiáine chun ár sciúch a fhliuchadh tar éis uair an
chloig
de shiúlóid i mbeirfean an mheán lae. Bhí braoinín uisce uainn go géar.

Seana-bhean de dhéine shéimh Pheig Sayers
fé chruitín údarásach a d'oscail doras ársa an tí feirme *Gasconne*.

An mbeadh *un verre d'eau* aici? Bheadh agus bucaod!
is d'iompaigh sí láithreach uainn i dtreo fhionnuaire chrón na cistine.

An mar seo a bhí le déircínteacht fadó? Gan aon éileamh mór a dhéanamh
ach a bheith i láthair in am an ghátair agus an chruinne ag athroinnt a coda?

Ar nós an tseana-fhráma rothair leis an leathroth búclálta
a bhronn m'athair ar an dtincéir mná mar aon le púnt siúicre,

is chuimhníos im gharsún gurb shin an fáth go mbíonn seana-fhrámaí rothair
ann
is gurbh shin an chiall go ndeintear rothaí a bhúcláil.

D'fhill bean an uisce gan mhoill le crúiscín lán na déirce agus dhá ghloine
á rá go mbeadh a thuilleadh is a thuilleadh ann dúinn dá mba ghá.

Agus fíon fuar an tobair bheannaithe ag beannú ár scornacha
sheas ár seana-bhean i mbéal an dorais–

a haoibh roicneach ag lonrú as an scáil
fé mar gu'b'í féin a bhí ag fáil na déirce ón mbeirt thincéir.

Lahas, 16 – 6 - 2005

Sleachta as an tsraith

SEIMEING SOIR

Ar fán in iardheisceart na Fraince

I

Tar éis dúinn seachtain
a thabhairt i seanmhuileann gaoithe
Leboulin, ar an ard idir

dhá ghort lusanna gréine,
nuair a dhúisímid ar maidin
bíonn ár gceann lán

de thimpeall éigin,
ár súile breac le baill bheaga bhuí.
Go moch maidin inniu

tá bús na n-éan fén ndíon
mar a bheadh sé á mheilt chugainn
go mall mín.

IV

I gceantar farraige Corbières,
neadaithe as radharc na dtránna
na n-eitleog is na *surfboards*,

sráidbhaile grianthuartha
aon-óstáin, glan amach
as *Film Noire*,

Maison Maître de chuid lucht ceannais
na bhfíonghort tráth,
a iompaíodh ina *Hôtel*.

Cónraí donndubha an troscán.
Na scáthláin Gotach.
As Islington do bhean a' tí.

As an mBronx dá fear, Fred.
"Strange people in this village.
In-bred!"

I dtaise na hoíche meirbhe
ár n-allas araon
ina aon allas amháin.

Laistíos dínn sa tsráid
Fraincis argotique na ndéagóirí,
a gcuid scútar ina mbeacha mire

síos suas.
Ar maidin triúr seana-shaighdiúirí
ag filleadh ón m*Boulangerie*

lena gcuid raidhfilí aráin.
Seasann tamall fénár bhfuinneoig thíos
i ndianchomhrá. Catalóinis.

VIII

Ón mbialann *terasse*,
fairim na *SDF*
istigh fé Phont Neuf,

iad umhaithe, leathbhogaithe;
gruaig chac capaill,
féachaint i bhfad ó bhaile

sna súile acu. Slataire dorcha
is fainge fionn gléigeal
ag diúl aon bhuidéil amháin;

scaoinse de ghadhar clamhach
ar téid ag umhlú rompu
ina mbruachbhaile cois Garonne.

Sé seo mo bhruachsa leis
ó scaoileas mo ghreim.
Níl de dhifear ach an *grand café crème*.

SDF: Sans Domicile Fixé

XIX

Ansan fuaireas jab
in institiúid oideachais *continue*
ag teagasc *Flamenco*.

Toisc ná fuil
aon chur amach agam
ar *Fhlamenco* thugas liom

cúpla feadóg stáin
agus bhí *Roddy McCorley*
ag a bhformhór laistigh de dhá lá.

Ansan thugas cúpla véarsa
den Amhrán Bréagach dóibh.
Seanbhean ina measc

de chuid Ariège thabharfá
an Leabhar gurbh í Máire Áine í
á rá, an tslí a deireadh sí

"Chonaic mé roc i gcluais goirt
's é ag bleán na bó,"
óna croí glan amach.

Nuair a theastaigh
ceol giotáir uathu
sheinneas leagan den Bhínsín Luachra

dhóibh á rá gur seancheol
de chuid Andalusia a bhí ann.
Nuair a theastaigh cúpla

steip *Flamenco* uathu
dheineamar seit le tionlacan portaireachta,
meascán de sheit

Chúl an Bhuacaigh
agus seit Na Machairí.
Cé d'aithneodh an difríocht?

Tráthnóntaí meirbhe
d'fágaimis an *salle de classe*
inár ndiaidh is théimís

ag spaisteoireacht cois locha,
nó sa choill, is chuireamar
aithne ar an iora rua

is ar an bhfia
is mhalartaíomar scéalta
áiféiseacha i dtaobh pleidhcí

gan fuaimint mar sinn fhéin.
Má chuaigh dian orthu
foghraíocht na ndúthaí thiar,

a thabhairt leo,
thugadar leo le fonn
tuiscintí ní ba luachmhaire fós,

ina measc, gur ceirín
don uile chréacht
an greann.

XX

Eadrainn na driseacha
uile casáin:
tír, tonn, tráthchlár.

Fáiscim tuilleadh
caiféine as taemhála
idir cipín plaisteach

agus taobh cupáin.
Tugaim claonfhéachaint
eile ar scáileán:

an t-árthach
tuirlingthe le fada
gan aon tásc fós ort.

Lasmuigh de *Phorte* 7
iliomad cineál taistealaí
tharam gan sos

ag brú trucailí rompu,
daoine ag breith ar a chéile
go golbhéarach.

B'in uaim tú ag sméideadh?
De gheit tá ár súile
i rádar a chéile.

Níl de dhris chasáin
anois eadrainn ach dris
an ghrá.

2004

THE FROST

What more could I want in life:
to come and go
whenever I choose

as the edgy night comes down
and frost spreads over the ground
and the stars are shrunk by the cold.

What more could I want in life:
to nestle in
under a pile of blankets

as the frost sits down outside
and the cold walks over the floor?
What more could I want in life:

a mug of strong tea at break of day
and a thick cut of buttered toast
sweetened with rasberry jam

and the country is white as a swan
and the day as hard as a scythe
and the mind is as sharp and as bright?

Translated by the author.

ALMS

for Moira

They simply weren't enough to slake our thirst, the wild cherries, after a
good hour
of walking in the oppressive midday heat. We badly needed a drink of water.

An old Gascon woman with something of Peig Sayers' good-humoured
harshness
under her worldly-wise hunch opened the door of the farmhouse.

Did she have *un verre d'eau*? A glass? Why not a bucket?
And she immediately turned away from us towards the kitchen, cool and
copper-coloured.

Might this have been how almsgiving once was? Not responding to some huge
demand
but being available as the need arose and the universe dealt its hand.

As when my father gave the tinker woman an old bike-frame with a buckled
wheel, along with a pound of sugar,

so that, as a boy, I thought that's why old bike-frames were in the world at all
and why there were such things as buckled wheels.

The woman of the house was suddenly back with a jug of alms
and two glasses, saying there was plenty more where that came from.

And as cold wine from a holy well blessed our throats
the old woman herself now filled the door mouth,

her smile a bright wrinkle
from the shadows, as if she had somehow been given alms by a couple of
tinkers.

Translated, from the Irish, by Paul Muldoon.

From SEIMEING SOIR

Wandering in the south of France

I

After a week
living in the old windmill
Leboulin, on the slope between

two fields of sunflowers,
our heads were thrumming
when we woke each morning

to do the rounds,
our eyes speckled with yellow flecks:
and early this morning

the birds chirped under the eaves
as if chipping towards us
slow and fine.

IV

In the coastal district of the Corbières
nestled out of view of the beaches
the kites and the surfboards,

a sunbleached village
one inn, straight out of
a *Film Noire*,

a Big House belonging
to the vineyard bosses
refurbished as an *Hôtel*.

Brownblack coffins of furniture.
Gothic screens.
The woman of the house from Islington.

Fred, her husband from the Bronx.
"Strange people in this village.
In-bred!"

In the heart of the sultry night
our sweats mingle
into one single sweat.

Below us in the street
the argot of the teenagers,
bee swarm of their scooters

up and down.
In the morning three old soldiers,
returning from the *Boulangerie*

with their rifles of bread,
stand to attention below our window,
intently talking. Catalans.

VIII

From the restaurant *terasse*
I watch the clochards
beneath the Pont Neuf,

weatherbeaten, halfcut,
hair the colour of horseshit,
a homeless look

in their eyes. A dark urchin
and a lanky whiteskinned stripling
sucking from one bottle;

a scrawny mongrel
on a rope, submitting to them
on this, their riverbank home by the Garonne.

And this too is my bank
since I let drift.
The only differ, my *grand café crème*.

XIX

Then I got a job
in an Adult Education Institute
teaching *Flamenco*.

Because
I knew damn all about
Flamenco, I brought

a clutch of tinwhistles
and most of them had *Roddy McCorley*
within a couple of days.

Then I gave them a couple of verses
of the Bragging Song.
An old one among them

from Ariège you would swear
she was Máire Áine
chanting the way she used to sing

"I saw a pleat in the ear of a field
and her milking a cow,"
from the heart straight out.

When they wanted
guitar music
I played some Kerry Slides,

saying that it was
the old music of Andalusia.
When they wanted to learn a couple

of *Flamenco* steps,
we danced a set to lilting mouthmusic,
a mixture of

The Buckgoat's Hole
and the Maharees set dance.
Who would know the difference?

Sultry afternoons
we used leave the *salle de classe*
behind us and go

rambling by the lake,
or through the woods, and got to know
the red squirrel

and the wild deer
and we told outlandish
tales of fools

as daft as ourselves.
If it was hard for them
to fathom the pronunciation

of our places out west,
they eagerly picked up on
insights more valuable,

amongst them, that the best poultice
for every wound
is humour.

XX

Between us obstacles
at every hand's turn:
land, wave, timetable.

I squeeze more
caffeine from the teabag
between a plastic stalk

and the cup's side.
I throw another glance
at the board:

your vessel
has long since landed
and still no word.

Outside *Porte* 7
every sort of traveller
surges by without a halt

pushing trolleys;
people grasp each other,
sobbing.

Is that you beckoning?
Suddenly our eyes
become each other's radar.

No obstacles
between us now
but love's sweet thorn.

Seimeing: *a play-on-words involving the similar pronunciation of* chemin *(French for* road *or* path) *in both Irish and the Gascon dialect in the Southwest of France.* Soir: east *in Irish and* night *in French.*

Translated, from the Irish, by John Montague.

These poems are published courtesy of Moira Sweeney.

Michael Davitt was born in Cork in 1950. He took a degree in Celtic Studies at University College Cork, where he came under the influence of Seán Ó Riordáin, Seán Ó Riada and Seán Ó Tuama. In the early 1970s he founded the Irish language poetry journal Innti, *which published some of the early work of Liam Ó Muirthile, Nuala Ní Dhomhnaill and Gabriel Rosenstock. He was the author of nine collections of poetry, most recently* Seimeing Soir *(Coiscéim, 2004) and* Dánta: 1966-1998 *(Coiscéim, 2004). He died on 19 June 2005 in County Sligo after returning home from a period spent in Gascony, France, with his partner Moira Sweeney.*

Michael Davitt
Lahas, France
March 2005

A CIVILIZING PRESENCE

Ted Hickey

4 March 1940 – 5 September 2005

We have come here today to remember a much-loved friend and to celebrate the abundance of his life. Ted Hickey is with us in spirit. But we miss terribly his physical presence, the subtle understated way he would arrive at a poetry reading or a gallery opening; the nonchalant thoroughness with which he would network the room, making all sorts of connections, making things happen.

Ted used to say that "making things happen" was his particular gift. It was certainly *one* of his gifts. He would come up to you and say: "Wouldn't it be a good idea if … " And that's how I, for instance, got involved in readings at the Ulster Museum by writers such as Joseph Brodsky, Miroslav Holub, Ian McEwan. Ted enticed the legendary Joseph Beuys to Belfast for the now famous sessions in the Museum. He was the first to bring De Danaan north of the border – for £125, plus expenses!

In the early seventies Ted discovered some notebooks by the great Irish landscape painter Paul Henry and persuaded me to edit them and publish them with Blackstaff Press under the title *Further Reminiscences*, with a preface by Ted himself. (That's when I first got to know him well.) Again, Ted suggested to Pat Murphy that she read the diaries of Robert Emmett's housekeeper and make a film out of them – which she did and she gave us *Anne Devlin,* a marvellous film. Ted was so refined and so astute. This showed itself particularly in his encouragement of young artists: for many he arranged their first shows or their first readings. (Marina Warner recently told Nora Hickey that it was Ted who arranged her first reading – here in Belfast at the Ulster Museum.) Felim Egan, Stephen McKenna, Rachel Brown, Poncho Monreal are a few of the artists Ted supported in their early days – Jack Crabtree, David Crone, Jim Allen …

He organised a small show in the Queen's Senior Common Room for my daughter Sarah when she was still a student, and he continued to encourage her. So I know at first hand how enriching his engagement could be. How many openings did Ted miss? Very, very few. Hardly any. Indeed, although he was terribly ill, he attended the most recent opening at the Fenderesky Gallery last Wednesday.

As Keeper of Fine Art at the Ulster Museum Ted made some astute purchases: most of those works are now many times more valuable than they were when he acquired them on behalf of us all. And he made sure that key artists from our own community were represented in the Museum's collection and in other important public collections. After retirement Ted continued to steer private and institutional buyers in the direction of the artists he valued.

His own home is full of beautiful pictures. He had a superb eye.

As a fellow bureaucrat I sat on a few committees with Ted. The atmosphere became more good-natured and kind-hearted as soon as he turned up. He didn't speak unless he had something to say, and everything he said was relevant. There was no need for Ted to raise his voice, so he didn't. His very presence was a reproach to what is impoverished and unproductive in bureaucratic life. With Ted around there was less chance of being suffocated by the managerial ethos.

In the Authorised Version's translation of the Psalms there's a lovely recurring phrase that describes pretty well Ted Hickey's *modus operandi* – loving-kindness. For Ted there was a trinity of cares and attachments: his family and his friends and the arts.

Two days ago in the Hickey household I talked with his daughters. They said that absolutely nothing was missing when they were at home with their father: it was all happiness and fun. They would cherish for the rest of their lives his stories, and his songs, and his mimicry - his ability to adopt a different persona, to take on in his impersonation the whole mind-set of another human being and not just the lingo and the accent.

Ted was the adored only man in a house full of women. Yesterday evening I was overwhelmed to watch his coffin being carried down the aisle on the shoulders of six women – by Elizabeth and Helen, and by his four daughters – "my girls" as he dotingly referred to them.

The warmth of Ted's family life radiated outwards to those of us who are lucky enough to have been his friends. He was a very exceptional friend, the soul of generosity. He loved to bring together friends from different walks of life and from different times and places. His spirit was energised by these interconnections. His life was a tapestry of friendships. Those sweet lines by WB Yeats come to mind:

> Always we'd have the new friend meet the old
> And we are hurt if either friend seem cold …

Yes, we miss his physical presence. Ted was, shall we say, dentally disadvantaged. He struck you at first sight as being somewhat dishevelled. But then you noticed the original clothes – the leather hat, the classy tweeds, the trim waistcoat, the stylish neckwear. Ted was a rumpled man about a town, a tousled dandy. He was every inch an aesthete. He believed absolutely in the centrality of the arts in our lives, and that meant including the arts of the weaver and the knitter.

When you met Ted you met a complete person. His opinions were never second-hand. He made up his own mind about everything. And it was a brilliantly well-stocked mind. He was enormously well read, and relished keeping himself up to speed on contemporary Irish novels and poetry. I'm sure that most people here recall Ted recommending a book to them, sending them off with a reading list. Last week Ted was reading John McGahern's *Memoirs*.

Ted ran a traditional music club in the Queen's Senior Common Room for many years. Irish music was central to his life. He had a lovely light tenor voice. At the end of this service Elizabeth has arranged for us to hear, through the magic of recording, Ted singing "The Lass of Aughrim," his favourite song and a highlight in his favourite story, James Joyce's "The Dead".

Decades ago, when the brilliant archaeologist Tom Delaney died in his mid-thirties, Ted organised a memorial concert with a massive line-up of musicians, singers and poets. We should do something similar for Ted as a way of thanking him for making so many exciting and beautiful things happen. To quote the man himself, "Wouldn't it be a good idea if … ?" Yes, we owe him so much. Ted Hickey *was* civilisation.

This eulogy was delivered by Michael Longley at St Brigid's Church, Belfast, 8 September 2005.

AMONG OUR CONTRIBUTORS

Chris Agee / Gary Allen / Neal Ascherson / Eileen Battersby / Sven Birkerts Wendell Berry / John Burnside / Rachel Giese Brown / Angus Calder /Moya Cannon / Ciaran Carson / Harry Clifton / Patricia Craig / Andrew Crumey / Gerald Dawe / Michael Davitt / John F. Deane / Greg Delanty / Michael Donhauser / Hans Magnus Enzensberger / Brian Friel / John Gray / Eamon Grennan / Michael Hamburger / Francis Harvey / Seamus Heaney / Kathleen Jamie / Julia Kristeva / Helen Lewis / Michael Longley / Seán Lysaght / Deirdre Madden / Sarah Maguire / Fred Marchant / Enda McDonagh / Medbh McGuckian / Askold Melnyczuk / Samuel Menashe / John Minihan / Zakaria Mohammed / Alfonso Monreal / John Montague / Paul Muldoon / Nuala Ní Dhomhnaill / Micheál Ó Conghaile / Bernard O' Donoghue / Liam Ó Muirthile / Cathal Ó Searcaigh / Tom Paulin / Sir Martin Rees / Tim Robinson / Gabriel Rosenstock / Raoul Schrott / Paul Seawright / W.G. Sebald / Gerard Smyth / Gary Snyder / Susan Sontag / William Trevor / Daniel Tobin / Michael Viney / Casey Walker / Hans van de Waarsenburg / Bruce Weigl / Charles Wright

and many others …

BACK ISSUES

Inaugural Issue: Belfast in Europe (Vol 1, No 1)
The Justice Issue (Vol 1, No 2) *Empire* (Vol 2, No 1)
The Earth Issue (Vol 2, No 2)

IRISH PAGES is printed on Challenger offset paper, thread-sewn, and set in Monotype Perpetua to a design by Keith Connolly of Tonic Design.

SUBSCRIBE NOW

£16stg/€26/$28 *(for one year)* £24/€39/$42 *(for two years)*

(For postage outside Ireland and Britain, add £4/€6/$6 per year for Europe or £6/€9/$9 for the rest of the world)

Name ____

Address ______________________________________

____

Country ____________________ Postcode ____________

Email ____

Send as gift (*with card from* ____________________) to above address.

Enclosed is my cheque/money order to IRISH PAGES for the amount of __________

Please charge my ◯ Visa ◯ Mastercard

Card Number ____________________________________

Expiry date __________________ Signature __________________

Subscribe now by posting this form to:

IRISH PAGES, The Linen Hall Library, 17 Donegall Square North, Belfast BT1 5GB
Email: irishpages@yahoo.co.uk Tel: ++44 (0) 2890 641644
or visit our website at www.irishpages.org